# The Right Way to Write, Publish and Sell Your Book

## Your Complete Guide to Successful Authorship

By Patricia L. Fry

Matilija Press
PMB 123
323 E. Matilija St., Ste. 110
Ojai, CA 93023

Web: www.matilijapress.com
Blog: www.matilijapress.com/publishingblog

i

# The Right Way to Write, Publish and Sell Your Book

## Matilija Press
## PMB 123
## 323 E. Matilija St., Ste. 110
## Ojai, CA 93023
## Web site: www.matilijapress.com
## Blog: www.matilijapress.com/publishingblog

**Copyright © 2006 and 2007 by Patricia L. Fry**
First Printing 2006
Second Printing 2007, revised
**All rights reserved**
**Second Edition**
**Printed in the United States of America**
**ISBN 978-0-9773576-2-8**

Publisher's Cataloging-In-Publication Data
(Prepared by The Donohue Group, Inc.)

Fry, Patricia L., 1940-
    The right way to write, publish and sell your book : your
guide to successful authorship / by Patricia L. Fry. — 2nd ed.

    p. ; cm.

  ISBN: 978-0-9773576-2-8

1. Authors and publishers—Handbooks, manuals, etc.  2.
Authorship—Marketing—Handbooks, manuals, etc.  3.
Books—Marketing—Handbooks, manuals, etc.  I. Title.

Z283 .F79 2008
070.5

**Book and cover design by Dennis Mullican**
**Editorial assistance by Bonnie Myhrum**

ii

Dedicated to
hopeful authors everywhere.

# Also by Patricia Fry

How to Write a Successful Book Proposal in 8 Days or Less
Successful Writer's Handbook
Over 75 Good Ideas for Promoting Your Book
A Writer's Guide to Magazine Articles for Book Promotion and Profit
Young Writer's Handbook
Write On! Journal-keeping for Teens
The Ojai Valley: An Illustrated History
Nordhoff Cemetery: Book One
Nordhoff Cemetery: Book Two
A Thread to Hold, The Story of Ojai Valley School
Quest For Truth, A Journey of the Soul
The Mainland Luau
Entertaining Hawaiian Style
Creative Grandparenting Across the Miles,
Youth Mentoring, Sharing Your Gifts With the Future
Once in a Lifetime: Adventures in Dubai

## Ordering information
www.matilijapress.com

# The Right Way to Write, Publish and Sell Your Book

## Table of Contents

**About the Author** ......................................................... **x**

**Preface** .................................................................. **xii**

**Testimonials** ............................................................ **xiv**

**Disclaimer** .............................................................. **xvi**

**Introduction** ........................................................... **xvii**

Publishing—The Raw Truth

A Few Encouraging Words

**1: Stop! Don't Write That Book...Yet** ..................................... **1**

Step Away From the Keyboard, Now!

Dismiss Those Discouraging Words

Myth Busters for Hopeful Authors

You Want to Write a Book Because?

Get in Touch With Your Unrealistic Expectations

**2: How to Find the Very Best Publisher for Your Project** ..... **16**

Five Authors' Mistakes

Why Choose a Publisher Now?

Manage the Maze of Potential Publishers

Can You Name That Genre?

Your ABC List of Publishers

How to Meet a Publisher Face-to-Face

How to Get the Most From a Meeting With a Publisher

Your Thirty-Second Commercial

How to Work a Book Festival So it Works for You

**3: The Good, the Bad and the Ugly Facts About "Self-Publishing" Companies** ................................................................ 44

POD Publishing History

Is POD Getting a Bad Rap?

How Much Does it Cost?

What is the Lure of the POD?

When is POD the Right Choice?

**4: Bite the Bullet and Write a Book Proposal** ...................... 56

The Query Letter—An Introduction

What is a Book Proposal, Anyway?

The Nonfiction Book Proposal

How to Write a Book Proposal for a Novel

How to Write a Cover Letter

Sample Cover Letter

The Title Page

Steps to Selecting a Perfect Title

Titles for Fiction Books

Now Create a Magnificent Synopsis

Sample Synopsis

About the Author—That's You!

About the Novelist

Sample, About the Author

**Book Proposal Part II**

**5: Write the Right Book for the Right Audience** ............... 84

Choose a Marketable Topic

Who is Your Target Audience?

Your Target Audience for Fiction

Your Bonus Audience

Sample Marketing Section

What's Your Competition?

Sample Market Analysis

## Book Proposal Part III
## 6: Dazzle em With Your Marketing Savvy ........................... 99

But I Write Fiction

What's Your Platform?

Build Your Platform

Build Marketability Into Your Book

What's Your Plan?

Sample Marketing Strategies

## Book Proposal Part IV
## 7: Okay, Now Organize Your Book .................................... 116

The Chapter Outline

Techniques for Creating Your Chapter Outline

Sample Chapter Outline

## 8: How to Approach and Work With an Agent or a Publisher 131

What Does an Agent Do for You?

Tips for Choosing and Working With an Agent

How to Find a Publisher on Your Own

Give Em What They Want

The Query Letter Explained

Sample Query Letters

A Word About Rejection

What Happens When You're Issued a Contract?

## 9: Get Ready, Get Set, Write ............................................. 160

Read What You Write

How to Get Beyond Overwhelm

Hone Your Research Skills

Interview Techniques

How to Discipline Yourself to Write

Do You Need an Editor?

Tips For Choosing an Editor

Introduction to Self-Editing

Let's Become Familiar With the Parts of a Book

How to Finish a Book

Criticism—Take it Like a Wo/Man

## 10: The Self-Publishing Option ........................................... 195

Why Self-Publish?

Is Self-Publishing for You?

Exploring the Pros and Cons of Self-Publishing

Self-Publishing Basics

Your Time-Line for Producing a Book

## 11: Book Promotion Basics for the Bold and the Bashful . 213

Set Reasonable Goals and Keep Raising the Bar

What You Must Do to Promote

Bookstore Sales

How to Work With a Bookstore

Exposure Versus Sales

Book Signing Tips for Authors

Specialty Stores

Tips for Getting Book Reviews

Don't Overlook the Library Market

Working With Wholesalers and Distributors

Amazon.com

Fulfillment Services

## 12: Book Promotion—Reach Out Beyond the Bookstore 241

Create Your Own Web Site

Your Book Trailer

Blog for Exposure and Sales

Promote Through Fantastic Handouts

Press Releases, Media Kits and Sell Sheets

Sample Press Releases

Make News

Solicit Free Advertising

How to Make Sales Using Your Mailing List

Produce a Newsletter

Network, Network, Network

Get on Radio and TV

Hone Your Speaking Skills

**13: Book Promotion—Get Creative** ................................... **264**

Give Customers More Than They Expect

Sell Books Through Articles and Excerpts

Let's Go Sell Books at a Book Festival

Seek Out Special Venues

Seasonal Promotion

Boost Sales—Produce Spin Offs

Dealing With Promotion Burn Out

**14: Bookkeeping Tips for Authors** ..................................... **283**

Do You Know Where Your Manuscripts Are?

Record-Keeping for Uncle Sam

Donating Books is Good Business

You and the IRS

Welcome to the Shipping Room

Copyright Law and Contracts

15: **The Writer's Life** ............................................................ **296**

16: **Resources for Hopeful and Already Successful Authors . 302**

# About the Author

Patricia Fry has been writing for publication since 1973 and earning a living as a freelance writer, author and publisher for nearly twenty years. Hundreds of her articles have appeared in about 260 different magazines including *Writer's Digest, Authorship, Canadian Author, Freelance Writer's Report, Spannet, SPAWNews, PMA Independent, Writer's Connection, Entrepreneur, Woman's Own, Country Journal, Catholic Digest, The Artist's Magazine, Pages, The World and I, The Toastmaster, Executive Update, Cat Fancy, Los Angeles Times, Kiwanis, Your Health* and many, many others.

She is the author of 25 published books and counting. She established her publishing company in 1983, before it was fashionable, affordable or even convenient to self-publish. Over a dozen books have been produced through Matilija Press to date. She has also worked with traditional royalty publishers and co-publishers. This author has recently contributed to several other published books including, *Confessions of Shameless Self-Promoters* by Debbie Allen, *The Obvious Expert* by Elsom and Mark L. Eldridge, *Book Marketing From A-Z* by Francine Silverman and *Feminine Writes* produced by the National Association of Women Writers.

Patricia is the president of SPAWN (Small Publishers, Artists and Writers Network) www.spawn.org and, in fact, was in on the ground floor when Mary Embree founded this organization in 1996.

In 1998, she was chosen a local Living Treasure in the literary category. She fulfilled her obligation by developing a program to take into the schools called, Write for Life. A few years later, she carried this theme into a highly successful workshop which she presented for a group of homeschooled children. By the end of their eight weeks together, the students had designed and published a book of their works.

Patricia writes the monthly *SPAWN Market Update* for the SPAWN Web site and responds to members' and site visitors' writing/publishing-related questions. She speaks at conferences throughout the world and teaches writing/publishing-related classes both face-to-face and online. She works with clients on their writing/publishing projects. Her corporate clients include Toastmasters International, a local school district, a world-known private boarding school and two southern California water districts. She has written copy for political campaigns, Web sites, resumes and class projects. She also works in a variety of capacities with hopeful and fairly savvy authors.

It is with pleasure that Patricia shares with you, through this book, her passion for writing and her knowledge of the publishing industry. For, in order to survive in this business, you must have a good measure of both.

Visit Patricia's informative blog often:
www.matilijapress.com/publishingblog

# Preface

My driving force—my motivation—for writing this book is **you**: the hopeful author, the inexperienced author and even the fairly savvy author. You email me through the SPAWN Web site or my own Web site. You call me on the phone. You stop by my booth at book festivals. You come to my presentations at workshops and conferences. And you all ask one of three questions:

1. I'd like to become a writer. How do I get started?
2. I've written a book, how do I go about getting it published?
3. What's the best way to promote a book?

Or you come to me complaining:

- Publishers keep rejecting my manuscript.
- I can't get my books into major bookstores.
- My publisher is doing nothing to promote my book.

I enjoy helping people to succeed in reaching their goals. So I generally spend twenty or thirty minutes sharing my humble offerings and expertise with folks who approach me or contact me. I delight in the opportunity to give hopeful authors and freelance writers the basic information they need and enough resources to help them through the first stages of their projects. It does my heart good when someone thanks me for my time and expertise (which doesn't always happen).

Instead, I get more questions—questions that I have either responded to adequately or for which I have provided resources. But some people don't want to do what it takes to become successful. Many hopeful authors are seeking the easy path. They want to accomplish in a few weeks what it has taken successful authors years to achieve. They want to grab the brass ring without ever getting on the carrousel horse.

It takes work and time and energy to succeed. YOURS!! Not mine; not that of other successful authors. My colleagues and I can teach, mentor and assist you, but you must do the work or you won't truly reap the benefits of success.

Not only do I mentor and help freelance writers and authors, but I'll also work with them for a fee. Generally, I edit the works of others. I also teach and coach the writer/author in the process of writing more concise sentences, searching for an appropriate publisher, learning the process of self-publishing or promoting his/her book. I provide the information, the tools and the resources and I encourage my clients to use these offerings in order to improve their skills, become keen researchers or take charge of promoting their own books. Occasionally, I work with a client who wants me to do everything. And what does he or she learn from the experience? What do they gain? Nothing as tangible as skills and tools. This author might eventually have a published book with his name on it, but still lack an understanding of the publishing industry and how to navigate it.

While this book provides thousands of information bites, resources, lessons and examples, it is not designed to take the place of hard work. This is an educational guide for authors, but it is not going to get you published—not unless you USE what you learn here to move your career forward.

There is no magic potion for hopeful authors. But there is a learning curve. There are certain things that you must experience yourself in order to meet your publishing goals. This book is designed to show you how to get that experience without making too many of the obvious mistakes.

Throughout these pages, you will bathe in the wisdom of publishing experts. If you heed the warnings, study the lessons, apply the tools and pursue the resources, you have a definite chance of reaching your professional goals.

# Testimonials

For a complete list of testimonials and entire book reviews go to: www.matilijapress.com/mediacoverage.html

"Landing a publisher is harder and has become more competitive than ever before. This wonderful and comprehensive book is the reality check aspiring authors need to get a leg up, get noticed, and get that Yes!" **Peter Bowerman**, award winning author. *The Well-Fed Writer* and *TWFW Back for Seconds*. www.wellfedwriter.com

"To most authors, book writing, publishing and promoting are a new business. Get this valuable resource. It is far less-expensive than making a mistake." **Dan Poynter**, *The Self-Publishing Manual*.

"This is exactly what every author needs: pages and pages of straightforward information on how to make their book a success regardless of the publication method." **Dehanna Bailee**, *The ABC's of POD: a Beginner's Guide to Fee-Based Print-on-Demand Publishing*. http://dehana.com

"Patricia Fry is probably one of the most well-known writing gurus. When she tells you how to write, publish and sell a book, her advice is well worth listening to." **Magdalena Ball**, *The Compulsive Reader*

"Patricia Fry's book, *The Right Way to Write Publish and Sell Your Book* is a must read for every new authors. This book has valuable information for authors no matter what avenue of publishing they choose." **Jill Barrett**, Saint Louis Writer's Guild.

"People who want to write and publish their own books frequently ask me for advice. Happily, I can now direct them to *The Right Way to Write Publish and Sell Your Book*. This book walks both the novice and the experienced author through the writing, publishing and book promotion phases from start to finish." **Alan Aruba**, Bookviews.

*"The Right Way to Write, Publish and Sell Your Book* is an impressive compendium of facts, advice, insights, tips, procedures, guidelines, anecdotes, information and processes about successfully writing and then

selling what you have written. Consider this a **Must Read** for anyone serious about earning their living by writing books." Midwest Book Review.

"*The Right Way to Write Publish and Sell Your Book* is a solid five star book. I highly recommend it. This is an awesome reference book that you'll turn to again and again." **Beth Ann Erickson**, Filbert Publishing.

"*The Right Way to Write, Publish and Sell Your Book* can cut some handholds and footholds in that mountain to ease your climb to successful authorship." **Charlene Austin**, Writing Road.

"Patricia has a wonderfully helpful guide in *The Right Way to Write, Publish and Sell Your Book*. She's frank, she's precise and she's thorough." **Gretchen Craig**, *Writing for Dollars*.

"Patricia Fry has rightfully been regarded as a maven when it comes to counseling authors in the art of publishing and selling their books. Taking a subject as broad as writing, publishing and selling your book, as Fry does in her book, *The Right Way to Write, Publish and Sell Your Book*, takes some doing, but Fry pulls it off with a combination of personal anecdotes and a writing style that is enlightening and accessible." **Norm Goldman**, Editor and publisher of *BookPleasures*.

"Sage advice for neophyte authors. Fry's friendly, wise, and information-packed book can mean the difference between utter frustration and a successful writing career." **Marilyn Ross**, publishing consultant/author, *The Complete Guide to Self-Publishing* www.selfpublishingrsources.com

"*The Right Way to Write, Publish and Sell Your Book*, especially helpful for the new book writer, presents an overview of the book publishing process as well as tips and suggestions for getting a book written and into print." **Dana Cassell**, *Freelance Writer's Report*.

"In *The Right Way to Write, Publish and Sell Your Book* you'll learn what it really takes to write and sell your book, find the right publisher, write a winning book proposal and promote your book. If you're new to publishing and you would like a book that shows you the ropes, pick up a copy of this book today." **Alyice Edrich**, *The Dabbling Mum*.

# Disclaimer

The information in this book was written, compiled and published as a reference for those interested in or involved in the writing, publishing and book promotion process. It is not meant to be used in place of professional legal or financial advice and it comes with no guarantees of success. This book is a guide designed to help the writer, author and small publisher discover his/her own path to whatever measure and definition of success he or she might seek.

Since the publishing industry and the Internet are in a constant state of flux, we can't guarantee that the resources listed will always be current. It is our intention to offer you the most updated information available and to give you the tools to locate the additional resources you need.

# INTRODUCTION

## Publishing—The Raw Truth

More people today than ever before are becoming authors. Unfortunately, most of them fail in their quest for success. The Book Industry Study Group (BISG) reports that in 2004, over seventy-five percent of titles in print sold fewer than 100 copies. According to a Jenkins Group survey, seventy percent of books published in this country do not make a profit. Why?

- Uninformed authors approach the publishing process all wrong.

- Even excellent, worthy books go unnoticed when the author isn't industry-savvy.

- Inexperienced authors tend to quit promoting their books when the going gets tough.

It used to be that authors wrote books and publishers produced, promoted and distributed them. After participating in a few book signings, the author was free to go back to his home office and write his next bestseller. In order to be a successful author today, however, you must have a significant understanding of the publishing industry and be willing to establish a sense of intimacy with your book. It's imperative that you become involved in the promotion of your book and, in some cases, the production process.

Technology has fueled dramatic changes in the publishing industry—and the news isn't all bad. Hopeful authors are faced with greater challenges today, it's true; but there are also more options and opportunities.

According to self-publishing guru, Dan Poynter, in 1970, there were only about 3,000 publishing companies. Today, there are somewhere around 85,000—many of them small/independent publishers who have established a company through which to produce their own books. However, I've reported on dozens and dozens of new traditional royalty publishers over the last seven years in the monthly *SPAWN Market Update*. Yes, there are a lot of publishers out there—more than just the big six. So why is it so difficult to land a publishing contract? In a word, *competition.*

Some years ago, I heard it said that over eighty percent of the public believe they have a book in them. With expanded publishing options, more and more of these people are actually writing their books. And millions of them are currently seeking publishers. Is there room in this industry for all hopeful authors? Probably not. But, according to R. R. Bowker, a whopping 291,920 new books were published in 2006.

My aim is not to discourage you, but to illustrate that there's more to becoming a successful published author than simply writing a good book. Besides a measure of talent and skill, it takes a bit of industry savvy, the ability to engage your left brain (participate in the business aspect of publishing) and the willingness to take the necessary steps. While writers, if they wish, can luxuriate in a world of creativity, authorship is a business. Once you decide that you want to be published, you must don your businessperson's hat.

What happens if you don't heed this advice? You've probably already witnessed some of the consequences. You hear Elaine from your writers' group whining incessantly because she can't find a publisher for her magnificent manuscript. Yet she stubbornly refuses to follow publishers' submission guidelines. She hasn't written a book proposal. She is sending out an inferior, ineffective query letter or she has bypassed this step altogether and is submitting an unsolicited manuscript. By refusing to learn or acknowledge publishing protocol, she's setting herself up for failure.

What about Brian, the guy in your online discussion group who is furious because his publisher isn't selling more copies of his book? He doesn't understand that promoting his book is his responsibility.

Many inexperienced authors go into publishing with more ideals than information.

Authors want their book to fly off bookstore shelves by the bushels—they dream of collecting big royalty bucks—but they aren't willing to lift a finger to make it happen.

In today's publishing climate, a traditional royalty publisher won't issue you a contract unless you have a marketing plan firmly in place. And the more credentials you flash, the better. A publisher isn't going to sink his money into your project unless he's at least ninety-eight percent certain that it's a risk worth taking. As the author, it's your job to convince him or her that you can and will do your part. Don't let people like Elaine and Brian discourage you from fulfilling your publishing dreams. Obviously, they've chosen to spend more time complaining about the process than to understand it.

## A Few Encouraging Words

Even though you might not see it as such at first, this is a book of encouragement. And it is a reality check. Those of you who will ultimately succeed in meeting your writing/publishing goals are those who can step outside your comfort zones and embrace the information, guidelines and resources within these pages.

I started writing articles for magazines in 1973. I wrote a book five years later and landed a traditional royalty publisher on my first try. I self-published my second book in 1983. While I'm not exactly a pioneer in the field of self-publishing, I did it before self-publishing was fashionable, convenient or reasonably priced. The book you're holding is the revised second edition of my twenty-fourth published book and my eighth writing/publishing-related title.

There were no readily available guidelines for authors when I entered into the world of publishing. Heck, I didn't even meet another author until I discovered the Internet in the early 1990s. I feel as though I suffered my professional growing pains alongside a transitioning publishing industry.

Things were simpler in the 1970s and 80s. Long-term standards kept the industry fairly steady. Competition was just tough enough that good literature was the rule instead of the exception. And then along came the digital revolution, and practically everything changed. In order to be successfully published, you must change, as well. And this means do not sit down and write your book as a first step. There is much to be learned and much to do before you start writing.

As an author who has gained a measure of recognition within the writing/publishing community and as the president of SPAWN (Small Publishers, Artists and Writers Network), I often receive emails from frustrated authors. One of them said, "My book is good. All I need is to find someone who will believe in my story and in me." It was obvious that she wanted me to give her a shortcut to success.

I explained that finding the right publisher is an all-consuming activity that takes time, study and energy. I encouraged her to enter into the competition with more knowledge than hope. And I outlined some very specific steps she could take toward locating and landing an appropriate publisher. I recommended that she write a book proposal and I offered her some good resources. She thanked me for my response and said, "But, I just want someone to believe in me and my book."

She obviously has no desire to approach this task as a professional. Like Elaine, she has established her level of comfort and is unwilling or unable to step outside of that realm. Ladies and gentlemen, hers is one book that you won't find competing against yours anytime soon.

I often hear from authors who have made some bad choices. Hundreds or thousands of dollars later, they wonder what to do. As I said, there are more publishing options than ever before. Many hopeful authors choose the quick and easy road to publishing. They hand over their manuscripts and large sums of money to the first company that agrees to publish it. In most cases, this is one of the growing number of subsidy "self-publishing" companies that readily appear during a Google search. That was the case with Jeff.

After receiving form rejection letters from several medium-sized publishers and being ignored by a few mega-publishers, Jeff saw an ad for AuthorHouse and contacted them. He said, "They accepted my manuscript and boy did that make me feel good. So, of course, I signed a contract with them. It has been six months and the only books sold are those that I sold personally—about a dozen to relatives and co-workers. Even the local Borders Bookstore won't carry my book. I'm frustrated and I don't know what to do."

I helped Jeff develop a marketing plan for his book, which he reluctantly pursued. He told me later, "I really thought that, when I finished writing the book, my part of this was over. And here I am marketing and distributing the thing."

Reality check for hopeful authors: **Book promotion is your responsibility**.

I meet hundreds of authors every year online and at book festivals and writers' conferences who are completely unaware of their publishing options and the ramifications of their choices. In this business, ignorance can be costly. Hopeful authors need to know that there are the major publishing houses, of course, and subsidy or fee-based POD (Print-on-Demand) "self-publishing" services. But there are also hundreds of small to medium-sized royalty publishers who are eager for a bestseller, and niche publishers seeking fresh, new projects. You could produce an ebook or you can publish the book yourself. You might even solicit funds to help support your project. No kidding, I've had publishers ask me if I could arrange for corporate funding to help them pay production costs on one of my manuscripts. And I've known self-published authors who solicited funds for the production of their books. Some do this by selling back-of-the-book advertising pages.

Which publishing approach is best? It depends on your project and it depends on you. There are advantages and disadvantages to each of these publishing methods. What might be an advantage to one hopeful author could be a definite disadvantage to another. Before making a decision, I urge you to consider the following:

- How important is it that the book be published?
- Can you afford to take a financial risk?
- How quickly do you want/need the book published?
- What level of quality do you desire for the finished product?
- How much control do you want and how much are you willing to relinquish?
- How far and wide do you want your product to reach?
- Is this book of local, regional, national or international interest?
- What is the size and scope of your target audience?

- Do you have a head for business?
- Are you able and willing to promote this book?
- What is your platform—your way of attraction readers?

Perhaps you're like a lot of the hopeful authors I meet—you've already made some mistake in your preliminary publishing ventures. Don't despair. There is hope. There's hope for you and me and for the future of American literature. Hope comes in the form of knowledge and responsible publishing and promotion. This book will guide you to that end. So get ready for the journey. Relax, breathe deeply, engage your right and left brain and open your mind, for successful authorship is a whole body experience.

# Chapter One

# STOP!

## DON'T WRITE THAT BOOK…

# YET

## Step Away From the Keyboard, Now!

You probably didn't expect to read this statement in a book about how to become a published author. Of course, I want you to write the book that's rolling around in your head and your heart, but not quite yet. There's work to be done before you put pen to paper or fingers to keyboard. First, you need information so you can develop a strategy.

You wouldn't open a retail sporting goods store or start a telecommunications company unless you had at least a basic understanding of the industry. You'd become familiar with the competition, you'd understand the needs of your customers, you'd develop a marketing plan and you'd probably make sure you had some financial backing. Like it or not, publishing is a business and your book is a product. While writing can be a marvelously delightful creative endeavor, the process of publishing involves a generous dose of marketing savvy and business sense. Launch blindly into the publishing field and use a scattershot method of producing and promoting a book and you'll likely fail. There are hundreds of thousands of disappointed authors out there who can back up this statement.

In 2004, there were 1.2 million titles in print in the U.S. and over seventy-six percent of them sold fewer than 100 copies.

As I said in my Introduction (which you should read, by the way), it is estimated that nearly eighty-one percent of all adult Americans have the desire to write a book. More and more of these people are actually doing it. Technology is certainly in the author's favor. Anyone who can construct a sentence, can turn out a manuscript. If you have a computer and printer, you can even produce a book. Those who don't want to *be* the publisher can *hire* a publisher. If you're diligent (or lucky) and have a viable manuscript, you have a good chance of landing a traditional royalty publisher. The opportunities for hopeful authors are amazingly vast. Most new authors, however, short-circuit their chances of publishing success by going about the process of producing a book all wrong.

Okay, you've written a book and you want to have it published. What more is there to consider? Nothing, if you wrote the book to give as gifts to your immediate family members and a few friends. If you want your book to be noticed by the masses, however, you will need buyers. You know, customers—folks who will purchase your book. It's only after publication—when sales are practically nonexistent—that many first-time authors realize they must have made some mistakes.

One disheartened author told me recently, "I was so eager to get this book published, I'm afraid that I didn't take time to learn the ropes. Now I have forty-two boxes of books in my garage and no idea how to sell them. I guess I was naïve to think that I could distribute them through bookstores, because that is just not happening. I learned too late that bookstores are not there for the author—that is, unless your publisher is Simon and Schuster."

What? Bookstore managers aren't eager to carry newly published books? Why? Consider this:

One reason is logistics. There are currently 1.2 million titles in print in the U.S. and even the largest bookstores can accomodate only around 150,000 titles. That's just over twelve percent of all titles in print. Also consider this:

There have probably always been poorly written, shoddily bound books produced, but never as many as since the most recent technological revolution. Along with some wonderful books, a proliferation of low quality books began appearing throughout the mid to late 1990s— most of them coming from fee-based POD (Print-on-Demand) "self-publishing" companies and lackadaisical independent publishers. What choice did credible bookstore managers, book reviewers and distributors have? How would they avoid endorsing inferior products while embracing and recommending only those books of superior quality? Rather than taking the time to consider the merit of each individual book, many of them decided to accept only books published through traditional channels. They would exclude books produced by subsidy publishing services and independent publishers.

Some bookstore managers, reviewers and distributors even shun books produced by legitimate royalty publishers if they use digital printing technology. This has closed doors to traditional marketing opportunities for many digitally produced and self-published books.

I met Frances at a writers' conference in St. Louis where I spoke on book promotion. She had published her novel through one of the many fee-based POD "self-publishing" companies two years earlier and was still struggling to recoup her investment. She paid extra for one of the promotion packages they offered, but said, "I've sold fewer than 100 books and that was without their help. They haven't actually sold any." According to Frances' calculations, she needed to sell 100 more books in order to break even. But she was at a loss as to how to do it. She bought lists of bookstores nationwide and mailed flyers to 1,000 of them without success. She contacted every bookstore within a hundred-mile radius of her home and managed to place a few books on consignment. She had also arranged for a few book signings which weren't all that successful.

Frances told me, "If it wasn't for the fact that I need to replace that money, I'd forget the whole thing and chalk it up to a bad decision. But I'm facing retirement and I need the money. If I had it to do over again, I would never have gotten involved in publishing."

I wanted to support Frances and offer her something of value at the same time. I suggested a trade—a copy of my book, *Over 75 Good Ideas for Promoting Your Book*, in exchange for her novel. And then I pointed out a few of the promotional ideas in my book that might help her sell her book. Frances was a paraplegic and her novel featured a paraplegic couple, yet she hadn't even considered soliciting reviews in disability magazines or giving readings at rehabilitation hospitals and nursing homes. I suggested that she write a provocative press release and send it to newspaper editors, radio talk show hosts and Web site hosts nationwide. There are approximately one million Americans using wheelchairs—or one in every 250 people. This should be a significant enough number to warrant national coverage for a book related to personal disabilities.

The last I heard, Frances had sent out review copies to several magazine and newspaper editors. Her book was being featured on a couple of appropriate Web sites. She had done some radio interviews by phone and was scheduled to make a TV appearance locally. Her total sales to date were 350 and counting.

Few first-time authors think beyond the bookstore when considering book promotion. Even fewer consider book promotion at all until they're faced with a book that no one is buying.

NEWS FLASH!!! It is up to the author to promote his/her book and the time to start planning your promotional strategy, fellow writers, is BEFORE you write the book.

Before you invest your time, energy and money into the project, you need to know whether there is a market for the book. Is your idea valid? Is there a need for this book? Is there room for another book on this topic? Exactly who is your target audience? Who do you want to influence or affect? What books would compete with yours? This is also the time to think about building promotional opportunities into your book. (Learn how to make your book more salable in Chapter Six.)

## Dismiss Those Discouraging Words

You may feel as though I'm trying to dissuade you from pursuing your writing/publishing dreams. On the contrary, my purpose in writing this book is to guide you toward a successful publishing experience. In so doing, I must squelch some of your preconceived ideas and burst your bubbles—at least those bubbles that are blocking your success.

Some readers will decide not to follow this guide and a few of them will stumble blindly into a sweet publishing deal that makes them a lot of money. I've seen it happen. I've also watched inexperienced authors blow their money and their chances for success by refusing to adhere to some measure of publishing protocol. Unfortunately, the latter is the more common scenario.

There are people out there who *will* try to discourage you from writing a book. Sour Sallys and Gloomy Glens will tell you that the manuscript market is saturated. They'll say that the big publishing companies monopolize the bookstores and that it's next to impossible to get your book reviewed through the most prominent channels. Is this true? Well, yes. But should this stop you from bringing out the book of your dreams? Emphatically, NO!

Giving up is not the answer. Recently, I sat on a panel at a writers' conference with four others who had varying degrees of publishing experience. Three of them were authors with one book each. One had self-published (established his own publishing company) and two were POD (subsidy) published. The fourth panelist worked for a small distributor of science fiction and fantasy books. There were about forty hopeful authors in the audience hungry for direction and encouragement.

Each panelist spoke from his/her own limited experience. One professed that having a Web site was the only way to sell books.

5

Another spoke vehemently against bookstores, big publishers and the whole damned publishing scene. The third author said, "Traditional publishers won't give you the time of day. Your only hope is the subsidy publisher." And the distributor told several long stories about the process of distributing books. My message that day was, *become and stay involved.*

I asked audience members to recall that sense of intimacy they each experienced with their book while writing it. I urged them to carry that over into the publishing process. I said, "Stay connected to your book during every step of the way and this means understanding the publishing industry. You must make several decisions throughout the writing and production process. Be sure that they are informed decisions, not emotional decisions based on desperation. Know what you want to accomplish and learn how to make it happen."

I cautioned this group of authors against turning their projects and wads of cash over to strangers simply because they don't want to bother with the learning curve. I stressed that an informed author is more likely to become a successful author.

The fact is that self-published authors are generally more successful than fee-based POD (subsidy) published authors. I often nudge hopeful authors, who believe they have exhausted their chance of landing a traditional royalty publisher, toward the self-publishing option. Why? Because when you self-publish—when you become an independent publisher—you develop a more intimate connection to your project which is more apt to carry over into the major, major task of book promotion.

I urged this audience of hopeful authors, "Don't hand over your hard earned money to the first POD publisher who offers you a contract. First, make sure that you have an excellent, marketable product. How? Write a book proposal. Then either approach traditional publishers with your proposal or self-publish, but not before you have spent some time studying the publishing industry. Take charge of your future. Become informed and stay involved."

Representing SPAWN (Small Publishers, Artists and Writers Network), I participate in several book festivals each year. Our booth typically attracts many writers at various stages of their passion. We do our best to respond to their questions and provide pertinent resources. At a recent book festival in Santa Barbara, California, while I was engaged in a straightforward discussion with a fledgling author about the importance of writing a book proposal, someone who was standing on the fringes of the conversation interjected her advice. She said, "Forget about writing a book proposal. Just sit down and write. That's how you become a writer, by writing."

Sure, you should write, write and then write some more. But I am here to tell you that writing the book is not the first step in producing and publishing a successful product. Hers is valid advice for someone who has writer's block, who can't think of anything to write about, who dreams of becoming a writer some day or who wants to become a more skilled writer. But this is bad advice for someone who is ready to write a nonfiction or even a fiction book with high expectations of it being widely sold and read. In this case, writing a book proposal is a logical first step.

There are too many people out there professing to be writing or publishing experts and who are more than willing to share their advice. Hear them out, but also be a proactive researcher. Consider the source. Is this person speaking from a wide base of knowledge or limited experience? Study the publishing industry. Pay attention to the experts—those with proven track records.

As you will discover while studying this book, there are abundant opportunities for authors outside of the antiquated publishing mold. There are numerous publishing options and countless avenues for book promotion and distribution. If you're still following the publishing model established in the 1960s and 70s, you are in for a culture shock. It's time that you learn some new concepts and strategies. My intent is not to offer encouragement where there is no hope, but to inspire you to think and to do the research necessary.

> Follow your dream with your eyes wide open and your expectations reasonable.

For those of you who are still questioning today's publishing climate and your chances of breaking in, I'd like to bust some popular myths for your benefit. Read on.

## Myth Busters for Hopeful Authors

**Myth #1:** It's impossible for a first-time author to land a traditional royalty publishing contract.

**Myth Buster:** You'll hear people say this and you may even see it stated on writers' online forums. And then you'll read in a newsletter or in a book such as this one that there were 291,920 books published in 2006 (Bowker). Believe it or not (actually, I prefer that you believe it), thousands of those books were published by traditional royalty publishers. Do your homework and produce a viable product and you, too, could land a traditional royalty publisher.

One student in my online book proposal class had her first book published by Houghton-Mifflin. Yes, Virginia, there is a royalty publisher for your excellent book— that is, if it is timely enough, unique enough and has a wide enough audience.

As an aside, this aforementioned newbie author changed the focus of her book during the book proposal process—a decision that may have been instrumental in landing the prestigious publisher. Too often, an author approaches a nonfiction book from the wrong perspective or one that is too broad. Writing a book proposal helps you to find the appropriate focus for your book before you begin writing it. (Read more about writing a book proposal in Chapters Four through Seven.)

**Myth #2:** Most publishers accept manuscripts only through agents.

**Myth Buster:** Wrong. There are oodles of publishers who prefer to deal directly with the author. My student—the one who landed a book deal through Houghton-Mifflin—did so without the assistance of an agent. *Writer's Market* (a reference book for writers and authors) lists over 1,000 publishing companies. More than ninety percent of them do not require that you engage an agent.

**Myth #3:** If I have an agent, I will definitely get published.

**Myth Buster:** Not necessarily. Unfortunately, while there are some very good agents, there are also some who are ineffective and even unscrupulous. (Read more about locating and successfully working with an agent in Chapter Eight.) And even a good agent can't always second-guess publishers.

I hear hopeful authors complaining about their agents—"She's not doing anything for me." But sometimes it's just a matter of poor judgment on the agent's part. Maybe your manuscript isn't as timely or well-written as she initially thought.

**Myth #4:** I don't have to worry about fine-tuning my manuscript. If the publisher is interested, he will have it edited.

**Myth Buster:** Don't EVEN go there! It may surprise you to know how many hopeful authors believe this. Of course, publishers hire editors and, if accepted, your manuscript will probably go through a stringent editing process. But it is your responsibility to present to the publisher the very best possible manuscript. You need to hire a good editor *before* you submit your work to any publisher. Adopt this motto: *Make a good impression the first time and every time.* This goes for every email, letter and manuscript you send to publishers, book reviewers and even fellow authors. You are a writer; let it show.

**Myth #5:** Bookstores won't carry self-published or fee-based POD published books.

**Myth Buster:** Have you contacted any of your local, independent bookstores about your self-published or POD (subsidy) published book? Have you approached specialty bookstores related to the topic of your book? Do you stop by independent bookstores to introduce yourself and your book when you're traveling? Stop focusing on the mega-bookstores and see if you can entice their smaller counterparts to carry your book. In fact, I recommend that you do business with independent bookstores the next time you want to purchase a book. They are your friends. Support them and they will be able to support you.

**Myth #6:** No one will review self-published, Print-on-Demand and subsidy published books.

**Myth Buster:** Here again, authors tend to focus on one segment of book reviews—prepublication reviews through prestigious library journals. These are difficult to get even when you've gone through the right channels. Some of these reviewers are opening avenues for self-published and POD published books for a fee. From what I hear, however, authors/publishers are not getting their money's worth for these paid services.

In the meantime, there are tens of thousands of legitimate magazines, newspapers, newsletters and Web sites hungry for good books to review. You're probably already aware of magazines related to your book topic. Contact the editors of these publications and offer them a review copy. Visit online directories to locate other possibilities. This is another case of thinking outside the box. I've had my writing-related books reviewed by close to 100 different magazines, newsletters and Web sites. Of course, each review generates book sales while building on my credibility in this field.

**Myth #7:** Writing the book is the hardest part of the process.

**Myth Buster:** Did you believe this to be true while you were involved in researching and writing your book? Now that you have finished your book, you feel differently, don't you? To avoid *author shock*, always, I mean ALWAYS write a book proposal first. Once you've properly and thoughtfully completed a book proposal, you will be, at least, somewhat prepared for the work and the stress that lies ahead. As Dan Poynter, the author of *The Self-Publishing Manual*, wrote in his testimonial for my book, *Over 75 Good Ideas for Promoting Your Book*, "Writing the book is the tip of the iceberg; promoting is the larger part under the water. And, whether you sell out to a publisher or publish yourself, the author must do the promotion."

## You Want to Write a Book Because?

Have you ever asked yourself why you write? I often interview writers who thank me for asking this question because it causes them to reflect and helps them to set more meaningful goals. We don't always consider the reasons why we write (or paint or sculpt). We just do it. Likely, you're in touch with what inspires you to write—your muse. But what motivates you to write for publication: money, prestige, fame, a yearning to share your joy or grief, the desire to help people or to facilitate change or a need to establish credibility in a particular field?

I write for publication in order to justify my passion for writing. I tell people that *I can't not write*. Since I have to earn a living, I've established a business around my love of writing.

I'd been selling articles to magazines for a dozen years when something happened that made it necessary for me to get a job. I hated working for someone else—on their agenda. I yearned to go back to my writing. I missed writing so much that I became despondent. When I realized that working would probably be the reality of my future, I knew that I had to find a way to write no matter what else was going on in my life.

I started getting up at four o'clock every morning and I'd write for two hours. I'd take my meditation walk, get dressed and arrive at work by 8:30. I also wrote on weekends. I completed my book, *Quest for Truth, A Journey of the Soul* in eight months on that schedule.

My soul was replenished, but I wanted more. I had to figure out a way to create a viable business around my passion for writing. And I began spending those early morning hours and weekends submitting articles to magazines. The assignments began to roll in and paychecks eventually followed. Several months later, I took a leap of faith and quit my job. I've been writing fulltime ever since.

> Are you living your writing dream or do you just keep dreaming?

I've worked with clients who go from writers' conference to writers' group to online discussion group and back again without ever really writing or submitting anything. They come to me requesting help with turning their dream into a reality. I always ask, "Why do you want to write?"

Most writers have this innate (or is it insane) desire to be read/heard—maybe even understood. Elizabeth K. Burton is the author of *Dreams of Darkness, Shadow of the Scorpion* and *The Ugly Princess*. She writes to be read. She says, "I love telling stories; if I make money at it, all the better. It's getting it out to the readers that compels me."

Some writers are eager to fill a void. Sande Cropsey wrote her children's book because she perceived a need. She was already writing plays and short stories when, one December, while watching Christmas specials with her children, she realized that none of the popular Christmas stories involved trains. "What is Christmas without trains?" she reasoned. And she created *Tinker's Christmas*, a children's storybook featuring a train.

Many authors today write books designed to help others. They've endured something or learned something they feel is of value to a segment of the population. Sharing, for most of them, serves two purposes. In the process of helping others, they are helping themselves. Writing is a way of purging, after all.

I met one author online who was promoting a book for a very specialized audience—dialysis patients. She said, "I wrote this book in hopes of reaching a very select audience and to offer some help based on my own personal experiences."

Other authors write in order to establish credibility. An experienced realtor might attempt to build on her reputation by writing a how-to book for potential clients. Technology experts often write books related to their field of expertise. I build professional credibility with each of my writing/publishing-related books.

Once you've decided to write a book and you know why you are writing, how do you choose what to write? Will you follow your heart and write a children's story, a book of poems or a novel? Perhaps you'll lead with your head and write a how-to book related to your business or your favorite hobby. Many professionals suggest writing a nonfiction book, first. Yes, even if your heart's desire is to pen the next great novel, consider breaking into the publishing field with a nonfiction book. Why?

A nonfiction book is easier to write and it's easier to sell both to a publisher and to readers. It doesn't have to be a huge tome. Produce a simple booklet featuring something you know well: a children's guide to recognizing constellations, 100 things you can fix with fishing line, what to do when you find an injured bird, a knitting guide for youngsters, tips for writing love notes or the history of your local Independence Day celebration, for example.

Whatever your genre or topic, in order to obtain some level of success, you must enter into the project with ample knowledge and appropriate expectations.

Julie began writing for relaxation while working in the corporate offices of a banking company. She enjoyed writing so much that she decided to quit her job and write fulltime. It wasn't hard for Julie to choose her topic—she writes suspense novels related to the banking industry.

I find it interesting how authors choose their topics. But sometimes the topic chooses the author, as was the case with Cindy. Her book captures her experiences as an island dweller living in a substandard cabin with an array of animals (only some of them domesticated). Cindy wanted to share her unusual experiences with others. She told me, "I was bubbling over with this story. It became terribly important to me to share the lessons I learned as well as to entertain, enlighten and inspire anyone who might venture to drop out."

## Get in Touch With Your Unrealistic Expectations

Most authors have an ideal or a standard by which they measure success. For some, success means becoming a published author. For others, they haven't succeeded until they've sold 100,000 copies of their book. I'm sure that some of us are never satisfied with what we've achieved. The more we obtain, the more we desire. Isn't that what goal-setting is all about? Set a goal. Reach the goal. Raise the bar. It works for me.

> The Author's Guild has determined that a fiction book is successful if it sells 5,000 copies and a successful nonfiction book sells 7,500 copies.

Publishing isn't necessarily a money-making venture. If you self-publish a book that sells 5,000 copies, you might realize $25,000 to $75,000 in profits. But if you had collected royalties on that book, your earnings might be just $5,000 to $20,000. Keep in mind that sales could spread out over a five or ten year period.

> Embracing unrealistic expectations generally results in an unsuccessful and very disappointed author.

How does a hopeful author establish realistic expectations? By understanding something about the publishing industry. This is not to say that I can teach you how to predict which book ideas will pay off in big bucks and which won't. Even the most experienced publishers sometimes miss the mark. But at least they make educated decisions. They're not apt to lead with their emotions (as an author will often do) or take an unknown risk. Understanding the possibilities will give you enough wiggle room to help keep your expectations well within the realm of reality.

A book of poetry, for example, is extremely difficult to sell. If you want to share your poetry for the pure joy of sharing, that's okay. Just understand that this will be more a labor of love than a commercial venture through which you will receive enough royalties to retire on next year.

Having said that, however, I'd like to recommend two books designed to help poets sell their work: *Poet Power, The Complete Guide to Getting Your Poetry Published* by Thomas A. Williams, (Sentient Publications, 2002) and *How to Make a Living As a Poet* by Gary Mex Glazner (Soft Skull Press, 2005).

The author of a children's book said to me recently, "The experience of publishing fell far short of what I initially thought it would be and that was largely due to my unrealistic expectations and perceptions about publishing. Marketing is so far removed from the experience of writing that it is like this constant stranger who speaks a different language with which I am neither equipped to nor have the desire to understand. Had anyone explained to me the ins and outs—the ups and downs—of marketing, I'm not sure I would have ever published."

Too many authors fail solely because they give up. Authorship is not designed to be a hobby. It isn't something that you can successfully manage as an afterthought. It demands your full attention. Your future in writing and publishing is almost completely up to you. If you do the necessary research and work—if you exercise persistence, perseverance and patience while maintaining realistic expectations—you will experience success.

# Chapter Two

## HOW TO FIND
# THE VERY BEST PUBLISHER
## FOR YOUR PROJECT

Most new authors make at least one of five mistakes when attempting to choose a publisher.

### Five Authors' Mistakes

1: **Inexperienced authors write a book that is not publisher-friendly**. In other words, they write the book to suit their own emotional or altruistic needs without considering its commercial value. Once the book is completed, they try to find a publisher. What's wrong with this approach?

Most manuscripts that are written without concern for the target audience are not marketable, thus would not be profitable. A publisher may reject a manuscript featuring your grandfather's World War II experiences, but would welcome a book focusing on blacks in the armed forces during that time period. Your book on selling buttons through eBay may not appeal to a publisher, yet the public might be screaming for one featuring the most unique items ever sold online.

If you had written a complete book proposal first, your project would probably be more appropriately targeted. And if you'd submitted a query letter before writing your book, the publisher could have more appropriately directed you, greatly increasing your chances of becoming a published author.

**2: Newbie authors frequently send their manuscripts to the wrong publishers.** Much like doctors, these days, publishers specialize. More and more publishers accept either fiction or nonfiction. Some specialize in children's stories or textbooks, while others focus their energies (and their finances) on true crime, poetry, romance, cookbooks, how-to, self-help or business books.

There's no such thing as one publisher fits all. You wouldn't send your collection of poetry to DAW Books. However, the editors at Loft Press might be delighted to receive it. These editors would reject your fantasy or science fiction manuscript on the spot, but those at DAW Books might welcome them. The publisher at Paulist Press doesn't want to see books in any of these genres, but send them a good children's or young adult book with a Catholic theme and you might score with them.

**3: Eager authors often set their hearts on being accepted by a mega-publisher.** In so doing, they miss out on more realistic publishing opportunities. I'm not trying to discourage you from starting at the top. I have no quarrel with you giving the big guys a whirl. But please develop a backup plan. Vow that if Random House and Grand Central Publishing (formerly Warner Books) turn you down, you will lower your sights and opt for publication with one of the many smaller publishing houses. Have you heard of Potomac Books, Inc.? They publish sixty nonfiction titles per year and offer a five figure (maximum) advance against royalties. Steeple Hill Women's Fiction publishes around eighty fiction titles per year. They also pay an advance against royalties. Massachusetts-based Cowley Publications produces as many as twenty titles each year and they pay ten to fifteen percent royalties. They publish Christian and spiritual nonfiction books and poetry.

**4: The most common mistake authors make when contacting publishers is to ignore their submission guidelines.** In fact, many inexperienced authors don't even study them. While there are basic standards for contacting publishers, there are also differences in submission requirements among publishing houses. Most publishers want to see a query letter first. If they are interested in your concept and impressed by your credentials, they will generally request your book proposal. Of course, there are exceptions to every rule and this is why it's crucial to locate and study the guidelines for each publisher before approaching him or her. (See details for locating submission guidelines on page 24.)

5: **Too many hopeful authors neglect to make a clear, concise and clean presentation.** Some inexperienced authors believe that a publisher can see through a poorly written query letter to the magnificence of their story. Others are so eager to get their works into the hands of a publisher that they simply don't finish dotting all of their i's and crossing all of their t's. I'm here to tell you that your chances of winning a contract with any publisher are extremely slim when you submit an error-riddled, disorganized, rambling query letter, book proposal or manuscript.

In order to be successful in this business, you have to stop looking at your project from an emotional place and start thinking like a professional. Don't worry; you can adopt a business persona without losing your creative edge. In fact, if you want to be published, it's necessary to shift from artist to businessperson on demand.

Publishers are bombarded with hundreds and sometimes thousand of query letters and book proposals each month. Pelican Publishing Company receives over 5,000 submissions per year and they publish just sixty-five titles. Frederick Fell Publishers receives 4,000 queries each year and they publish only forty books. Last year, Strider Nolan Publishing received around 2,000 submissions and they publish only five to ten titles. The news isn't all bad, however. Check out some of the smaller publishing companies. Windward Publishing publishes six to ten titles and they receive just 120 queries and fifty manuscripts per year. Scriblerus Press publishes anywhere from one to five titles and they receive only 100 submissions throughout the year.

Whether you decide to approach a mega-publishing house or a smaller one, vow to give nothing less than your most polished presentation. Think about it: what is the point of leading with your second or third best shot when there may be 3,000 other authors soliciting this publisher with equally good ideas and highly polished presentations?

Last year, a hopeful young author asked me to evaluate his query letter. He'd been sending it out to publishers for several months and wondered why none of them had expressed an interest in his project. I was able to give him several reasons.

- His query letter had numerous grammatical errors and misspelled words.

- A couple of his sentences made no sense at all.

- The letter read more like a casual note to a friend than a sales pitch to a publisher.

- He neglected to say anything meaningful about himself.

- He didn't provide information as to the age group for his children's book.

- Instead of giving the publisher a solid reason why this book was a good investment, the author wasted an entire paragraph explaining how much he and his friends like the book.

## Why Choose a Publisher Now?

Locating and landing a publisher can take time. Most hopeful authors, after devoting several months or years to writing the perfect manuscript, don't want to spend another several months in search of a publisher. It is at this juncture that many authors make their first major mistake. They go with the first publisher who expresses an interest in their project without considering the consequences or cost. If you have a few appropriate publishers in mind *before* writing your book, you could save time, money and heartache.

A publisher might have some specific requirements that you need to know about before writing the book. One successful author forged ahead with her book without considering her publishing choices. It took her only five or six months to find a publisher, but he wouldn't publish her book without a major rewrite. This extra work might have been avoided had she put more effort and thought into a publisher before writing the book.

Choose a publisher before you write the book and you may get an advance. A publisher might pay you a fee to write the book. This amount would then be deducted from future royalty earnings. Generally, a publisher will pay half of the advance when you sign the contract and the remainder upon satisfactory completion of the manuscript. While publishing advances are sometimes thousands of dollars, it is rare for a first-time author to receive more than $500 or $1,000.

Here's what you need to know before you start writing:

- What are your publishing options for this particular book? Are there publishers who produce books like yours and if not, are you willing to self-publish (establish your own publishing company) or go with a fee-based POD publishing service such as AuthorHouse or iUniverse.

- What is the general word count for a book like the one you want to write? Some publishers have word count requirements. One publisher might want no more than 50,000 words, while another won't publish anything less than 80,000 words. There are strict word count guidelines for children's books based on the age group. And few, if any, publishers will invest in an oversized novel by an unknown author.

- What does the publisher need or expect from you? Does the publisher of your choice want to see the completed manuscript, a synopsis and two sample chapters or just a query letter? What specific information does the publisher require about your project—about you?

Of course, there are writers who just want to write. If you write purely for the joy of it—if you don't have any professional aspirations— please pass this book along to someone who cares and go back and join your muse at the keyboard. If, on the other hand, you are writing for publication—you have a deep desire to be widely read or you hope to earn a living or retire on book sales/royalties—let a publisher drive your project.

## Manage the Maze of Potential Publishers

I receive the same question from hopeful authors many times each year. "How do I find a publisher?" Another even more important question might be, "What is a publisher?"

A **traditional royalty publisher** assumes the expenses involved in publishing a book and gives the author a percentage of each book sold. Depending on the policies of the publishing house, royalties are figured on either the retail or the wholesale price and generally range between five and eighteen percent.

**Subsidy** or **vanity** and **co-publishers** produce your book for a fee. Some of them do not have very good reputations. The most common gripe against these publishing services is that they do shabby work. I once worked quite successfully with a co-publisher on a commissioned book. This local company had an excellent reputation and they produced a quality hardcover book for my corporate client.

**Fee-based POD "self-publishing" companies** charge you anywhere from a few hundred to many thousands of dollars to produce your book and then they print the number of copies that you need as you request them. These companies are extremely popular right now, but they are also the brunt of numerous complaints. I maintain that this is due mostly to the authors' lack of industry savvy and unreasonable expectations. (Read more about fee-based POD publishers in Chapter Three.)

**Self-publishing** means that you establish a company through which to produce your book and you arrange for and pay for all of the necessary components—copyright, ISBN, bar code, cover design and so forth. You audition printing companies and hire one for your project. You also promote, distribute and shop your books. (Read more about self-publishing in Chapter Ten.)

Traditional royalty publishers are everywhere—not just in high-rise buildings in New York City. They reside and work in practically every state in the U.S. So how do you find out about them?

Start in your home library. You probably have books on the topic or in the genre that you will be writing. Look at those books. Who published them? Visit your local bookstores and locate recently published books similar to the one you have in mind. The publisher's name and contact information is usually on the copyright page and/or the back cover of the book.

New authors typically say, "But there is nothing out there like my book." Then determine where your book would be placed in bookstores. What section will it be in? Go there in search of potential publishers.

## Publishing Industry Reference Books

Extend your research for appropriate publishers, their contact information and, in some cases, their submission needs and requirements by studying some of the world's most comprehensive and useful publisher reference books:

> ●*Writer's Market* is located in the reference section of your public library, for sale for around $30 in most bookstores and online for an annual fee of $29.99 at writersmarket.com. The print book is updated annually and distributed each September.

> ●*Literary Market Place* is located in the reference section of your public library. Purchase this volume for around $300 or access it online at literarymarketplace.com for $399 annually or a weekly fee of $19.95

> ●*Books in Print* is located in the reference section of your public library. You can also purchase this book or the CD or access it online at booksinprint.com. This book and the use of the database are also very expensive.

The publishing industry seems to be in a constant state of flux these days, so make sure that you access the most updated volume available. And always check the data you glean. Information in print guides can be more than a year old. Databases aren't always kept current. With every convenient resource comes the possibility of error. What is an author to do?

1: Verify publisher information by visiting the publisher's Web site.

2: Locate or request a current copy of the publisher's submission guidelines.

3: Call the publishing house for address verification or to confirm the name of an acquisitions editor.

**Publishing Industry Periodicals**
Stay on top of industry news, changes and trends through periodicals. Subscribe to *Publisher's Weekly* for around $200 per year. Or subscribe to their free daily enewsletter at publishersweekly.com. You'll find their archives at publishersweekly.com/enewsletterarchive/2286.html. Some budding authors spend an hour or so at their public libraries each month reading current issues. I strongly suggest that authors subscribe to publishing-related newsletters, as well—those newsletters that commonly report changes within the industry. This is the best way to learn about new launches and failed publishing businesses. You'll be privy to editorial changes and new contact information. Here are the newsletters I recommend:

- *SPAWNews,* a free monthly enewsletter produced by SPAWN—Small Publishers, Artist and Writers Network. (spawn.org)

- *SPAWN Market Update*, a meaty monthly online newsletter posted on the SPAWN Web site for members only. Join SPAWN at spawn.org.

- ***SPAN Connection***, a monthly print newsletter produced by SPAN—Small Publishers Association of North America—for members only. (spannet.org)

- ***PMA Independent***, a print newsletter for members of PMA, The Independent Book Publishers Association. (pma-online.org)

Join authors/publishers online discussion groups to help you stay abreast of industry trends and changes. Most are free. Visit writerspace.com, freelancewriting.com, absolutewrite.com, writer.com, writing forum.com, authorme.com. Join SPAWN ($45/year) and participate in SPAWNDiscuss and the SPAWN forum. Find others by doing a Google search.

**Tips for Locating Publishers' Submission Guidelines**
Once you have found several appropriate publishers, visit their Web sites for more specific information. Print out a copy of their *submission guidelines* (or *editorial guidelines* or *writers/authors guidelines*). Sometimes the guidelines are difficult to find. If you don't see a link button to the submission guidelines, click on "About Us" or "Contact Us." If you don't see the guidelines on either of these pages, look for a link within a link. Put your cursor on the available link buttons and see if a menu appears. Read the selections on the menus.

If you cannot locate the guidelines at all, email the editor and ask for a copy. Or send a letter of request for submission guidelines in the mail along with a self-addressed-stamped envelope (SASE). That is, an envelope with your name and full address as well as enough postage for the return trip.

**What Can You Learn From a Publisher's Web Site?**

✐ **What type of books does he publish?** Read the submission guidelines, but also look at the publisher's online catalog and see if your book idea seems to be a fit. If this publishing company is a definite possibility for your project, review some of their books as a guide to writing yours.

Be aware that publishers sometimes change their lines. I came across a publisher last week who is known for publishing adult fiction. Now they are seeking young adult fantasy manuscripts.

When I began the research necessary to revise this second edition book, I discovered many changes among publishers and have noted them throughout this book.

✒ **What is his contact information?** Go to the "Contact Us" page to find out this publisher's mailing address, phone number and email address.

✒ **What does the publisher want from you?** Does he prefer receiving a query letter first, a book proposal or the complete manuscript? Will he accept this material via email or USPS only? Is he open to receiving submissions all year around or only during certain months? Locate this information in the submission guidelines or, perhaps, on the "Editorial Page." Here, you'll get an idea about the attitude of the publishing house—does it seem author-friendly or staid and remote? The site may also give clues as to the amount and nature of promotion this company does for its authors. (See examples in Chapter Six.)

Many publishers post explicit details on their Web sites indicating the commitment they expect their authors to make with regard to promoting their books.

✒ **What's the name of the acquisitions editor?** Always address the appropriate individual when submitting your query letter or book proposal. A large publishing house may have several editors—each with a different focus. Note which editor is most suited to your project.

✒ **Who are some of this publisher's authors?** You may want to contact them and inquire about their working relationship with this publishing company.

### Tips for Using Google to Locate Publishers' Web Sites

What if you can't find a Web site address listed for this publisher? Do a Google search. Here's how:

✎ Type the name of the publishing company at the Google prompt and click the search button. If they have a Web site, their listing will generally appear on the first page.

✎ Use Google to locate additional publishers that may not appear in the resource materials you've studied. To find publishers who accept books in your particular genre and topic, type "fiction publisher," "novel publisher," "publisher dog books," "publisher fantasy," for example.

## Can You Name That Genre?

Genre is a French word for *kind, class, form* or *type*. If you're confused by what comprises a specific genre, you're in the majority. Even publishers sometimes lack unison when it comes to defining a genre.

While some say that genre is the classification of a book, others argue that it is a species within the category. One thing for sure is that there are many more types of books recognized now than ever before.

Is your book a novel, novella, romance, historical fiction or a how-to book? Is it considered commercial fiction, chick lit or true crime? Perhaps it's a young adult novel or a self-help book. As I said, more and more publishers specialize and the specialties have become even more diverse. It is sometimes difficult to define your genre, but it is important to do so in order to attract the right publisher. How would you pigeonhole your manuscript?

### Fiction Categories

*Commercial Fiction* encompasses books featuring popular contemporary issues for a general audience. Commercial fiction might include westerns, romance and mysteries. Books in this category are generally highly marketable works that interest a wide range of readers.

Look at books published by the major publishers in America. These are generally good examples of commercial or mainstream fiction. Think John Grisham and Danielle Steele.

*Literary Fiction* typically appeals to a smaller audience than does commercial fiction. Books in this category are less conventional and more creative. Not only are the stories generally more complex, the writing style is less rigid. It is said that literary fiction creates challenges for the reader instead of offering pure entertainment. Think *Da Vinci Code* and *Memoirs of a Geisha.*

*Mainstream Fiction* could describe either commercial or literary fiction if the book presents a modern day scenario relating to a universal theme. Mainstream fiction usually appeals to a more diverse audience. When you see books on the bestseller list, these are generally considered mainstream fiction. Think James Michener, Amy Tan, Carol Oats and Sue Grafton.

A *Novel* is a story featuring everyday people and encompassing at least 50,000 words. A novella is a short novel of just 7,000 to 49,000 words. Your novel or novella might be considered mainstream fiction or commercial fiction. It could also be categorized a romance, western or mystery. There are young adult novels, adventure novels, Christian novels, detective novels, gothic novels and historical novels, for example.

**Fiction Genres**
*Historical Fiction.* The author uses fictional characters to tell a story related to actual historical events. Sometimes he uses real characters and fictionalizes some of the events. St. Martin's Press publishes historical fiction, as do Pelican Publishing Co., Hill Street Press and several publishers of children's books.

*Science Fiction* features future-based plots using scientific principles and theories. Think *Star Trek.* If you're seeking a publisher of science fiction, consider Del Rey Books, Fat Cat Press and Bancroft Press.

27

*Fantasy* is a departure from reality. Publishers of fantasy include several children's book publishers and Greenwillow Books, HarperCollins, Sable Publishing and Baycrest Books.

*Romance* is considered escapist fiction by some. For the most part, romance books are formula love stories. Publishers seeking manuscripts in this genre include Barbour Publishing, Red Dress Ink, Love Inspired and Twisted Shift.

*Mystery* books usually focus on murder. Publishers include Arrow Publications, Medallion Press, Bancroft Press, Bantam Dell Publishing Group and at least one hundred others.

*Chick Lit* is a relatively new genre. Stories usually border on modern literature for and about single women. Helen Fielding's *Bridget Jones' Diary* is a good example of chick lit.

Additional genres and sub-genres include horror, thriller, techno-thriller, suspense thriller, political thriller, futuristic, time-travel and paranormal.

**Category—Nonfiction**
Nonfiction is, of course, factual—just give me the facts ma'am. Nonfiction is more widely read and there are hundreds more publishers for nonfiction than fiction books. Genres include the following:

*Creative Nonfiction* might also be referred to as literary nonfiction. It's a form of storytelling focusing on actual happenings. A memoir written with flair could be considered creative nonfiction, as might a personal essay or a biography. Those who publish creative nonfiction include New Horizon Press, Seal Press and Katco Media.

*Narrative Nonfiction* is a nonfiction account that is narrated throughout.

Your nonfiction manuscript might be classified as a how-to, self-help (or prescriptive nonfiction), humor, historical, ethnic, New Age, juvenile, reference, science or regional and the subject might be parenting, pets, medicine, gardening, hobbies or computers.

Let's say that you are writing the true story of a murder that occurred in your town in 1894. This book would probably be classified as a nonfiction true crime book. But it's also a history.

A book telling how to prune rose bushes would be considered a nonfiction how-to book on gardening.

Your book on how to be a less stressed parent is nonfiction. It is a self-help book and the subject is parenting.

Some manuscripts need further definition in order to target the right publisher. Would you contact a publisher of history books, romance stories or regional materials for your book featuring a turn-of-the-century romance set in your hometown? Maybe all three! The story of your ancestors striking it big in Nevada's silver mines might interest a publisher of memoirs, a regional publisher or a publisher of history books. Contact University of Nevada Press, Grand Canyon Association or Soho Press. If the story carries a spiritual message throughout or the miners had paranormal experiences while working the mines, you might focus on religious or New Age publishers such as Barbour Publishing or Hay House.

While several publishers produce how-to books, your manuscript might not appeal to any but the most specialized publisher. The good news is that sometimes it's possible to pinpoint your ideal publisher almost immediately, but only if you can clearly identify the category, genre and subject of your book.

Here are a few examples of publishers who specialize: BuilderBooks publishes how-to books, but only those related to home building and the construction industry. They would not be interested in seeing your book on how to teach wheelchair dancing. Nursebooks produces books on subjects related to nursing. There is a remote possibility that they would be open to your book on wheelchair dancing. Contemporary Press produces fiction only, so don't approach them with your book on how to win a decathlon, unless you decide to write a fiction story around the lifestyle of a decathlon competitor. Breakaway Books, however, might accept either of your decathlon ideas as they only publish books (both nonfiction and fiction) that relate to sports. Copper Canyon Press specializes in poetry only. DAW Books, Inc., an imprint of Penguin Putnam, publishes fantasy and science fiction. Barefoot Books is always seeking excellent children's books.

If you're still not sure how to classify your book, find books similar to the one you propose. Look on the top left corner of the back cover. Some of them have the classification (genre) and subject printed there. It might say, writing/reference, history/autobiographical or cooking. I have books in my own library with such notations as religious/philosophy, self-help/inspirational, parenting/personal finance, women's studies and just plain, fiction.

## Your ABC List of Publishers

It's unlikely that your first choice of publishers will accept your book, especially if you are a first-time author. However, it is possible and I want you to try. It has happened to me a couple of times and I've known others who have landed their first choice of publishers. The more thoroughly you research publishers and the more stringently you adhere to their guidelines and requirements, the more likely you are to receive a positive response.

## BUILD YOUR "A" LIST OF PUBLISHERS

Who is the ideal publisher for your project? Most authors start at the top of the publishing chain. And that's okay. Keep in mind, however, that few of the large publishing companies will entertain a proposal without representation by an agent. (Read how to find and select an agent in Chapter Eight.)

### Advantages of Landing a Big Name Publisher

- You pay no publishing costs.

- You are validated as an author.

- There's prestige associated with this partnership.

- Your book will most likely be available in bookstores.

- Your book has a greater chance of becoming a bestseller.

**Disadvantages of Landing a Big Name Publisher**

- You will wait for a year or more to see your book in print.

- Your book may have a very short lifespan. Typically, major publishing houses give a book a year or less to prove itself. If it isn't paying its way, they will not reprint it.

- Communication is often difficult. The company is so large that your itty bitty problem or miniscule request can become quite insignificant. Even though your contact person may ask you to pass along ideas for promoting your book, your emails and letters are often ignored.

- You have to rely on someone else to get your books to signing events on time and to send out review copies within deadline. Even the largest publishers are sometimes lax when it comes to amply supporting an author's promotional efforts.

- You are expected to help promote your book.

- You earn only a small percentage on sales.

## CREATE YOUR "B" LIST OF PUBLISHERS

Your B list might include some of the many appropriate medium and small traditional royalty publishing houses. Time spent researching these publishers is definitely time well spent.

### Advantages of Working With a Small- to Medium-Size Publisher

- You pay no publishing costs.

- You are validated as an author.

- Your book will most likely have a longer shelf life. Liguori Publications, a large publisher of Catholic books, but a relatively small publishing house, is still selling my book, *Creative Grandparenting Across the Miles*, eight years after publication. Island Heritage Publishing continues to distribute my book, *Entertaining Hawaiian Style,* after six years.

- The publisher will participate to varying degrees in promoting the book.

- The publisher may have access to important promotional avenues such as bookstore sales.

- Smaller publishers seem more loyal to their authors. Liguori has published three of my books.

## Disadvantages of Working With a Small- to Medium-Size Publisher

- The publisher is less well known—there may be minimal name recognition.

- You could wait for a year or more before seeing your book in print.

- Author/publisher communication is sometimes a problem. I hear the following complaints from authors: "She doesn't return my phone calls." "I give him promotional leads and he doesn't follow through."

- You must rely on the publisher to ship your books to a bookstore for a signing or to get copies to you in time for a book festival. I've heard from some authors who have found their publishers disappointingly unreliable.

- There's a greater chance that a new publishing company will go out of business.

- You are expected to promote your own book.

- You earn only a small percentage on sales.

## DEVELOP YOUR "C" LIST OF PUBLISHING OPTIONS

**Subsidy/Vanity/Co-Publisher**

You could pay a subsidy, vanity or co-publisher to produce your book. In most cases, you own the books and, depending on the company, you may get some assistance with promotion. Different companies offer different packages. I know of one co-publisher who becomes a royalty publisher after the author has sold 1,000 copies of his book.

**POD Publisher**

The general description of a fee-based POD publisher is a subsidy publisher that uses digital technology to produce books when you need them. The POD subsidy publisher (or fee-based POD publisher or POD partnership publisher or self-publishing company) is a popular means of book publication these days. Some POD companies try to confuse you by advertising that they are royalty publishers or that they will help you to self-publish your book. I urge authors to exercise caution when considering a subsidy publisher. I can't stress enough the importance of heads-up research before signing any publishing contract. Read Chapter Three for a more detailed explanation and evaluation of this modern day publishing model.

**Advantages of Co-Publishing or POD Publishing**

- You are guaranteed that your book will be published.

- You'll have a book in weeks rather than months or years.

- Your book stays alive for as long as you promote it.

- If you sell enough copies, you may be able to interest a traditional royalty publisher in your book.

- In the case of the POD publisher, you don't have to store boxes and boxes of books.

**Disadvantages of Co-Publishing or POD Publishing**

- It is generally costly.

- Yours may be one of the countless POD books that are riddled with errors.

- Your book won't be welcome in bookstores unless you can bring in enough customers to warrant them carrying it.

- You may be asked to sign away the rights to your book for a period of time. (One POD publisher holds your copyright for seven years.)

- You are expected to do the majority of the book promotion with very little help. What help you do request from the company will cost you.

- Some reviewers generally reject POD published books.

- Books are often priced above market value, making them difficult for you to sell.

**Self-Publishing**
You establish a company through which to produce your book. You obtain your ISBN, bar code, etc. You arrange for the page layout and cover design work. You hire a printer. You accept total responsibility for writing, producing and marketing your book. (Learn how to publish your own book in Chapter Ten.)

**Advantages of Self-Publishing**

- You'll definitely see your book in print

- You could have a product in weeks instead of months or years.

- You are in charge of every aspect of production and sales.

- You can keep the book alive for as long as you promote it.

- You have a book to show around to publishers. If it does well, you may land a royalty publishing contract. (It happened to me three times!)

- You keep all of the profits.

- You have legitimate tax breaks.

**Disadvantages of Self-Publishing**

- Self-publishing is costly (but usually not as expensive as subsidy publishing).

- You are in charge of every aspect of production and sales; promoting a book is extremely hard work.

- You are also the distributions manager, shipping clerk, PR person and bookkeeper.

- Some bookstores and book reviewers may shun your book.

- Unless you use POD printing technology, you may have to store boxes and boxes of books.

**Ebook**

An ebook is a digital book posted online for consumers to purchase and print out, download onto a handheld electronic device or read online. While some feel that ebooks are the wave of the future, others do not believe that their time has come.

I have published two ebooks and, while I like having the electronic option available for those who prefer it and for my overseas customers, I do not actually sell many ebooks. Some publishers are sold on the ebook, however. The latest reports published by the International Digital Publishing Forum (IDPF) indicate that the number of ebooks sold during 2005 was up, but that was only because there were over 5,000 new ebooks published during the year. Eighteen of the major publishers claim that, collectively, they sold over a million and a half ebooks in 2005.

**Advantages to Publishing an Ebook**

- There is no or very little cost. Generally $0-99.

- You do not have to store or ship books.

- You can make changes to an ebook at any time.

- You keep all of the profits, except for any royalties you pay to Web hosts of sites where the ebook is sold.

**Disadvantages to Publishing an Ebook**

- They are still not well received.

- You are not taken seriously as an author when you produce only ebooks. (Self-publishing of print and ebooks will be discussed in depth in Chapter Ten.)

# How to Meet a Publisher Face-to-Face

There are numerous writers' conferences, book festivals and trade shows held all over the world throughout the year. Many writers attend these events as a way to meet publishers. Attendees at a writers' conference can generally engage in a casual conversation with a publisher after his or her presentation. Some conference organizers will arrange a meeting for you with a publisher for an additional fee. This is as much to the publisher's benefit as the author's. Publishers are as eager to find good material as you are to locate a publisher for your project.

To locate conferences near you:

✐ Do a Google search. Type in "writer's (or writers') conference," "publishing conference," "writing conference," "writer's (or writers') conference California," "writers' (or writer's) conference Virginia."

✐ Check with your local arts council or writers groups for conferences held in your area.

✐ Ask your librarian for information on local writers' conferences.

✐ Keep an eye on the arts section of your local newspaper.

✐ Read writing/publishing-related magazines and newsletter. (See a list in Chapter Sixteen.)

✐ Access the Shaw Guide Directory of writers' conferences: http://writing.shawguides.com

## How to Get the Most From a Meeting With a Publisher

Your first introduction to a publisher is usually through a letter or an email. And every writing professional will advise you to make a good first impression. This is even more crucial when you have that rare opportunity to meet a publisher face-to-face. I'm not trying to make you so nervous that you faint at the mere sight of the publisher. Heaven forbid! But I strongly encourage you to give this opportunity your best shot. How?

Before the event:

✐ Find out which publishers will be at the conference.

✐ Do a little research to learn what type of books they publish and what titles they have published, lately.

✐ Prepare and practice reciting a brief description of your project. I call this your thirty-second commercial. (See pages 39-41.)

✐ Create a promo package including a brief synopsis or overview of your proposed book and information about yourself. What is your writing background, why are you the person to write this book and what is your platform? (Read more about platform in Chapter Six.) Include your complete contact information: full name, address, phone number as well as Web site and email address.

If you are at all assertive, you will most likely have the opportunity to speak, at least, informally with a publisher. If not, and you decide to send him your query letter or proposal later, mention that you attended his presentation and tell him what you gleaned from it.

## Make a Good First Impression
When you meet a publisher, be gracious and professional, not timid and desperate. Come across as a potential business partner with an excellent product, not an emotional writer who believes he has just completed the book of the century.

Every conference is operated a little differently. You might get anywhere from sixty seconds to twenty minutes with a publisher. Whether you are fortunate enough to have an *audience* with a publisher or you just happen to get a brief opportunity, the best advice I can offer is, be prepared.

The more well-prepared you are, the better your chances of talking to the publisher. And this might not occur as a planned event. Your opportunity may come about while standing in the buffet line or on the way to the airport. So be at the ready.

Why not invite the publisher to lunch or for coffee and pie after the last workshop? When I travel to other cities to speak at conferences, while there are usually people who know me, I rarely know another soul. I enjoy meeting new people and I always appreciate a lunch or dinner invitation.

When you finally manage that chance meeting with a publisher, use your time wisely. Introduce yourself and your project with clarity. Make it interesting. Describe your proposed book through your intriguing thirty-second commercial.

Initiate questions and respond succinctly. Some publishers seem to ask all of the wrong questions, such as: "Are you related to the Fry who used to live in Tucson, Arizona?" or "Did you travel all the way from California to attend this conference or were you already in the area?"

Who wants to waste time engaged in small talk when you have a book to pitch? Never fear. Just focus on your mission. And the more well-prepared you are, the more successful the exchange will be.

Before ending the conversation, hand the publisher something to take with him. Generally, this would be an overview of your book, something about you and your contact information. Keep the package small enough to fit easily into his coat pocket or her purse. You can fold 8.5 x 11 pages in half and put them in a 6 x 9 envelope or fold them in thirds and use a number10 (letter size) envelope.

Have the handout ready to hand out. Don't ruin a perfectly professional moment by rummaging through your purse or briefcase in search of the material. As I keep saying, preparation is key.

Unless you've paid for time with the publisher or you're buying him dinner, after a conversation of from three to eight minutes, thank the publisher and excuse yourself. You might stay within hearing distance, though, to glean additional information that might be passed along to others who are waiting their turn to speak to the publisher.

If you have that rare opportunity for a formal meeting with a publisher, count your blessings. You may have anywhere from fifteen to thirty minutes of uninterrupted time. This is your moment. Make it count.

You'll probably be more nervous during a formal meeting than the informal, chance meeting. But if you prepare well, you will do just fine. Remember that publishers are always looking for good manuscripts and adept, energetic, professional authors who can make them fly.

## Your Thirty-Second Commercial
Some publishing coaches recommend that authors develop a one- or two-sentence description of their book—something that they can recite should someone ask. This is a valuable exercise to help you more

succinctly define your project. It is also a good idea for those brief opportunities with a potential publisher, agent or customer. But a prepared thirty-second commercial gives you even more marketing ammunition.

Why should you develop a canned speech? While you may love talking about your book, it's not always appropriate to carry on and on about it in public. You may have limited time to make a pitch and you definitely want to make a positive impression. Think about it, don't you appreciate it when a friend or acquaintance describes a movie or provides instructions clearly and concisely rather than rambling on and on?

A short, prepared speech can be used at a class reunion or business meeting where you have snippets of time to discourse with classmates or colleagues. If you should be fortunate enough to have an audience with a publisher or even talk to a publisher on the phone, you want to be ready with a brief description of your book.

It isn't as easy as it sounds to create and rehearse a thirty-second commercial. But it is an excellent exercise. When someone asks me about my book, *The Ojai Valley, An Illustrated History*, I might say: "This is the only comprehensive history ever written about the Ojai Valley. I start the book with the geology of the valley and the native American cultures. This is an intense historical account of the valley through the 1920s, including all of the firsts: the first store, the first jail, the first train, etc. I also profile dozens of early pioneers. The book is heavily illustrated with old photographs, which makes it even more interesting." I might tell a potential publisher or customer that I spent five years conducting research for this 360-page book, which includes interviews with close to 100 people.

You may want to tweak your spiel depending on who you are talking to. In the case of the Ojai history book, if I'm speaking with a potential customer who has just purchased a business in Meiners Oaks (a rural community in the Ojai Valley), I tell her about the chapter on the development of Meiners Oaks. I might say: "Did you know that in the

1920s, developers buried gold coins to entice visitors here to look at the property? Old timers claim that some of the gold was never recovered."

For my book, *The Mainland Luau*, I might say to a publisher: "It's a guide to presenting an authentic Hawaiian luau in your own backyard no matter where you live. I've included eight different methods of cooking a whole pig and I give complete instructions for doing this. I've featured some delicious and fun authentic Hawaiian side dish recipes—some having come from the collection of an elderly Hawaiian-Japanese friend. The Chicken Hawaiian recipe was first served to me at a wedding years ago on Waikiki Beach. In this book, I show you how to make fresh flower leis, how to decorate for the party and I even give you a Hawaiian language lesson."

If given the opportunity to speak to a publisher or agent about my unpublished manuscript on fatherhood and fathering, I might say: "This book explores the history of fatherhood in America and chronicles how the different styles of fathering and fatherlessness are affecting our children today. This is a guide for loving, involved fathers and it's a wake-up call for estranged and dropout dads. This book is designed to create a lifeline to the millions of children who are suffering for the sins and the short-comings of their dads."

## How to Work a Book Festival So it Works for You

You can also meet publishers at book festivals and book trade shows. The larger the event, the more publishers in attendance. You probably won't meet major players in the publishing world at hometown book fairs and festivals. But there are almost always small to medium-size publishing houses represented at these events.

A book festival is where authors, publishers, writing/publishing organization leaders and booksellers rent booths for the day or the weekend to promote their books and themselves. It is a great place to meet publishers, and a good opportunity to network with other authors.

If you have a book in the works and you want to meet publishers at a book festival in your area, plan ahead. Learn who will be there. Find this information published in your local newspaper or online at the festival Web site. As a last resort, pick up a copy of the festival program and booth map the morning of the event. Sit down somewhere with a latte and a muffin and study the program. Read about each publisher and note those who are likely candidates for your book. If in doubt as to what the publisher produces, visit the booth and see what he's promoting. If this publisher doesn't produce books in your genre, ask him or her for references.

Visit author booths. Ask who published their books, if they like working with the publisher and how their books are selling. Sometimes an author is embarrassed to talk about book sales. A better question might be, "Are you pleased with the results of your publisher's efforts?"

A festival booth can get busy. Never lose sight of the fact that the reason this publisher or this author is there is to sell books. If you approach them to talk about your book, please be considerate of their time. I love talking with freelance writers, authors and publishers who visit my booths at book festivals. But I resent people who try to monopolize my time for more than a few minutes when there are potential customers attempting to browse.

Make contact with the publisher. State your polished and rehearsed spiel. Be prepared to respond to a few questions. Ask him or her if you can send your manuscript or book proposal. Before you exit, pick up the publisher's/author's business card or a brochure and ask if you can leave him or her some of your information.

Have your material conveniently ready. Do not slap your backpack down on the table of books and begin a thirty-minute search for each piece of your handout. Believe me, I have had more than one such individual invade my space at book festivals. How amateurish is that? Be professional. Make the transaction as smooth as possible.

When you get home, jot this publisher a note, send an email or, if you were invited to do so, send your book proposal or manuscript with a

42

note reminding him that he met you at the Austin Book Festival or the Central Coast Festival of Books.

Even though book festivals are generally rather casual events held out-of-doors, have an air of professionalism about your persona. You can dress in casual clothing and still portray a business-like appearance. How? Be neat, tidy and well coiffed. Avoid dressing in baggy sweats. Clean jeans are okay when worn with a crisp cotton shirt or blouse. Remove dark sunglasses when talking with a publisher or an author. It's impolite to keep your eyes shaded during a conversation. Lightly shaded glasses are okay. My regular glasses turn darker in the sunlight, but not dark enough to keep people from seeing my eyes.

By now, you're getting the idea that authorship is not as easy and straightforward as simply sitting down and writing a book. There are crucial decisions to be made, thus the need for the information and perspective that fill the pages of this book. As I tell hopeful authors, *publishing is not an extension of your writing.*

A major new player in the publishing game is the fee-based POD "self-publishing" service. To find out what they bring to the table, read on.

## Recommended Reading
*Writers Market*, Writer's Digest Books (a new edition is published each September).

# Chapter Three

## THE GOOD
## THE BAD
## AND THE UGLY
# FACTS ABOUT
## "SELF-PUBLISHING" COMPANIES

They are called POD publishers, fee-based POD publishers, POD partnership publishers, POD subsidy publishers and "self-publishing" companies. Who are they? Where did they come from? What do they do?

First, you should understand the distinction between POD publishers and POD technology. POD stands for print-on-demand—a digital process used to print books and other materials one product at a time. While companies using offset printing techniques generally won't take on jobs of less than 1,000 copies, those using POD technology might print as few or as many as you want—from 1 to 999 or more. Some traditional royalty and independent publishers use POD technology for their book projects. I've used POD printing companies for some of my books. The major benefits are a quick turnaround and fewer books to store. The downside is you generally pay more per book, thus decreasing your profit margin.

Russ and Kathlyn Spencer use POD services to produce their *Windshield Adventure* series travel guidebooks. Not only do they have the convenience of ordering books on an as needed basis, they can easily make editorial changes each time they place an order. When a landmark they've featured in one of their travel books burns down or a country store changes hands, for example, they can adjust their file before the next printing.

But what is a POD publisher?

## POD Publishing History

The new wave of POD subsidy publishing companies came about in the late 1990s. Before this, there were basically three ways to publish a book. You could attempt to land a traditional royalty publisher, you could use a subsidy publisher (pay to have your book published and purchase X number of copies of that book) or you could self-publish (establish your own publishing company). With the event of digital technology, a few innovative businesspersons took the print-on-demand concept and linked it with the old subsidy publishing model and started a new sort of company. Others soon followed. These forward-thinking businessmen and women began promoting the heck out of their companies and they were promptly noticed. They succeeded in opening doors for hopeful authors who might otherwise never realize their dream of publishing a book.

Within a decade, the number of POD publishing companies has increased significantly. Dehanna Bailee lists over ninety such companies in her free access POD publisher database. And I hear about new companies sprouting up nearly every month. Even the inexperienced are jumping on the bandwagon. One woman I know published her first book in 2004 and has since begun advertising her services as a POD publisher. It's scary, isn't it?

Some POD publishers advertise themselves as *royalty* publishers. Yes, they pay royalties on books sold, but only after you put up the money to have the book produced. A traditional royalty publisher does not charge authors publishing fees. Some POD publishers trick the author into believing that he is entering into a self-publishing agreement. No, no, no. Self-publishing means that you obtain the ISBN and bar code. You hire the page and cover designer. You arrange for the printer. You are in charge. It is your publishing company and you reap the benefits. The only similarity between signing with a POD publisher and self-publishing is that you are responsible for promoting, selling and distributing your books. (Read more about self-publishing in Chapter Ten.)

# Is POD Getting a Bad Rap?

As stated above, as a self-published author, you may choose to have your book printed using POD technology. Technology is improving to the point that it is becoming more difficult to tell when a book is digitally printed. POD books are continually rejected, however. Why? The poor quality stigma lives on. While the technology has improved, some POD publishing companies and self publishers are still bringing out poorly written, poorly designed books. Because of a few indiscriminant publishers, many bookstores have a policy against carrying any POD produced books and many book reviewers will not review them. Even some writers' associations won't grant membership to fee-based POD published authors.

Elizabeth Burton is executive editor at Zumaya Publications, a traditional royalty publishing house that uses POD technology. She says that the POD publishing scourge has affected her company's ability to do business. She explains, "Local bookstores refuse to even take our books on consignment for no other reason than the way they were printed. We've been told that our books lack editing—by people who not only haven't read any of them, but refuse to do so. Why? Because they believe that POD books are written by people not good enough to get a *real* publisher and are badly prepared for printing."

Burton is on a mission. She says, "I'm trying all sorts of things to persuade bookstore owners that they CAN stock one or two copies of our books and they should because ours are of comparable quality to anything they'll get from New York—and in some cases, better."

Important transitions have occurred within the publishing industry before. Maybe, with crusaders such as Burton, the POD blight will disappear.

Since POD publishing companies came into being, there have been hundreds of complaints launched against many of them. I believe this is primarily an author issue. Few newbie authors take the time and exert the effort necessary in order to truly understand the publishing industry or even a single publishing agreement. This is why I strongly advise: buyer beware—buyer be well-informed. Before entering into any publishing contract, know what to expect and what is expected of you from start to finish.

If you are contemplating hiring a POD publisher, I highly recommend that you access Bailee's database. She lists the features, services and costs of around ninety such companies. I urge hopeful authors to research a company before signing with them. Bailee makes it easy for you to make important comparisons. Go to dehanna.com/database.htm. I also recommend Mark Levine's new book, *The Fine Print,* in which he rates seventy-five of the largest fee-based, POD "self-publishing" companies.

Generally, fee-based POD publishing companies will accept any manuscript submitted to them with the possible exception of pornographic or racist material. Having your manuscript accepted by one of these companies is not necessarily a statement of its value or worth. This premise was tested once by a disappointed POD published author. She deliberately submitted an unfinished, inferior manuscript with numerous organizational flaws and blatant errors to a well-known POD publishing company and promptly received a letter of acceptance. It read, in essence, "We are happy to inform you that your wonderful manuscript has been accepted for publication with XYZ Publishing."

Fee-based POD publishers do little (and some do nothing) to promote your book. Think about it, once you've paid a fee to have your book produced, what is the incentive for the publisher to promote it? Most of them have add-on packages inviting you to pay extra for promotional services, however. One SPAWN member claims that he paid his POD publishing service $4,500 for three months of promotion. To say that he was unhappy with the results of this service is an understatement. "I didn't even break even," he laments.

According to Robert Olmsted at Dan River Press in Maine, "Anyone with a job can have a book published, but having a book published is not what authors need. Readers are what authors need. Paying a subsidy does not get an author even one reader."

> No matter what type of publisher you land, you must promote
> your own book. An author's ignorance of the book promotion
> process will keep even a good book from the public eye.

There are a wide array of publishing contracts issued by the large variety of POD publishing houses. Typically, for your money, you get an International Standard Book Number (ISBN), bar code, standard page layout and cover design package, printing and a percentage of each book sold. Generally, you will be asked for additional money if you want editing services, custom page and/or cover design, special formatting, promotional packages and the printing of any graphics and photographs as well as any corrections or changes you request.

As I said, this is a typical scenario. There are numerous creative options. I join most other professionals in saying, before you sign a contract with a POD publisher make sure that you understand it. For example, some of these contracts contain statements similar to this one: "We will make your books available to bookstores nationwide." Sounds good, right? But it is a little misleading. You'd like to think it means that your book will be shipped by the truckloads to Barnes and Noble and Borders Bookstores everywhere. What it actually means is that if a bookstore manager contacts the publisher requesting a book like yours, they would certainly tell him or her about your book. They'll fill bookstore orders, should a customer request a copy.

At least one POD publisher charges $800 extra for what he calls *returnable insurance*. The managers of this company are convincing authors that all they need in order to get their books into bookstores is proof of this returnable insurance. But, trust me, unless you do something to generate a lot of bookstore sales, your POD published book will not be available in major bookstores anywhere.

I did my own survey involving a cross section of bookstore managers to find out how valuable the returnable insurance is to an author.

Apparently, not very. While most of the managers I spoke with appreciate the *returns* concept, this is not enticement enough to sway them to accept books by authors who lack a following.

One independent bookstore owner told me that most POD publishing companies with a return policy do not pay cash money for returns, they offer credit. He said, "The last thing I want from a POD is credit."

## How Much Does it Cost?

My research shows that the price you can expect to pay for a basic package with a POD publisher averages around $800. Royalties average thirty-eight percent for retail sales/direct sales. With this in mind, you would have to sell roughly 100 copies of a $20.95 book in order to break even. According to figures from some of the most well-known POD publishers, their authors' sales average just 100 books.

Of course, your publishing experience could vary dramatically from the average. The highest price I found for the services of a POD publisher was $7,200. The cheapest is $120 and this includes ten books. This is an ideal package for folks who just want to produce a memoir for family members.

Many authors refuse to pay a POD publisher the extra fee for editing services. This is fine with me if, instead, you hire your own excellent editor. The going rate for editing services through a POD publisher is $30-$60 per hour or $5-$7 per page. Hire your own editor and you'll pay about the same. I've heard from numerous authors who were extremely disappointed with their POD publishers' editing services. One author told me that she feels she paid editing fees for proofreading skills. But her disappointment didn't end there. She was eager to have this book published without spending additional money, so she okayed the edits. She says, "When the proof copy came to me for my approval, it was full of the original errors." At this point, she had few choices— pay an additional fee to have the errors corrected or let them stand in order to meet her publishing deadline.

> Keep in mind that POD publishers aren't in the business of selling books. Their main focus is selling their services.

One of my clients decided to go with a POD publisher. At first, he was happy with the contract and the publisher. Everyone was treating him well. He sings a different tune now. He had practically single-handedly sold the first run of 1,000 copies of his book, but the publishing house was not paying the agreed-upon royalties. He said, "When it came time for them to start paying royalties, they were all of a sudden unavailable. They're breaking every clause in the contract. It has been a nightmare trying to deal with them. Thank heavens my contract is up and I can move on. But if I do, I wonder if I'll ever get paid. I figure they owed me around $6,000. They've only paid me $400, so far."

There are some excellent books produced by fee-based POD publishers—there's no doubt about that. But many of the worst books on the market also come through these channels. Let's examine who's to blame. I fault a company that produces books indiscriminately. But I also hold careless, uninformed authors responsible. It's a shame to see what these combined efforts have contributed to (or taken away from) literature. They've tainted the reputation of all POD published and self-published books.

Think about it, the many poorly written and sloppily constructed books that are being published today are creating obstacles to the success of your potentially great book. Bookstores won't handle your POD published or self-published book because of them. The major reviewers won't review your book because of them. Few people will consider your book on its own merit. If you are POD or self-published, you already have a strike against you.

## What is the Lure of the POD?

Why are so many people hiring POD publishers for their book projects? There are many reasons. Most inexperienced authors don't know how to find or approach traditional royalty publishers. Some aren't aware of the numbers of publishers seeking quality manuscripts. Others just grab the first opportunity that comes along and POD publishers are out there advertising in all of the most prominent places. Hopeful authors who notice these ads in prestigious magazines, newsletters and at the top of the Google search list, see no reason to look any further.

POD publishers make the process of publishing seem easy. This is extremely attractive to an author who has spent several months or a couple of years researching and writing a book. Suddenly, you have found someone who believes in your project, seemingly, as much as you do. And they vow to handle every detail of production for you. All you have to do is send money. Most hopeful authors find the publishing maze all too overwhelming and the POD model seems like an easy way to approach success. In the end, many authors are left feeling compromised and disillusioned. But it's not necessarily because the POD publisher did anything wrong. It has more to do with the author's ignorance and unrealistic expectations. Most authors, who are facing the world of publishing for the first time, neglect to do sufficient research.

You wouldn't enter into an investment scheme without studying your options. You don't buy a car without conducting research. Why would you invest in an unknown, unfamiliar field such as publishing without having some understanding of the industry?

One first-time author sent his novel manuscript to just six traditional royalty publishers. When he didn't receive a contract within a short time, he went a different route. He says, "I found one of the POD publishing houses online. I did not research at all. They were so very nice upfront. After they had my money, it all changed. Why did I choose this route? I had never heard of this concept before and I thought it was the answer to my prayers."

This author now has numerous complaints. He says, "They charged me $300 extra for an editor that I thought was part of the deal. She did only a mediocre job and it took her so long to complete her work that it delayed publication of my book by four weeks. They ruined my pictures, my font, my dedication page and my about me page. They left out pictures and started text half way down the page. They left blank pages in the middle of the book, they changed font style mid-sentence, they put commas in the middle of the title on the cover of the book and they put the title in quotes. The headings and footers are not coherent with the text. It's a mess. Now they want me to pay to make the corrections."

This brings up another problem among many new authors. As writers, we are usually pretty good with words. We know how to use our favorite word processing programs. But how many of us are also adept at page layout and design? There's a technique to preparing a manuscript for a printer. I don't do Adobe PageMaker. Nor do I know how to operate my Microsoft Word page design program. Since I know there are definite tried and true methods of manuscript preparation, I always hire someone to design my books and to communicate accurately and expertly with my choice of printers. I wonder how many of the numerous design problems I hear about in fee-based POD published books occur because of miscommunication and the author's lack of knowledge.

Is the POD publishing concept here to stay? Probably. But I predict that there will be fewer such companies in the future. Those companies that survive will refine and polish their services and it could also follow that bookstores, distributors and reviewers will begin accepting books on merit, not by publishing status. Well, I can dream, can't I?

POD technology will prevail as we become more concerned with saving trees. Some predict that one day you will be able to buy a book in the form of a plastic card. You'll put the card into a slot in a vending machine and a bound book will come tumbling out.

I wrote the previous paragraph in October of 2005. Eight months later, *Publishers Weekly* ran an article (written by Judith Rosen) announcing the "Espresso Book Machine," an invention designed to print and bind a 300-page paperback book with a four-color cover in three minutes. Jeff Marsh invented the machine five years ago, and it is currently being tested in three sites across the U.S. The machine installed at the World Bank in Washington, D.C., for example, is programmed to print your choice of 200 titles.

## When is POD the Right Choice?
I suggest using a fee-based POD publisher ONLY if:

- You have some understanding of the publishing industry.

- You know what is expected of you once you become a published author.

- Your project is simple—without photographs, graphs and tables, for example.

- You hire your own editor.

- You prepare the manuscript accurately for the printer and stay on top of quality control.

- You demand close communication with your company representative and stay informed each step of the way.

- You have developed a marketing plan for your book which you are willing and able to implement.

- Your book is pretty much non-publishable through traditional channels.

I met a man with a basically unpublishable project two years ago at a book festival. He was a first-time author with a novel that encompassed more than 800-pages. He asked me, "How do I find a publisher for this book?" I explained the basic process of locating a publisher and he said, "I've done that. I've even had publishers interested in my book, but they all tell me that I need to cut it down. They won't publish a book of this size by a first-time author. How can I find a publisher for my book?"

I said the obvious, "You cut it down."

He responded by saying, "I can't cut it down. That will ruin the story." And, again, he asked me to tell him how to go about finding a publisher for his novel.

This man is a candidate for a fee-based POD publisher, but I would recommend this only if he is willing to do his homework: spend at least a couple of weeks or months researching the publishing industry, study contracts from several POD publishing companies, have an intellectual properties attorney review any contract he's considering, hire an experienced editor, hire an experienced book designer and have a complete understanding of his responsibility for promoting the book.

I know some authors who use POD publishers quite successfully. One is a professional in her field and she periodically produces books related to her industry. She frequently speaks on topics within her expertise and promotes her books at the same time. She also promotes them through a company newsletter. She has accurately targeted the audience for her books and uses specific methods to reach them. When she needs a supply of books quickly and doesn't want to take on the responsibility of self-publishing, she hires a POD publishing house.

I know another author who has published four niche books through the same fee-based POD "self-publishing" company. Unfortunately, these are some of the many books produced through this channel that are extremely poorly written and designed.

Your decision to go with a POD publisher should be based on your ultimate objective for your book and/or your career. Here's your check list for deciding. Be truthful and thorough in your responses.

- What is the purpose for writing this book?

- What do you hope to accomplish with the book?

- Have you explored, evaluated and carefully considered all publishing possibilities?

- Can you make an informed decision? I strongly urge you not to make any decision until you can.

While writing is usually emotional, the decisions related to producing a book should be all business. It's when we are desperate to have our book published that we make mistakes. Lead with your head when looking at publishing options. Educate yourself. Become informed. Don't hand over your money and your future without knowing exactly what you're getting into.

## Recommended Reading:

*The ABC's of POD: A Beginner's Guide to Fee-Based Print-on-Demand Publishing* by Dehanna Bailee (Blue Leaf Publications, 2005).

*The Fine Print* by Mark Levine (Bridgeway Books, 2006).

## Chapter Four

### BITE THE BULLET
### AND

# WRITE A BOOK PROPOSAL

The first time a colleague suggested that I write a book proposal, I reacted as if she had asked me to go skydiving. I saw no reason to write a book proposal when I had a perfectly good manuscript. I didn't know what a book proposal was. Just the term intimidated me. It sounded like way more work than I was willing to do.

Since that time many years ago, I have written over a dozen book proposals of my own and I've helped write dozens more for clients.

> In today's extremely competitive publishing climate, a book proposal for a nonfiction manuscript is essential and is recommended for fiction.

### Why Write a Book Proposal?

✐ Publishers do not generally issue contracts based only on a great book idea or outstanding writing skills. The information in your book proposal helps them to more realistically evaluate whether your project is a good business investment.

✐ A well-organized, complete book proposal helps you to ascertain if you actually have a publishable book.

✐ A well-researched book proposal helps you to understand your responsibilities as a published author.

✎ A good book proposal is an extremely useful guide to writing the book.

Many a book has changed direction during the book proposal process. And this is a good thing! Forge ahead and write the book and you may miss an opportunity for success. It's through the book proposal process that you learn whether or not your great idea is truly a great idea. That's why I suggest writing a book proposal *before* writing the book.

The only possible exception to this "book proposal first" rule is the novel. If there's a story bubbling up inside you and your muse is sitting on your shoulder shouting in your ear, go ahead and write. Take advantage of every creative moment. But don't forget to consider your audience. There may be steps you can take and editorial decisions you can make to enhance your readership base while in the writing process. So it is wise to at least understand what goes into a book proposal before you start writing the book.

Once you have finished writing your marvelous story, stop. Don't fine-tune the manuscript until you've developed a complete book proposal. Why? There are many reasons, but my favorite one is the fact that, during the process of writing the proposal, you may discover ways to build promotion into your book. If you finish your story before considering possible promotional avenues, you may miss some great opportunities to create an even wider audience for your fine work. (Read more on this concept in Chapter Six.)

Publishers and agents need certain information to help them determine whether or not this book will make them some money. It may surprise you to know that not every publisher is looking for the next bestseller. Some are hoping to discover a stable, long-term product. One publisher told me during an interview last summer that he was interested in publishing books that he could be proud of.

Melvin Powers at Wilshire Book Company confided in me a couple of years ago by saying, "We are searching for books that will be successful in the marketplace. We need you to write what we can sell." But all publishers are not the same. Powers may be one of only a handful of publishers with outlets for your 60,000-word book on horsemanship, for example. Harold Carstens over at Carstens Publications wouldn't know where to begin promoting a book on horses. But bring him a book on model airplanes or railroads and he'll have plenty of valid marketing ideas.

Elder Signs Press doesn't accept nonfiction, at all. But submit a proposal for a good adventure story, mystery or science fiction book and some of your own marketing ideas and they may issue you a contract.

A book proposal is the first step in writing a book. It is through the process of writing a book proposal that you will define the scope of your book and respond to the publishers' most burning questions.

## The Query Letter—An Introduction

You may wonder, "Can't I write a query letter instead?" In a word, No! A query letter is your introduction. It's your first chance to make an excellent impression. But, I recommend creating a book proposal even before writing a query letter. Why? Most publishers, after reading your intriguing query letter, will request a book proposal. You want to have yours ready. But more importantly, the focus of your book could change during the book proposal process. Don't send a query letter for a concept that could soon become obsolete.

Why write a query letter when you have a perfectly good book proposal? There's no need to unless the publisher requests it—and most do. Some publishers receive hundreds of submissions each month. Reading a query letter consumes a fraction of the time it would take to read an entire manuscript or even a proposal. This is why most publishers prefer to screen projects through the query process.

Whether you prepare the book proposal first or last, you will, at some point, be required to write a one to two-page query letter. A successful query includes a provocative lead (whet the publisher's appetite), a brief synopsis (describe your book), a little about yourself (your writing experience, credits and expertise in the area of your book topic) and something about your platform (how will you attract readers). As a next step, the publisher will most likely either request your book proposal or pass on your idea altogether. (Read more about writing a query letter in Chapter Eight.)

## What is a Book Proposal, Anyway?

A book proposal is a business plan for your book. A well-designed book proposal is a remarkable tool for convincing a publisher of your project's worth. Think of it as a sales pitch for your book.

I know, I know, you are not a salesperson, you are a writer. And the more pride you take in your writing ability and your great idea, the more difficult it becomes to find a publisher. A publisher may not be particularly interested in how well-written your book is—at least initially. His primary concern is marketability. What is the potential for sales? Is this a good investment of his time and money? Yes, publishers are more interested in their bottom line than in your talent or, by the way, your feelings. A publisher wants to know:

- Who and how widespread is the audience for this book?

- How does your book compare with similar books?

- What makes this book different?

- How will you promote the book?

- What are your credentials (related to this topic and as a writer)?

- What is your platform—your way of attracting readers?

A book proposal is pretty much required for a nonfiction book and requested more and more often for novels, poetry, children's books and other fiction. The only exception to this rule might be if you are Hillary Clinton or if you have secret dirt on someone of celebrity status.

A book proposal is also a useful tool for you. It helps you determine whether your original focus for your book is on target or if you need to tweak it. Here's how a book proposal can help you write the book:

59

> ✎ A book proposal will tell you whether you have a book at all. If you can't write a synopsis or come up with a chapter outline, you don't have a handle on your book idea, yet.

> ✎ A book proposal will give you information about your competition. You might find that there are numerous books on raising kittens, but few featuring stories about the trials of rearing feral kittens. Armed with this knowledge, you might decide to shift your focus.

> ✎ A book proposal helps you to clarify the audience for your book and define the numbers of potential buyers.

> ✎ An effective book proposal is a guide for writing the book.

> ✎ A book proposal helps you to better understand the scope of your book so you can more succinctly and successfully pitch the book to agents and publishers, and promote it to consumers.

> ✎ Through the book proposal process, you will become more educated about the publishing industry.

The first book proposal is the hardest one to write. Once you break through the barriers of fear, insecurity and lack of knowledge, you've created the mold and future proposals will go together more easily.

While I always recommend writing a book proposal, and it is standard for publishers to request a book proposal, especially for a nonfiction book, there are publishers who will cut to the chase and ask for the complete manuscript. This is why I and other publishing professionals will tell you to always get a copy of publishers' submission guidelines. And comply with them. (For a complete guide to obtaining and using publishers' submission guidelines read Chapter Eight.)

## The Nonfiction Book Proposal
A nonfiction book proposal consists of the following:

- Cover letter. (Generally, one page.)

- Title page. (One page.)

- Table of contents. (One or possibly two pages.)

- Synopsis or overview. (One and a half to around four pages.)

- Marketing section. (Who is your target audience?) Two to four paragraphs.

- Promotional ideas. (How do you suggest this book be promoted and what will you do to promote it?) Two to six paragraphs.

- Details about your platform. (How widespread is your following— people who know you as an expert in your field or as an author? What promotional activities do you have in place?) Use as much space as it takes. Impress the publisher.

- Market analysis or comparison of competitive works. Compare your manuscript with five or six books. (One or one and a half pages.)

- About the author. (What makes you the best person to write this book?) One to three paragraphs (Be sure to add your list of published books and books in the works).

- Chapter summaries. Approximately 100-400 words per chapter.

- Sample chapters (if requested).

- Samples of illustrations, photographs, etc. (if appropriate).

## How to Write a Book Proposal for a Novel

There are fewer parts to a fiction book proposal. You will include:

- Cover letter. (Generally, one page.)

- Title page. (One page.)

- Synopsis or overview. (Two to four pages.)

- Promotional plan, including your platform.

61

- About the author.

- Endorsements (Some publishers request endorsements—testimonials about your proposed book from experts in the field or, in the case of a novel, experienced and well known authors.)

- Sample chapters, if requested, or first 100 pages.

## Presentation and Formatting

While it might be tempting to fancy up your book proposal so it stands apart from the rest of those in the perceived slush pile, most professionals advise against this. You want your book proposal to stand out from the others, but your focus should not be on packaging. The way to get the publisher's attention is with a professional presentation, not frills and fireworks.

Christine Holbert of Lost Horse Press told me during a recent interview, "Forget everything you've been told about creative packaging for your manuscript (or book proposal); when I receive a manuscript tied with ribbons and flowers and lollipops, my first reaction is to throw it vigorously out the window. Do, however, send a neatly typed, double-spaced, clean, uncrumpled manuscript along with an SASE."

Use plain white 8.5 X 11 paper, typed, double-spaced on one side of the page. Some experts suggest double-spacing every page of a print book proposal except the synopsis. I single-space lists: listings of my published books and books in the works, for example. And, of course, the cover letter is single-spaced. For greater reading ease, use 12-point Times New Roman and leave 1 to 1 ½ inch margins.

I'm not one to get too stressed about something as seemingly unimportant as the size of the margins and how far down the text starts. These preferences may vary from publisher to publisher, anyway. The point of these picky requirements is so that the finished product is easy for the publisher to read. Too much space around the text may mean an unnecessary number of pages. Too little margin space makes for an unattractive, cluttered, difficult-to-read page.

I was shocked to learn recently that some people are still submitting handwritten manuscripts. A publisher told me that she receives one every few months. And just today, I received an email from a woman asking me if she could send her handwritten manuscript to a publisher. Now I know why publishers still state on their submission guidelines what seems obvious to most authors—"typed, double-spaced," etc.

While it is okay to use a paperclip or a binder clip to hold the pages of a book proposal together when submitting it, publishers do not like staples or three-ring binders. A box is okay for a large (100-page or so) proposal. Otherwise, use one paperclip or binder clip to hold the entire proposal. Do not separate and clip the various sections.

Number the pages. It is also a good idea to type your name and the title of your book at the top left hand corner of each page. This helps the publisher to keep all sections of your proposal together.

Make a neat and organized presentation. Do not paste Post-it notes all over the proposal with arrows for the publisher to follow. Do not write in the margins and do not draw on the pages of the book proposal.

Your primary concern in preparing a book proposal is that you conform to the form and style that the particular publisher has requested and that it is presented in the most convenient mode possible.

Some publishers prefer to receive proposals via email. Before clicking "send," check their submission guidelines. Does the publisher want the proposal embedded in the email or sent as an attachment? I single-space email proposals. I also use a font and a type size that is easy to read. Recently, I received a manuscript from a potential client as an email attachment and I promptly returned it with a note of reprimand. She used purple type on a mauve-colored background and it was difficult to read. Take pity on those of us who spend our days staring into the computer or reading reams of manuscript pages.

## How to Write a Cover Letter

The cover letter identifies and introduces your book proposal package. Use your letterhead. If you don't have letterhead, type your name and contact information at the top of the page. Include your Web site address (if applicable to your writing skill and/or the topic of your book). Date the letter and address it to the appropriate editor/publisher. (Read more about approaching a publisher in Chapter Eight.)

Your cover letter should:

- be single-spaced.

- remind the publisher if he/she requested your proposal.

- describe your book in one or two paragraphs.

- introduce you as the author and include a brief list of your qualifications for writing this book. (Or mention that this information is included on page eight, for example, of the proposal.)

- say whether the manuscript is completed or not. If not, what is the projected delivery date? (When do you think you could submit the complete manuscript?)

- ask for what you want—"Please review the book proposal and let me know if you would like to see sample chapters or the complete manuscript."

- be signed by you.

- note enclosures by listing each part of the book proposal. Or provide a separate table of contents with page numbers.

## <u>Sample Cover Letter</u>

Today's Date

Acquisitions Editor Name
Publishing Company
Address
City, State, Zip

Dear Mr. (or Ms.) Name:

Per your request of June 10, 2002, I've enclosed my proposal for *Hope for Parents and Teens: Stop Bickering and Start Understanding.*

As you will notice, this book is for both parents and teens. Parents will read it from the front cover to the middle and their teens turn the book over and read from the back to the middle.

Within the pages of this book, I'll provide information that will help parents understand what is happening with their teens biologically, hormonally, physically, emotionally and intellectually. I'll discuss the value of communication and, with counsel from family life experts, guide parents in how to keep the lines of communication open with their teens. I'll provide exercises that will help parents to honestly recall who they were in their teen years so they can better understand the needs and desires of their teen. For example, while parents are concerned with raising well-adjusted, well-rounded, productive offspring, their teens are focusing pretty much exclusively on their social life, school, having fun and exhibiting the proper image to their peers.

I'll help the teens to understand at least some of what's going on from their parents' point of view. I'll offer them ways they can help make their transition from child to adult less traumatic for everyone, especially themselves. Teens should realize first that they are loved and wanted. They need to know that parents also have feelings and fears. I'll suggest that they take more responsibility in the decision-making process by asking themselves, "What do I want in my life? What sort of life do I want as an adult?" If he's honest, he'll realize that 99.9 percent of the time his answer is the same as that of his parents, thus so will his decision about, for example, whether or not to have pre-marital sex, try drugs, hang with a particular group of kids, etc.

I expect this book to meet your Submission Guideline requirements of 50,000 words. I have three chapters written and can send you the complete manuscript by December of this year.

Please let me know if you're interested in seeing more.

Sincerely,
Patricia L. Fry
matilijapress.com
Encls: Book Proposal (Author Credits included in Book Proposal)

## The Title Page

Include a title page similar to a title page in a published book. Type the title of the book centered about one-third of the way down the page. Below that, type, "by" and your name. At the bottom of the page, type your projected word count.

Okay, I know what you're thinking, "Hey lady, how do I know the number of words I will have until I write the book?" This brings up another of your responsibilities—determining the appropriate word count for the type of book you're writing based on the publisher's requirements.

Here again, you need to read publishers' guidelines. Generally, a nonfiction book encompasses 60,000 to 100,000 words or 240 to 400 typed pages. However, while one publisher won't publish anything over 60,000 words, another might want at least 90,000 words. There are publishers who produce series of booklets encompassing just 120 pages while another might publish only substantial hardcover books of 300 pages or more.

When double-spacing and using 1 ½ inch margins, you can figure approximately 250 words per typed page. Your 195-page manuscript is going to run around 48,000 words. If you need 60,000 words, you'll have to come up with around 240 pages.

Change the projected number of words on your book proposal according to the guidelines of the particular publisher you are contacting. If ABC Publishing is looking for novels of between 60,000 and 80,000 words, estimate your projected word count at around 75,000. If this is the publisher who requests your manuscript, you will write it to conform.

## Steps to Selecting a Perfect Title
A title is extremely important so take your time in choosing one.

> While intriguing titles sell novels, a nonfiction title should define the book.

Anyone seeing a copy of my 360-page book, *The Ojai Valley, An Illustrated History*, knows that it is a comprehensive history of the Ojai Valley and that it is illustrated with old photographs.

The title for my book, *The Mainland Luau*, may not conjure up accurate images. Add this subtitle and it becomes more concise: *How to Capture the Flavor of Hawaii in Your Own Backyard*. When Island Heritage took over the publication of this book, they simplified the title: *Entertaining Hawaiian Style*. The subtitle is: *The How-to Book of Hawaiian Luaus*.

I like most of my book titles, but I really missed the boat with one of them. While I was writing my true metaphysical adventure, I came up with what I thought was a gang buster, dynamite title: *Quest for Truth, a Journey of the Soul*. A few people tried to talk me out of it, but I stubbornly stuck to my convictions. I thought this title was intriguing and even descriptive. If I can ever sell the remaining 1,000 copies of this fascinating book, I will reprint it with a new title.

FYI, this book tells the story of my experiences working with a hypnotist who used hypnosis and past-life regression therapy with his clients. I was commissioned to write a book about his work. In the process, I succumbed to hypnosis, I experienced what seemed to be some of my own past-lives and I participated in incidents of instantaneous healing. Before I could write his book, the hypnotherapist died and years later, I decided to write my own story.

Better titles for this book might be, *Days of Our Past Lives, Who's Waiting For You on the Other Side?* or *How I Changed My Life Through Hypnosis.*

When contemplating your title, think about the audience you want to attract. Let's say that your book features the practice of dressing dogs. Yes, there are people everywhere who purchase large wardrobes for their dogs and delight in dressing them for outings and occasions. If you want to attract people who already dress their dogs and people who might if they knew more about it, *Doggie Dress-Up* is probably a good title. If your book is a collection of stories about Hollywood celebrities who dress their pets, you could call it, *The Best Dressed Dogs in the West*

The working title for the book you are reading is, *The Right Way to Write, Publish and Sell Your Book.* It is a bit long and maybe a tad misleading. This is definitely more than a guide to being published. It is more than just a book on book promotion. It is designed to walk hopeful authors through the process of publishing and beyond. Some might think it is just for those who want to self-publish, however.

*Write Right* is a nice title, but it implies grammar and writing techniques more than publishing. What about, *How to Get Noticed in Today's Publishing Climate?* Naw, there's so much more to producing a book than just finding a publisher. I'm now thinking about a new title. What about, *A Guide To Successful Authorship?* Readers, you may have just witnessed a moment of creation.

Protect yourself. Before writing your title in stone, check book titles that are already in use. This ought to be fairly easy now with the advent of the Internet and our friend Google. You can do a quick search at amazon.com. But the best gauge of what's in print and what's soon to be in print are current editions of *Books in Print* and *Forthcoming Books in Print.* Both of these volumes are generally found in the reference section of your local public library. Or you can pay to view the most updated version of these volumes online. (See Chapter Sixteen.)

You may also want to check your perfect title to make sure it hasn't been trademarked. When I wrote *Creative Grandparenting Across the Miles,* my working title was *Long-Distance Grandparenting.* The publisher changed the title. When he sent review copies to my list of resources—those organizations and individuals who had provided some of the material for the book—he got a surprise. One of the organizations was known as *Creative Grandparenting* and, in fact, they had trademarked that name. I don't know what sort of deal the publisher made in order to continue using the title, but I guess we're lucky that we didn't have to destroy all of the books and start over with a new title.

## Titles for Fiction Books

Novelists have more creative license when it comes to selecting a title. However, I still recommend that you consider your readers. You, too, want to attract the appropriate audience. If yours is a mystery, include the word *mystery* in your title or subtitle. If it falls under the chick lit category, use a title or subtitle indicating that this is a girly story. How? Presumably your book features issues of interest to women—romance, comfort food, buying and owning shoes, dating men and so forth. Make sure that this is evident in the title. Here are some titles for current chick lit books: *The Guy I'm Not Dating, The Secret Life of Becky Miller, Undomestic Goddess* and, let's don't forget, *Bridget Jones' Diary.*

Some authors of historical fiction include a date in their title to show the era. Or they use terms signifying a historical time period. Others use subtitles to show genre. For example, *Queen Helene: A Historical Novel Set in England* or *Grossmont Heights: A Historical Fiction Novel.*

Study the titles of bestselling novels to get some ideas for your book. I think you'll notice that novels with unusual, catchy or intriguing one-

or two-word titles seem to fare well. For example, *The Broker, Predator, True Believer* and *Mary, Mary.*

## Now Create a Magnificent Synopsis

A synopsis is an overview of your book. This is where you describe your story or the theme and purpose of your book in one to four pages. What kind of book is this? What is your book about? What is the focus and scope of your book? Why did you decide to write the book? Who will be interested in this book? (Use statistics.) What proof do you have that there's an audience for this book? What makes your book different/interesting? Will you include expert quotes? Who are your experts? (If there are many experts, list a few of them in the synopsis and type the rest of them on a separate page.)

If the task of compiling a synopsis seems a bit overwhelming, try writing a one or two-sentence description. A brief sentence or two description might give clarity and spark ideas for the synopsis. Some authors discover their descriptive sentence only after writing the synopsis. Which one should come first? It's the old chicken and egg question all over again. I suggest writing the one that comes easiest for you.

### The One-Sentence Challenge

Here are some examples of one- and two-sentence descriptions:

*Over 75 Good Ideas for Promoting Your Book.* A collection of low and no cost ideas for promoting your traditionally published or self-published book. (By Patricia Fry, Matilija Press.)

*Fatherhood and Fathering, The Ultimate Guide for Today's Dads.* This book explores fatherlessness in America and its affect on our youth. It is also a guide for all fathers who want to be the best dad they can be. (Patricia Fry's unpublished manuscript)

*A Year of Sundays* is the true story of my year-long travels through Europe with my blind wife and our cat. (By Edward D. Webster, VanderWyk and Burnham Publishers)

*Ma Duncan,* a true crime featuring an uncommonly evil woman whose incestuous relationship with her son impelled her to have her daughter-in-law and unborn grandchild killed. (By James Barrett, Pentland Press)

It's not always easy to describe your book in one or two sentences. But this task will serve you in four important ways:

1. It will help you to focus on the scope of your book.

2. It will become the theme for writing your synopsis.

3. It may help you to decide upon a title and/or subtitle.

4. It will be extremely useful in the promotion of your book.

What can you say in one sentence that describes your book? If you can't describe your project in one or two sentences, you probably don't have a handle on the topic of your book. I suggest that you spend some time researching books similar to the one you have in mind and try to determine an angle or aspect that hasn't been covered.

Note: Keep these books in mind to use in your market analysis later in the book proposal process.

Some inexperienced authors try to cover too many aspects in their books. I met a woman this week who has written the story of her son's illness and death. The book includes information and tips for parents of terminally ill children and it provides a guide for parents who are grieving the loss of a child. She is confused as to how to describe her project to a publisher.

I suggested that she streamline her book. She might gear it toward parents who are caring for a terminally ill child–what to expect and how to cope, for example. She might write a book on grief and grieving for parents. These would be self-help or how-to books. If she wants to write a memoir, that should be the primary focus of the book.

**Let's Write That Synopsis**
A synopsis is like a book in that it has a beginning, middle and end. Your synopsis is generally the next thing a publisher sees after your query letter. Imagine this: He has opened the book proposal package, tossed aside your cover letter, title page and table of contents. You

now have your second best shot at attracting his attention and convincing him that your book is a great idea. Here's a guide to organizing a synopsis:

Get the publisher's attention with the first sentence. In my book proposal for *Youth Mentoring, Sharing Your Gifts With the Future*, I wrote:

> The statement, "It takes a whole village to raise a child" was never more true than today. More children come from broken homes. They spend more time either in daycare or home alone while their parents work. Fewer children have the day-to-day support of extended family members. And neighborhoods lack the networking systems that once helped to keep our youngsters safe.

Give facts and data to illustrate the value of the project. In the youth mentoring synopsis, I wrote:

> According to the Department of Labor, in 1995, nearly 70 percent of all mothers with children under the age of 18 worked. Over 62 percent of mothers with children under 6 work. America's young children are spending a lot of time in daycare. They're being raised by someone outside the family—learning the values of virtual strangers.
>
> A recent study reveals that 84 percent of children by the age of 6 have spent time in some form of daycare. The same study declares that the more time kids spend in daycare, the more aggressive they become and the more behavior problems they have.
>
> When these children reach the age of 8, 9 or 10, they become latchkey kids. Do you know how latchkey kids typically spend their afternoons? Safely locked inside their homes watching TV or playing video games and eating junk food. The result is a decline in the overall fitness of our children and an increase in childhood obesity. According to a recent study, 22 percent of children between

the ages of 12 and 17 are considered obese. What they're feeding their minds is another matter that obviously needs attention.

Those children who are allowed to roam the neighborhood after school without adult supervision are at risk of getting into trouble. The fact is that more vandalism, shoplifting, underage drinking, drug use and other crimes perpetuated by the younger set occur between 2 and 6 p.m. on school days.

Demonstrate the depths of your research. For example:

For this book, I'll interview the directors of the National Mentoring Partnership, Mentoring USA, Committed Partners for Youth, I Have a Dream Foundation, Mentor Consulting Group, Ojai Valley Youth Foundation Mentoring Program, One-to-One Mentoring, Big Brothers Big Sisters of America and about two dozen others. I've already received permission from the Search Institute to publish their 40 Developmental Assets and the results of their most recent national study.

Outline the contents of the book. What is the point of it? What do you hope it will accomplish? Will it teach, provide comfort, inform, educate, inspire? In my youth mentoring book proposal I wrote:

The bottom line is that America's children are in crisis and we can help by becoming formal or informal mentors. This book is for those adults who are already mentoring a child either formally or informally and want more information, support and help in their endeavor. It's for the educator, religious leader and community leader who want to do more to help children and need additional guidance. It's for those who are ready to give something back to society and want to do it through our children. It will assist folks who already spend time with their grandchildren or kids in the neighborhood and who want additional inspiration and ideas for successful mentoring. And it's for those who, perhaps, see a problem developing with children in their community or neighborhood and they want to get involved but don't know how. This book is for every adult who cares about kids.

What are the highlights of your book? Most books, whether fiction or nonfiction, have a climax or an important feature. Maybe your novel tells the story of two women from different ethnic groups and societal status who find themselves held hostage together in a war-torn country. The highlight of this story might be the deep regard and respect they develop toward one another, though they formerly resented and, in fact, hated such peoples before their capture. Be sure to clarify this in your synopsis.

Assume that the publisher is ignorant of the topic you are presenting. And in some cases he/she is. For the *Doggie Dress-up* book, for example, tell him what percentage of the $31 billion pet industry comprises clothing and grooming aids for dogs and how many dog owners dress up their pooches. Let the publisher know that you have done your homework.

For help in locating information and statistics, read the section on research tips and techniques in Chapter Nine of this book.

## Sample Synopsis

For the book that you're reading.

> Authorship is a whole body, mind and spirit experience. Most authors tap into the spirit—they write from the heart. They cannot expect to pursue publishing using the same process. They must strive to understand the industry and be willing to go into business mode. And so I profess that the first step in writing a book does not start at the keyboard.

Nearly 81 percent of America's population believe that they have a book in them. More and more of these people are actually producing books. In 1999, it was estimated that there were over 6 million manuscripts being circulated to publishers. Only a small percentage of them were published. Around 120,000 books were published last year.

Yes, there is a lot of competition. But there are also more opportunities. An estimated 8,000-11,000 new publishing companies are launched each year—some of them are eager to produce your book for a fee. New small and independent publishing companies are also on the rise. They are reported to be 50,000 strong. Of the 1.8 million books currently in print, 78 percent of them are from small and independent publishing companies. And what's to stop them?

Technology is certainly in their favor. Anyone who can type can produce a manuscript. And with self-publishing so convenient and inexpensive, the opportunities for wannabe authors are boundless. Most new authors, however, go about the process of producing a book all wrong.

The book I propose is designed to nudge the hopeful author toward success by educating, informing and coaching him, thus changing his approach to writing, publishing and selling a book.

Many new authors are happy to pay POD publishers to produce their books, but most are greatly disappointed in the results. Note: A fee-based POD publisher is a subsidy publisher who produces your book digitally—a purveyor of publishing services, if you will. They produce your book complete with the necessary ISBN, bar code, etc. for a fee. The POD publisher differs from the POD printer, who simply prints your book for a fee. Many publishers use POD printers for small runs.

How effective are fee-based POD publishers? According to my research, less than four percent of books published through POD companies sell more than 500 copies. In fact, the average author sells between 80 and 100 copies and collects a total of around $111.

Books produced by POD publishers are often inferior in quality and over-priced, thus extremely difficult for the author to market. If the author lowers the price to make the sale, he compromises his profits.

I know of a few experienced authors who use fee-based POD publishers and I don't have a quarrel with that. These professionals understand the publishing industry and they have a marketing plan in place. They simply want a supply of books without the responsibility of self-publishing.

It's the inexperienced authors who concern me. They are generally overwhelmed by the concept of publishing. They're confused and they're eager to see their book in print. The promise of help, guidance and hand-holding through it all is mighty tempting, even if there is a price tag attached. My primary gripe with these all-inclusive publishing contracts is that the author walks away as uninformed as when he started. The POD published authors that I meet have no sense of intimacy with their books. They still know nothing about the publishing process. And now they're stuck with an (often) over-priced book with less than professional packaging and no clue as to how to promote the darned thing. Bookstore owners won't stock it, it's next to impossible to set up a book signing and don't even think about contacting Oprah. What is an uninformed author to do?

*The Right Way to Write, Publish and Sell Your Book* will explain the book promotion concept and provide a treasure trove of promotional ideas for the timid author, the assertive author and every author in between.

A second step for many unsuccessful POD published authors is to hire someone to help pull them out of the quagmire. Some join organizations in hopes of getting marketing help. While many of the organizations and agencies have the information and resources they need, these authors aren't accustomed to researching on their own behalf. They reach out for help, but often discount the help they receive. They aren't prepared to take the steps necessary. I can't tell you how often I respond to desperate authors who are hungry for an easy way out. They want to sell their books in order to recoup their money and they don't want to lift a finger to do it.

Throughout this book, I'll strive to help hopeful authors understand the publishing business, because education is going to save them a lot of money and heartache. I will help them to establish realistic expectations and guide them in taking the right steps and choosing the right path. I will also talk about the consequences of making unwise publishing decisions.

As I said, writing is not the first step in producing a book. While reviewing my chapter outline, you'll notice that I suggest several steps before the writing begins. The writer must know if there is a market for his book. He must recognize whether or not his idea is a valid one. A hopeful author needs to understand his competition. I'll explain how to search for and recognize the hard facts.

Of course, an author can do whatever she wants with the information she gathers during the research phase, but she must be aware of the consequences of her decision. Here's where expectations come in.

I advise having a publisher in mind before starting the book. You may not land that publisher, but if you are focusing on the most appropriate publisher from the beginning, the direction of your project is probably correct.

This book will include four jam-packed chapters on writing a book proposal. My research stems from my own experiences as well as the research I've done over the years via interviews with publishers and reading books such as, Herman and Adams' *Write the Perfect Book Proposal* (Wiley). I have written numerous articles on this subject and I just produced a 72-page book based on a book proposal course I developed last summer. The book is called, ***How to Write a Successful Book Proposal in 8 Days or Less.***

As you will notice when reviewing the chapter outline, I don't talk about writing the book until Chapter Nine. I offer a segment on organizing your book—a skill that escapes many authors. And we'll touch on writing ability. Writing is complex and can be difficult. It takes skill, talent and an ability to focus. Many more people write books than can write good books. And, of course, some good books go unnoticed because of ignorance about book promotion.

While this book is designed for the hopeful author, the once or twice published author and even the experienced author will also benefit from the wisdom and expertise within these pages.

## About the Author—That's You!

The publisher wants to know who you are, what is your level of writing experience and what makes you the best person to write this book. This section typically encompasses anywhere from a paragraph to a page or so. I usually single-space this section because I list my previously published books and my books in progress. Lists work better when single-spaced.

If you have expertise in the topic of your book, mention that first. For example: "I've been playing doggie dress-up with my terriers for ten years." Or "I'm one of about thirty-five people in the United States who makes and sells clothing for dogs." Or "I earn my living as a groomer specializing in costuming and creative grooming for dogs."

Talk about your writing experience, especially where pertinent to this topic. You might say, "I've been writing articles for pet magazines and industry trade magazines for about five years, having been published in *Pet, Dog, Fancy Dog,* and in several online newsletters and Web sites. I write my own monthly print newsletter, *Dressing Doggie* for the doggie dress-up community."

Of course, the publisher wants to know about any previously published books. List each title, publisher, date of copyright (include every edition of each book) and add a little description.

List your books in progress to illustrate that the well isn't likely to run dry with this project. If this book is successful, the publisher wants to know that you can make a repeat performance. You never know when information like this is going to bring unexpected results. I've had publishers turn down the book I was pitching and ask to see proposals for books on my list of works in progress.

## About the Novelist

If the book you are pitching is fiction, you'll need to take a slightly different approach in your About the Author section. You'll need to convince the publisher that you can write. Tell him if you have expertise in the topic or genre of your book. You'll also want him to know that you understand and can meet deadlines, that you are flexible and easy to work with and that you are able and willing to promote your book. How do you assure him of your worth? Mostly by example.

Rather than telling the publisher that you are a great writer, prove it. Instead of promising that you will be an asset to his stable of authors, illustrate some of your past and current publisher or editor/author-relationship successes. Tell him about the ebook that RST Publishing produced in 2005 and the fact that you've sold 1,500 copies. Reveal your ongoing work with two well-known fantasy magazine editors over the last five years. Explain the positives that make up your platform— your way of reaching your particular audience. Perhaps you write a regular column for a fantasy newsletter, you have a slot on a well-known radio station or you travel frequently on business and could use this opportunity to promote your book throughout the U.S., for example.

If your story features someone with Down's syndrome and you have a daughter with Down's, tell the publisher this. Maybe your story is set in a major law firm and you worked for such a firm for many years. Let the publisher know this. He or she is interested in whatever you can bring to the table in the way of writing talent, contacts, knowledge and promotional savvy.

Based on my research in 2005, roughly half of all publishers of novels wanted to see a query letter first. One-quarter were asking for the complete manuscript and another quarter were adamant about your preparing a book proposal. I notice that more and more publishers of fiction are now requesting book proposals.

Note: The general rule of writing says to spell out one- and two-digit numbers. I use numerals freely in query letters and book proposals, however, in order to more readily catch the publisher's eye.

## Sample, About the Author
From the book proposal for this book.

> I've been writing for publication for over 30 years, having contributed hundreds of articles to about 190 different magazines. My articles have appeared in *Writer's Digest, Authorship, Writer's Journal, Freelance Writer's Report, Canadian Author, The World and I, Entrepreneur Magazine, Pages, Cat Fancy, Los Angeles Times, Kiwanis Magazine, Your Health, The Artist's Magazine* and many others. My

writing/publishing-related articles, to date, number around 200.

I'm the author of 22 books. (See list of published books and works in progress next page.)

I'm the president of SPAWN (Small Publishers, Artists and Writers Network), a nine-year-old networking organization. I work with clients on their writing projects. I've done editing for clients, writing, book proposal writing, promotion consultations and I've helped clients find publishers for their projects. One book proposal client just landed a contract with Houghton Mifflin. The editor there said that it was her outstanding book proposal that convinced them to acquire the book.

I teach online classes. My seminar topics include Book Promotion 101, How to Write Articles for Magazines, How to Write a Book Proposal and self-publishing topics. (See the list of the conferences in which I've participated in the Marketing Section, Page 5.) I also work with young writers. Earlier this year, I led a group of 12 homeschoolers in an 8-week course that resulted in a 136-page published book of their works which the students also designed.

I write the monthly SPAWN *Market Update* for the SPAWN Web site. Through this 8- to 14-page newsletter, I report on industry news. In order to stay current, I must be constantly in research mode—aware of trends and events. I also interview publishers and agents. I've completed 46 editions of the Market Update, to date.

While I have written on a number of topics over the year, there is nothing that I know better or love more than the subject of writing and publishing. It's obvious that I'm the right person to write this book. Not only does it include material that I know, but I have numerous contacts with other experts and the ability, contacts and energy to promote this book through a number of appropriate channels.

## Patricia Fry's Published Book Titles

*Hints For the Backyard Rider* – A.S. Barnes, 1978 (out of print)
*The Ojai Valley: An Illustrated History* (a 360-page comprehensive local history) – Matilija Press, 1983; $2^{nd}$ printing (revised) 1999.
*Nordhoff Cemetery*: Book One, Matilija Press, 1992
*A Thread to Hold, The Story of Ojai Valley School* (a 325-page comprehensive history of a local, world-known, 80-year-old private school) – Fithian Press, 1996
*The Mainland Luau: How to Capture the Flavor of Hawaii in Your Own Backyard* – Matilija Press, 1996; $2^{nd}$ printing, 1997 ($3^{rd}$ printing by Island Heritage)
*Entertaining Hawaiian Style* – Island Heritage Publishing, 1999
*Quest For Truth, A Journey of the Soul* – Matilija Press, 1996
*Creative Grandparenting Across the Miles, Ideas for Sharing Love, Faith and Family Traditions* – Liguori Publications, 1997.
*A Writer's Guide to Magazine Articles for Book Promotion and Profit* – Matilija Press, 2000.
*Over 75 Good Ideas for Promoting Your Book* –Matilija Press, 2000
*Write On! Journal-keeping for Teens* – Liguori Publications, July, 2001.
*Nordhoff Cemetery: Book Two,* Matilija Press, 2002
*The Successful Writer's Handbook* – Matilija Press 2002. An ebook featuring Fry's best writing-related articles.
*The Successful Writer's Handbook* – Matilija Press, 2003. Revised book published in print.
*Young Writer's Handbook* – Matilija Press, 2003
*Youth Mentoring, Sharing Your Gifts With the Future* – Liguori Publications, 2004.

Plus several private and corporate-generated publications

Note: Matilija Press is the author's own publishing company.

<u>**Patricia Fry's Books in the Works:**</u>

*Fatherhood and Fathering: The Ultimate Guide For Today's Dad.* This book is complete.

*The Grandparent's Survival Guide.* A book for the millennium grandparent.

*Hope For Parents and Teens: Stop Bickering and Start Understanding:* A unique book of hope for both parents and teens—parents read it from the front to the middle and the teen turns it over and reads it from the back to the middle.

*The Inner Vacation: How to Go Away and Return Really Refreshed and Recharged.*

*Alone But Not Lonely:* Keys to Healthy, Happy, Solitary Living. Shift Your Life to the Next Level Through Your Own Creativity: A guide to living in the now.

*Write From the Heart: Journal to Find Your True Path*

*7 Stages of Writing. From Infatuation to your Final Chapter*

While the query letter is your foot-in-the-door, the book proposal is the deal maker (or breaker). And you're not finished yet. In fact, you've just scratched the surface of the professional book proposal.

## Recommended Reading:

*Write the Perfect Book Proposal* by Jeff Herman and Deborah M. Adams, (John Wiley and Sons, Inc., 2nd edition, 2001).

## Chapter Five

### WRITE

# THE RIGHT BOOK
## FOR THE RIGHT AUDIENCE

You've described your wonderful book. Now you need to convince the publisher that there's a market for it—that it is a sound financial investment. The publisher wants information about the commercial merit of your book and he needs facts and figures, not your uninformed opinion or wishful thinking.

While there's no crystal ball to tell us which books will sell and which won't, there are techniques and tools for determining whether or not a particular book might have a future. We can guestimate by watching trends. The Association of American Publishers (AAP) comes out each year with a report on industry net sales. And they even break sales into categories.

If you are currently planning a book, you might consider writing a children's or young adult hardcover book as, according to a report by the AAP, sales were up thirty-one percent during the first part of 2007. And religious book sales were up by thirty-three percent. Both of these categories have been strong in the market for several years. Keep an eye on book sales by visiting the Association of American Publishers at publishers.org.

## Choose a Marketable Topic

Tom and Marilyn Ross are cofounders of SPAN (Small Publishers Association of North America) and coauthors of thirteen books including: *The Complete Guide to Self-Publishing* and *Jump Start your Book Sales*. Marilyn is also CEO of the Web site, SelfPublishingResources.com. They wrote in an article published in a 2002 edition of SPANet, "The first and most important step any potential businessperson takes is to decide what product or service to offer customers. Whether you're an author or publisher, you must determine your 'vehicle.' Some forms of writing hold more promise for commercial success than others."

I believe that many authors miss this important point. We don't think our projects through thoroughly enough. We just launch out and trust that everyone will love our book as much as we do. I have no problem with an author following his/her passion. Write the book that's in your heart. Enjoy the process. But if you hope to make money on that book, you must consider more than just your desires. You have to think like a businessman/woman. And this needs to be your mindset before your book becomes a book. If you intend selling copies of your book, choose a marketable subject.

As the Rosses say, "A marketable subject is vital both for commercial publication and self-publication." What makes a marketable subject? According to the Rosses, marketable books are "usually about hot, timely subjects." They say, "Choosing a marketable topic is the first step toward the bestseller dream to which all authors aspire."

In order to write a book that's hot and timely, you must stay alert. The Rosses use the story of the first crockpot cookbook to illustrate this point. "The author attended a trade show and noticed that several manufacturers were introducing these new devises. Presto! The lights flashed. Would cooks need new recipes and guidance on how best to use their new cookware? You'd better believe they would. Since *Mabel Hoffman's Crockery Cookery* came out in 1975, more than three million copies have been sold." (I happen to own one of those three million copies.)

The Rosses caution writers to differentiate between a fad and a hot topic. But I believe that even a fad can make you some money, if you're on your toes and bring it out at the right time. Of course, I would go along with the Rosses and advise focusing on a trend rather than a novelty. One way to do this, according to Tom and Marilyn is, "Ask yourself if a lot of people are likely to still be interested in it in a year or two. Think whether other ideas in this field have tended to flash and die or whether they've lasted at least long enough for a book on the subject to be written, published and find an interested readership."

The Rosses offer a few topics that were hot three years ago—some still are: spirituality and religion, money, diet and exercise. They say, however, "There are hundreds of books on these topics. It would make no sense to come out with another run-of-the-mill tome on dieting. If you are clever, however, you may find a new way to ride the wave of interest others have generated."

Address large segments of people such as grandparents, teens or the largest one of all, currently, baby boomers. What might their interests be? How about managing personal finances, volunteerism, aging gracefully, health and fitness for the senior, part-time self employment and how to write a memoir?

The Rosses urge writers to become "lurkers." By this they mean visit chat rooms, discussion groups, online bulletin boards. Find out what people are talking about, concerned about, wondering about. They write, "When you see a pattern emerge, you've just learned about a need you might want to fill."

And they offer this advice, "As you climb the sheer cliffs of publishing, look for tiny crevices that have been passed over by the big guys."

As you can see, there's more to producing a book than just fulfilling your desire to write from the heart. In order to become successful, you must also engage your brain.

## Who is Your Target Audience?
How difficult can it be to find readers for your terrific book? In America, readers support close to 20,000 bookstores and 118,000 libraries.

And amazon.com is the biggest thing going on the Internet. Reading is still one of America's favorite pastimes. Everyone enjoys reading a good book, right? Not necessarily.

According to the Jenkins Group, fifty-eight percent of adults claim they have not read a book since high school and forty-two percent of college graduates never read another book. Reality check! Your audience does not comprise all of humanity.

Knowing that, what segment of the population is most likely to be interested in your book? Everyone who reads? Tell a publisher that and you're practically guaranteed a rejection letter. Only the most naïve, inexperienced, short-sighted author believes that his book will appeal to everyone.

Targeting your audience can be just about as difficult as taming a wild buffalo. But there are techniques that will help. We often write something that we would like to or, perhaps, need to read. Thus, the audience for your book might be made up of people like you—people who enjoy a good novel, who want to learn to knit, who need help with an emotional problem or who collect cookbooks.

The fact is that most first-time authors give little thought to their audience until *after* they write their book. They have a book in them and they just want to get it out. I met one such author at a recent book festival. Gerald wrote a book focusing on what he perceived as scientific proof that there is no God. He wrote it and he paid to have it published. When I met him, he was borderline despondent. His book wasn't selling. He came to my booth asking for help.

Putting my personal convictions about the subject aside, I asked Gerald, "Who is your audience?" He quickly and confidently responded, "Everyone." I said, "So you think that everyone will want to read this book?" He said, "Well, everyone ought to." Isn't this how we all feel about our lovely and important words?

After some discussion, Gerald and I isolated his target audience— those with the same theory as his. This might include some scientists and philosophers, atheists, agnostics and those who are on the fence but leaning in the direction of Gerald's beliefs. We talked about where he would find these people. Together, we determined that it would be pretty much the same places where Gerald hangs out—lecture halls where speakers talk about this theory and Web sites and publications devoted to atheism and science versus theology.

This isn't what Gerald hoped to hear. He wanted a quick and easy entrance to bookstores as an outlet for his book. More than anything, he is interested in changing minds. Whether or not he took my advice and started soliciting appropriate magazines, newsletters and Web sites, I may never know.

If Gerald had written a book proposal, he would probably have altered the focus of his book. He might have realized that his approach— trying to convince readers to change long-held traditional beliefs— would turn off the very audience he wanted to attract.

You may dream of making a difference in the world through your book on living a more Christian life, for example. Your goal is to reach the sinful masses. In reality, however, your audience will most likely include Christians who want to do an even better job of being Christian— people like you. Your target audience probably read the same books and magazines you read. They attend church. They visit Christian Web sites. But it isn't enough to say this. The publisher wants to know how many people you're talking about.

Your job is to find out how many Christian churches there are in the world and calculate the combined attendance. How many Christian bookstores and Web sites can you locate? Again, find books similar to yours and ascertain the number of sales. This will help you to define and calculate your target audience.

What segment of the population will embrace your book? Who are you writing for? Who will seek out a book like yours for the entertainment value? Who cares about what you have to say? Who will benefit from reading your book?

As authors, we sometimes want to do more than just write. We want to make a difference. We hope to alter perspectives. We yearn to teach and to share. It's when we set out to change minds that we lose sight of our true target audience.

A McDonald's groupie is not likely to buy a book featuring vegetarian recipes, no matter how desperately you want to change his ways. You can pretty much cross this segment of people off your potential reader list—at least when discussing your target audience with a publisher. Focus, instead, on the more realistic audience—vegetarians and those who try to eat healthy meals. *Vegetarian Times* reports that there are around twelve million vegetarians in the U.S., after all, and that's a pretty large audience.

Actually, that's not exactly your audience. This number is simply a starting point. Now you must determine what percentage of vegetarians and vegans cook and from that number, how many of them buy cookbooks. Add to that, the general cooking, cookbook-buying public who also serve their families vegetable dishes.

Now determine if there are other books on cooking with vegetables. Does it look as though the market is saturated or is there room for one more? What makes your book stand out from the rest?

Think hard about this: will the differences attract or repel readers. If yours is the only vegetarian recipe book that features lemon grass in every recipe, it may not appeal to every vegetarian. But one focusing on converting old favorite family recipes to vegetarian dishes might provide just the hook you need. Or how about producing a guide to the best vegetarian restaurants in your state?

The audience for a how-to book is probably somewhat easier to ascertain than those for self-help books and books without a message. Your book on tax tips for authors would attract authors who are making or who expect to make money selling their books. Do you know how many people this is? Neither does the publisher. It's up to you to find out. Use statistics to illustrate the percentages and numbers representing key segments of people who might be interested in your book. Always double check that figure, if possible, and provide the sources for your statistics.

Find statistics in a current *Information Please Almanac* or at infoplease.com or askanexpert.com, through reference or informational books on the subject and/or do a Google search. (Learn more about conducting research for a book proposal or a book in Chapter Nine.)

A book featuring pet photography techniques would probably draw beginner and intermediate photographers as well as people who want to learn how to take better pictures of their pets. Seek out facts and figures to demonstrate the huge increase in camera use throughout the world. This figure, combined with those related to our fondness for pets, would certainly help to make a case for this book.

I happen to know that there are around seventy million pet cats and sixty million pet dogs in the U.S. alone. One in four households has at least one pet. While not all pet owners are interested in photography and not all photographers want to learn about photographing pets, demographics such as these give you a good starting place in determining your target audience.

Now see if you can more precisely pinpoint your readers. Is the theme of your book stepfamilies? Gather statistics representing the number of stepfamilies in the U.S. Maybe you're writing about a particular disease and how it has affected your family. Do some research to learn the scope of this ailment—how many other families are dealing with this illness?

Choose a subject that corresponds with something traditionally taught in school. Your readers might include potentially every fourth grade student in every school in California, for example.

Why would anyone buy a book on your chosen topic written by you? Do you have a following in this field? If so, this may be a plus. The fact that you have expertise may supersede the fact that there's a near glut of books out there on your subject.

Let's go back to the idea for a book on pet photography. Be sure to reveal your connections—you've been specializing in pet photography for ten years, you produce a newsletter and have 8,000 subscribers and you get 50,000 hits per month on your Web site. Not only does this demonstrate that you have a following, but that you know how to market yourself.

## Your Target Audience for Fiction

How does one target an audience for a novel? First, you might get some statistics related to the number of novels sold each year. Then see what you can find out about the public's interest in the particular type of novel you want to write or the subject of your story. Your novel featuring a band of mercenaries in a war zone circa 2020 won't appeal to all novel readers. Your audience might comprise those who have purchased similar novels, who rent war movies, who read futuristic stories and who visit related Web sites. Get these figures and tally them.

To acquire information about sales for books similar to yours, check amazon.com and other online bookstores. Ask the managers at several traditional bookstores how a particular book is selling. Snoop around at author and publisher Web sites. If a book is in its third printing, it is pretty clear that it is selling. Ingram has an automated system you can access by phone to learn how a particular book is selling. Call 615-213-6803 and punch in the ISBN. Mention your findings in the marketing section of your book proposal.

Not every book is in the Ingram database. You may get an author to tell you how many copies of his book he has sold. It would be convincing, indeed, if you could say, "Arthur Author's novel, *The War Within the War* (XYZ Publishing, 2004), sold 20,000 copies in the first ten months of publication." Or "Wanda Writer has sold over 100,000 copies of her romance novel." Do your best to provide numbers to illustrate the popularity of books like the one you are pitching.

Maybe you have a children's story running around in your head. You can even visualize the illustrations. Who is your audience? Is this a book for the preschool set, for 5-7-year olds or for pre-teens? I've met children's book authors who insist that their book is for all kids and, they say, "Adults will like it, too." No, no, no. Your audience is not all of humankind. Aside from, perhaps, the Bible, there is no such one-size-fits-all book.

To determine your target audience, study children's books—lots of them. Find books in a similar style and language level to the one you plan. What is the age recommendation for these books? This is your target audience, too.

## Your Bonus Audience

Sometimes you get a bonus audience when you produce a book. This has happened to me more than a couple of times. I wrote my local history book for Ojai residents who want to know the history of their hometown. But I sell as many books to newcomers, tourists and families of early pioneers every year as I do longtime residents.

One of my spin-off books, *Nordhoff Cemetery* (featuring our pioneer cemetery and the earliest burials there), sells not only to locals, but to folks from all over the country who are working on their genealogy and people who collect materials related to cemeteries.

I wrote *The Mainland Luau* for visitors to Hawaii. I figured that many of the tourists who had experienced a luau in the Islands would be interested in trying this at home. I was surprised to discover an equally large audience for this book living and barbecuing in the southern United States. The recipes intrigued both those wishing to capture the flavor of Hawaii through kalua roasted pork and those folks who love their hog barbecues.

While developing the marketing section for your book proposal, ask yourself:

- Who is my target audience?

- What do they need or want from a book like this—information, techniques, instructions, entertainment, inspiration?

- Do they have a problem? Do they want to make a lot of money? Do they need help understanding digital cameras, rose gardening, death?

- What do they worry about? What do they want to know?

- Why would they care about what I have to say?

## Sample Marketing Section

For my book on youth mentoring.

According to a recent AOL/Time Warner Foundation study, only 11 percent of all adults are involved in a formal mentor program. Another survey reports that 2.5 million kids have mentors but that there are over 15 million young people who still need or want a mentor. The good news is that 57 million adults have said that they would consider becoming a youth mentor. That would be enough for everyone in the United States between the ages of ten and eighteen to have at least one mentor.

This book is for those adults who are already mentoring a child either formally or informally and want more information, support and help in their endeavor. It's for the educator, religious leader and community leader who want to do more to help children and need additional guidance. It's for those who are ready to give something back to society and want to do it through our children. It will assist folks who already spend time with their grandchildren or kids in the neighborhood and who want additional inspiration and ideas for successful mentoring. And it's for those who, perhaps, see a problem developing with children in their community or neighborhood and they want to get involved but don't know how. This book is for every adult who cares about kids.

## What's Your Competition?

Now that you know how to focus your book and who will buy it, you need to find out what else is out there like it. What is your competition?

- Are there other books on this topic?

- How similar/dissimilar are they to the one you propose?

- What is special about your book?

- Why should the publisher invest his money in another book on this topic?

How do you check out the competition? Here's a guide.

**Step One**
Visit amazon.com and reference *Books in Print* as well as *Forthcoming Books in Print* to find listings for books similar to the one you propose. Visit local bookstores to locate additional books. Don't forget to check your own home library.

**Step Two**
Study books like yours and choose four to six recent books that are most similar. If the book is also popular, that's a plus. Note the title, author, publisher, publication date, page number, size, type (hardcover/paperback) and ISBN. To get sales figures on these books, call 615-213-6803.

**Step Three**
Compare each book to yours, noting significant similarities and differences in the design, scope, information, style and purpose. Perhaps yours is more well organized, is more comprehensive, provides an easy-to-follow guide, includes diagrams and graphs and/or has an index. Maybe your book for horse owners is unique in that it is for beginners

and it provides tips for trail riding skill and etiquette. Possibly yours is the only craft book with instructions for the popular hand crocheting technique for kids. Perhaps none of the other books you found on fatherhood and fathering feature true life anecdotes.

Never, never make the mistake of claiming that there is nothing out there like your book. There may not be another book on how to handle rattlesnakes without getting bit, but there are books on rattlesnakes, reptiles and taming wild animals. Your book on losing weight by living in the moment may be unique. But you can compare yours with others in the self-help section and those on dieting.

You must convince the publisher that there is a place for your particular book. Is there truly a need for another book on snakes? What would your book add to a perceived glut of books on weight loss? Is your book topic timely enough to be accepted and different enough to be noticed?

It could be that you came up with the idea for this book when other books on the topic didn't adequately address the questions you had. If so, tell this to the publisher.

Authors must guard against trying things that are too unique. There's a fine line between what will be accepted in the marketplace and what will be rejected. Thus, most publishers tend to shy away from things that are too different. Call your book idea *unique* and you might as well kiss that publishing contract goodbye.

I know a first-time author who planned to write a book about a particular scientist's study revolving around flotsam (wreckage and/or cargo found floating in our oceans). After doing her comparative study, she realized that there was more promise for a scientific account of the ocean's currents as it relates to flotsam. It's practically the same book, only with a different focus. Yes, she found a publisher.

Most publishers are reluctant to try something that hasn't been proven in the marketplace. Nor will they publish something that has been overdone.

Marilyn and Tom Ross suggest, "Look closely at the competition. Do the existing books leave a gap your book could turn into a target? If your book is to stand out from the pack, it must have a fresh angle, offer a unique approach or information to persuade a prospective reader to buy it rather than one of the others."

## Sample Market Analysis
For my book on how to be alone and happy.

Although the late 1970s and early '80s ushered in a minor flurry of books on aloneness, there aren't many of this nature being produced today. Following are data, synopsis and evaluations of those I found:

### Belonging: A Guide to Overcoming Loneliness
By William R. Brassel, Ph.D.
New Harbinger Publishing, 1994
This book is based on clinical research and includes therapeutic techniques designed to help depressed and reticent people (particularly women) break down their barriers to relationships. This differs from the book I propose in that it deals specifically with healing relationships and, unlike mine, is not easy reading for the lay person.

### Conquer Loneliness: Understand Your Loneliness and Banish it Forever! (Life's Little Keys—Self-Help Strategies for a Healthier, Happier You)
By Frank J. Bruno
Arco Publishing, 1997
This book encompasses 135 pages. It is a brief guide written by a psychotherapist designed to help people deal with being alone. Unlike Bruno's book, I will offer numerous anecdotes illustrating the various loneliness issues I discuss in the book. And my book will fill around 300 pages.

***Contemporary Solitude: The Joy and Pain of Being Alone***
By Joanne Wieland-Burston
Samuel Weiser, 1996
This book focuses on the negatives of being alone without offering solutions nor pointing up the benefits to finding solutions.

***The Healing of Your Aloneness Workbook: The 6-Step Inner Bonding Spiritual Process for Healing Yours***
By Erica J. Chopich Ph.D.
Evolving Publications, 1996
This workbook deals more with addiction and abuse issues. It may also be more spiritual than some people are comfortable with.

***Overcoming Loneliness in Everyday Life***
By Jacqueline Olds, M.D.
Richard Schwartz, M.D.
Harriet Webster
Birch Lane Publishing, 1996
These authors focus on cultural rather than individual loneliness and they suggest shared tasks as a way to overcome. Along with psychotherapy, medication and self-help groups, these authors say that the cure for loneliness lies in family and the greater community.

There are also books specific to the needs of widow(ers), divorcees, single parents, military spouses/ loved ones and retirees, which generally include only small sections on coping with loneliness.

The book I propose differs from what I've found currently on the market in that it teaches readers of all ages and in all situations how to overcome destructive feelings of loneliness by learning how to be successfully alone—how to find joy in solitude. While the focus of this book is curing loneliness through self-examination, awareness and inner work, there are chapters specific to the widow(er); divorcee; single parent; military spouse/loved one; those suffering empty nest syndrome; the nesters, themselves; retirees; someone moving to a new community and those suffering temporary loneliness such as feeling alone in a crowd or being alone during the holidays.

This book will teach the skills necessary to be successfully and blissfully alone, whether being alone is by choice or circumstance—skills that will transfer into more successful relationships and a richer life.

## Recommended Reading:

*The Fast-Track Course on How to Write a Nonfiction Book Proposal* by Stephen Blake Mettee (Quill Driver Books, 2002).

## Chapter Six

# DAZZLE EM

## WITH YOUR MARKETING SAVVY

Now that you have a marketable topic, you know who your audience is and where they are, how do you plan to reach them? "What?" you ask. "I have to promote my book, too? Won't the publisher do that?"

This is where the inexperienced, naïve, unaware hopeful author makes his biggest mistake. He expects the publisher to handle promotion and sales. Unfortunately, it doesn't work that way anymore. At least, not until you establish yourself as a bestselling author or can attract a large following for your line of books. Until then, the publisher is counting on you to actively generate sales.

Few people even consider the promotional aspect of authorship. Until we enter into the field of publishing, we have no reason to know what goes on behind the scenes. If you want a book, you go to the bookstore and buy one, right? You see others in the same bookstore buying books. And you assume that, once your book is published, it will have its spot in bookstores nationwide and enough readers will buy it to support your writing habit for years to come. Ahhh, wouldn't that be nice?

Well, enjoy the fantasy while you can for, once the book is published, you will be required to promote it.

The promotions portion is probably the most important aspect of a book proposal. A publisher wants to know that you understand the concept of book promotion and that you can and will participate in promoting your book. This section of your book proposal is important for you, too. You need to have a plan. You must understand what it takes to promote a book and be willing to commit to it. There is nothing easy about book promotion.

Too many authors disregard this aspect of a book proposal. They so believe in their project that they expect sales without effort. Don't fall into this trap. Reality check: you must be prepared to promote your book and you have to convince a potential publisher that you'll be successful in this endeavor.

## But I Write Fiction

Authors of fiction works will be expected to help with promotion, as well. While some publishers of fiction say it isn't necessary to provide them with a marketing plan, I suggest showing off your marketing savvy even for fiction. Tell the publisher that since your novel is set in the state of Georgia, you see this book as a good regional seller and that you plan to promote the book to historical societies at the state and city levels, at libraries, through museum gift shops and, of course, Georgia-based bookstores. You might let the publisher know that you'll be available to do book tours throughout the state and beyond once the book is published. If your heroine has diabetes, you might involve the American Diabetes Association in your promotional efforts. Maybe your romance is set in a senior home. You can surely promote your book by doing readings in such homes as well as through articles and excerpts published in senior-related magazines, Web sites and newsletters. Many newspapers have columns devoted to senior interests. Find out how many and assure the publisher that you will contact each of these editors to solicit interviews and book reviews.

### What do Publishers Really Want?

I interview publishers regularly for the *SPAWN Market Update* and I usually ask them, "What sort of authors do you most like working with?" They almost always mention those with time, energy, ideas and the ability and willingness to promote his or her book.

Some publishers even post their expectations on their Web sites or in their submission guidelines.

Mystic Ridge Books advertises that they want writers who are good self-promoters. Their submission guidelines ask authors to tell them how proactive they plan to be about getting publicity. And they want details. They state in their submission guidelines, "Authors must be willing to be aggressive and proactive regarding doing publicity and book-related events on their own. Books do not sell without author-self-motivated marketing efforts."

YMAA Publication Center guidelines say that author participation is mandatory.

The editors at Equilibrium Press say, "Please do not contact us unless you are willing to make promotion of your book a top priority."

The editors at JIST Publishing say, "Demonstrate your ability and willingness to help promote and sell the book after it is published."

Morgana Press states, in their submission guidelines, "Egomaniacs, curmudgeons, complainers, prima donnas and those with an overall bad attitude, sense of entitlement and a reluctance to promote one's own work are stongly discouraged from making submissions to Morgana Press."

Publishers today need your help in promoting your book. And many of them are seeking, along with excellent manuscripts, authors who are bold promoters and who are not afraid to be in the public eye.

**It's Never Too Soon to Think About Promotion**
From the time you first conceive your book idea, you should be thinking about promotion. In fact, I generally start a file folder for promotional ideas from the get-go, which I add to over the duration of the project and beyond. I might write myself a reminder note to contact school districts once my *Young Writer's Handbook* is completed. I may note a particular teachers' magazine editor who expressed an interest in reviewing the finished book. And I'll start collecting data on newspapers nationwide with literary arts and/or kids' columns. I'll want to send out press releases to each and every one in hopes of initiating reviews or interviews.

**Become Acquainted With Your Target Audience**

Once you have determined your target audience (per the guidelines in Chapter Five), you must take time to get to know them. What do these people read? What magazines do they buy? Where do they purchase books? What associations and groups do they join? Do they attend workshops, lectures, church? Do they travel, exercise, diet, have pets, knit, go fishing? What do they care about? Do they support a particular cause? You've used these prompts to isolate your target audience, now you must figure out how to reach these people. What ploys do you have up your sleeve to attract readers from your perceived demographic pool? How do you envision prompting these people to purchase your book? You'd better figure it out because the publisher wants to know. If you plan to self-publish, this information is even more vital to your success.

You don't have to go into great detail about every promotional idea that strikes you. The publisher just needs proof that you understand the job of promoting your book and are willing and able to take it on. Tell him about any important contacts you have.

## What is Your Platform?

We hear a lot about platform these days. What is it and why do you need one? Your platform is your way of attracting readers. It's an indication of your following. My platform for my writing/publishing-related books includes the fact that I have been in the business for over thirty years. I'm the author of twenty-five books, including eight related to writing and publishing. I am the president of SPAWN (Small Publishers, Artists and Writers Network). I present workshops at writers' conferences throughout the U.S. My writing/publishing-related articles number in the hundreds and appear frequently in a variety of industry publications. I teach online courses for freelance writers and authors and I have a Web site featuring information and resources for writers. Obviously, I've built a pretty solid platform based on experience, expertise and exposure.

Are you involved in an area of expertise related to your book? Do you have a reputation or a measure of influence within your community or beyond?

Karen Stevens is founder of All For Animals and the author of a book by the same name. She has a large following of animal advocates through her Web site and she also appears on a local weekly TV segment with the "Pet of the Week." She writes for several animal-related publications. A publisher would probably accept her book of animal stories based largely on her impressive platform.

Debbie Puente was working for a well-known kitchen store when she started pitching her book on how to make crème brulee. She gave the publisher a letter from the store buyer confirming that she would place the book for sale in all of their stores once it was published. This was a major factor in Puente receiving a publishing contract for *Elegantly Easy Crème Brulee and Other Custard Desserts*. While Puente didn't have a following or her own at that time, she had a connection to a business with a huge customer base.

Be sure to tell a publisher if you have a meaningful association within the area or field of your book subject. Maybe you're a CEO for a company that sells knitting supplies. What publisher wouldn't be interested in your book featuring the latest and greatest projects to knit or one called, *Knitting Nostalgia*?

Perhaps you spent ten years swimming with the dolphins at various water theme parks throughout the world. Your impressive contacts would surely help sell a publisher on your *Dolphin Stories for the Soul* book. This is especially true if you tell him that you still present special programs at water parks every summer and could promote your book to these audiences.

Maybe you can afford to hire a publicist, your brother-in-law produces a major catalog and has agreed to feature your book in it or you have a strong marketing background. These are all part of your platform.

Face it, even if you're well-known in your field and you've just written the best book of the century, it will take some effort to entice people to buy it. People will not come just because you wrote it. It will take time, work and strategy to get news of your book out there so it is noticed. Tell the publisher how much time you will spend promoting your book every day/week.

When Jim Barrett made the rounds with his second book proposal, he was on the verge of retiring. He told the publisher that he would be available to promote the book practically full time at that point. The publisher believed him and has not been disappointed. Barrett's connections and experience as a peace officer help to sell copies of his true crime book. But, he still must put in the time and energy to get the word out.

It's discouraging to know that seventy percent of all books published do not make a profit (Jenkins Group). What is behind the sales and success of the other thirty percent? A little bit of luck, perhaps. But mainly it is persistence and work.

Sure, a traditional publisher will offer some promotional assistance. He might include your book in the annual company catalog, showcase it on his Web site, offer review copies to three or four dozen reviewers and send press releases to his list of periodicals. The publisher may also set you up with his marketing agent once your book is published. When you locate someone willing to review the book or when you are scheduled to do a book signing and need books, you let this person know and he or she will make necessary arrangements. Some publishers will also arrange for shelf space for your book in bookstores. But if you aren't bringing in the customers, your unsold books will be returned.

Some of the main selling points for fee-based POD "self-publishing" companies are their promotional packages. Hopeful authors are thrilled to think that their publisher will go out of his way to promote their book. This may cost the author an additional $300 to $2,000, but is it worth it? Probably not. To date, I have not met nor have I heard of a

104

POD "self-published" author whose company sold more than a handful of his books.

The POD publisher may use a service to send out cookie cutter press releases announcing your book to a general audience. You could hire the service yourself for less money. But I'd rather see you send your own press releases to a more appropriate list.

The sad truth is that you cannot rely on your publisher or anyone else to take over full responsibility for promoting your book. Think about it, no one else knows your book as intimately as you do. And no one cares about it as much as you do.

## Build Your Platform

Begin building a platform even before you write the book. I realize that some of you have already written your book, and that's okay. You'll just have to play catch-up. How do you build a platform where none exists? Become visible within your field or genre. For example:

- Introduce yourself to appropriate Web site and organization leaders and ask how you can become involved.

- Write articles in your field or stories in your genre for appropriate Web sites, magazines and other publications.

- Make news in your field or genre and tell it to the media.

Do whatever it takes to get your name out so that your public knows you exist. Be creative. Be consistent, persistent and patient. Even with a fairly solid platform, it still takes effort and energy to promote to your audience.

## Build Marketability Into Your Book

Whether your book is a novel or work of a scientific nature; whether it will appeal to artists, is meant to entertain, is important to psychologists or significant to history buffs, you can build promotional opportunities into it.

## For Nonfiction
### Involve Others
Practically everyone likes to see his or her name in print. Most people will buy one or more copies of a book in which they're quoted. Mention a particular organization, charity, or company and they might actually help promote your book. Here are some ideas for involving people in your book:

- Quote experts in the text.

- Mention agencies and organizations in your resource list.

- Share true stories that relate to your subject.

- Create an acknowledgements page and list everyone who contributed to your book through information, resources, stories, etc.

- Ask experts in the field of your subject to write testimonials (or endorsements) for the back cover or pages inside the book.

- Include a bibliography, plenty of resource material and an index and you will entice another level of readers—researchers, the media and librarians.

### Get Permission
For a nonfiction book or even a book of fiction in which you've actually used true anecdotes, be sure to get permission to print a quote or a story. I generally type up the quote or the story exactly as I wish to publish it and send it to the individual along with a permission slip for them to sign. Most people simply sign. Others might make slight changes before signing. While I've never had anyone refuse to allow publication of their quote, I would rather get a refusal before the fact than a law suit after.

## For Fiction
Choose your setting carefully. Make sure that it is conducive to promotion. Select a city that is interesting—one in which the citizens

take pride. Provided your story portrays a positive view of the community, residents of this town are apt to welcome you for author events. Write about a rundown town where nothing is happening and the residents are depressed and you probably won't get friendly invitations to promote your book there.

Involve your characters in current issues: autism, gang activity, politics, the battle against terror threats or childhood obesity, for example. Why? This gives you additional ammunition for promoting. Your audience base, in this case, might go beyond the typical mystery or romance reader.

## Premiums and Incentives

Companies sometimes purchase large numbers of books to give away to customers. Your book might be chosen as a premium item if it mentions a certain product. A historical novel might be of interest to a bank or another large business in the area where the story takes place. My local history book has been purchased as curriculum at area high schools and as a research tool for projects being conducted by grammar school students. It's a primary resource used by museum docents, Chamber of Commerce employees, city hall officials and librarians countywide. Local realtors also regularly purchase copies of this book to give to their clients.

## Your Book as a Special Interest Item

Write a novel or a children's story that will appeal to a specific group of people. Give one of your characters an illness, a horse, a disability, a motorcycle, a convertible, a set of twins or an affiliation with a well-known agency, for example. The American Diabetes Association might be interested in promoting a book with a character that provides a positive diabetic model. Child health professionals and advocacy groups might purchase quantities of your book on how to help slim down our overweight kids. School administrators might purchase numbers of books that relate to subjects taught in their classrooms.

Several copies of Betty Middleton Britton's first book, *Promises! Promises! Adventures of Jose Joaquin Tico, Cataluna to California 1766-1802*, were purchased by the California school system for classroom use. Not only does this book reflect early California history, it gives an excellent Spanish lesson throughout.

Create an interest in your book for several segments of people. My book on solitude includes chapters for people who are alone for a variety of reasons: separation, divorce, death, relocation, empty nest and so forth. Presumably, this book will have a wider appeal than it would had I focused just on widowhood.

## What's Your Plan?

You truly won't know much about the process of promoting your book until you get involved. Most first-time authors find it is more work and more difficult than they had imagined. A book proposal forces you to think about promotion way before you ever write that book, thus to be more well-prepared.

What is your plan? Are you hoping that word of mouth will drive sales? Let's say that you tell everyone you know about your book and half of them tell one or two other people. If it is a subject of interest to them, one-quarter of those people may tell people they know. Some of them will buy the book—a few might even purchase extra copies as gifts. Okay, so a few months pass. Those who would read a book like this, have done so. The others have forgotten all about it. Sales have stopped. Now what?

Presumably, you don't have a storefront where you can display your product. But you have managed to get the Borders downtown to carry it because you are a local author. It is shelved, not with other books of this type, but on a special bookcase along with those by other local authors. Who's going to find it there? How will anyone know about it?

Think back to the information you gleaned while working on the marketing section of your book proposal. Where are your primary customers? What do they buy? Where do they shop? What do they read? What newsletters do they subscribe to? What's the best way to reach them?

Let's say that your ideal customer reads travel magazines. You'll want to offer excerpts from your book and write articles for such magazines. This would be great exposure for a book like Edward D. Webster's travel memoir, *A Year of Sundays*. As I understand it, those who travel, read travel magazines, but so do an equally large number of arm chair travelers.

Maybe you plan to do back-of-the-room sales during professional conferences throughout the world. This is a good promotional plan that many authors use to sell books related to their professional expertise. When you explain this to your potential publisher, be sure to give details: where, why, how often, numbers of attendees and so forth.

I recently worked with a client who had grandiose ideas for promoting his fitness book. Jonathan wrote in the promotional section of his book proposal that he was planning a conference next summer and that he would travel the world speaking to groups on the subject of his book. This looked good on paper, until it came to proof. I challenged him to offer the publisher something concrete. I asked him to describe the upcoming conference: Where would it be held? What celebrities would be there? How many people did he expect? He had nothing. I asked him to tell about similar conferences he has organized in the past. He admitted that he had never done anything like this before. I suggested he give a few examples of his successful speaking engagements. Well, guess what? He had no such experience.

Imagine how a publisher would view this portion of Jonathan's book proposal. Do you think he would take this author seriously? Would he trust that the author would follow through with these ideas? Wouldn't the publisher be more impressed and convinced if Jonathan could give some particulars—"The conference is tentatively called, *Feeling*

*Good, Being Fit.* I've reserved a hall at the Hilton Hotel in Los Angeles for June 30, 2008 and I have commitments from Suzanne Somers and Queen Latifa to be presenters. I've also contacted Richard Simmons, John Basedow and Dr. Phil McGraw. I expect this event and this line-up to draw at least 1,000 people. We have provisions for 1,500."

I would vehemently advise against Jonathan or anyone else inventing details such as these. I would suggest, instead, that he hold off sending his book proposal until he had something concrete to share with the publisher.

However, if he had a track record, he could use that as proof. He could say, for example, "I teach fitness workshops nationwide. For the last five years, I've presented workshops in twenty-five cities including Denver, Baltimore, Los Angeles, New York and Portland. Last year, I was a featured speaker at the Fantastic Fitness Fantasy Expo in Chicago with 800 people in attendance. I created a test book for this event and sold all 150 copies. I'm scheduled to speak in Seattle this spring before a group of colleagues at the World Fitness Council Conference and believe I could sell a thousand copies of this book there."

Don't blow in the wind, people. Give the publisher something to hang his bank account on. If you don't have anything, maybe you should postpone your book. Spend the next several months testing your idea, making contacts, developing a following, creating projects and even honing your public speaking skills. (Read more about public speaking in Chapter Twelve.)

You don't need to share all of your promotional ideas in your book proposal—just the best ones. Try to come up with a few really good short-term, get-this-book-off-the-ground ideas and a couple of great long-term ideas. Those initial ideas might include: sending review copies and brochures to key organizations that might be interested in using your book as a premium or employee incentive. Perhaps you've already reserved a booth at a trade show related to your topic.

Long term ideas might include spending two hours every day sending press releases to newspapers, starting a charity related to your book topic or launching a radio talk show. Radio personalities, such as the ever popular Dr. Laura Schlesinger and Bill O'Reilly, sell a lot of their books to their listeners.

If your expertise relates to the theme of your book and you have enough personality and skill to pull it off, consider launching a local radio show. If you're good and if you're lucky, it could even become syndicated. Possible topics might include cooking, travel, pets, computers, finance, automobiles, senior or family issues, child-rearing, health or even writing.

**Strategies for Promoting to Your Audience**
I know a published poet who landed a spot on a writing show on public radio. This led to her own one-hour show. As often as she can, she mentions her book of poetry.

Blogging (Web logging) is all the rage now. From what I hear, people really do take time to visit their favorite blogs regularly to keep up with the patter on their topics of interest. So don't rule this out as a means of book promotion. (Read *Promoting Your Book Through Your Blog* at spawn.org. Click on "Articles.")

Many authors write newsletters to promote their books. Azriela Jaffe produces a free monthly email newsletter for subscribers who are interested in how to build a successful business while managing the challenges of marriage and family. She does counseling, coaching and speaking in the area of her expertise and she is the author of several books on the topic. Each monthly newsletter includes tips, ideas and inspirational stories as well as information about her published books and services.

Newsletters and e-newsletters have been informing readers rather inexpensively for a long time. Even insurance companies, hospitals, utility companies and investment companies send newsletters to their customers.

Jaffe warns, however, "I don't think you should write a newsletter just to sell books. The reason you do a newsletter is to position yourself as an expert in your niche, to expand your reach and to give something of value to your customers."

## Keep On Promoting

I tell hopeful authors that your book will sell for as long as you are willing to promote it. So consider book promotion a commitment similar to that of raising a child. You created the book; now you're responsible for it. Nurture it and it will flourish. Neglect it and it will falter and fail.

Keep in mind that it isn't necessary to convince a publisher that you can turn hardened nonreaders into book buyers with your marvelous book and sell 50,000 copies in the first year. Most publishers are savvy enough to know that, even though there are an estimated forty-four million dog owners in the United States, only a percentage of them will actually purchase a book on dog ownership. Let's say that you can convince a publisher that you could potentially sell 10,000 books. He might be interested in taking the risk. After all, a $5 profit on 10,000 books is a cool $50,000.

## Should You Hire a Publicist?

Sure, if you can afford to and if he or she is experienced in working with authors. Hire a good publicist and you will sell books.

Don't think that hiring a publicist is a way out of promoting your book, however. They don't do the promotion for you. Typically, a publicist will spend her time and energies making appropriate contacts. You will be expected to follow through. A good publicist will keep you very, very busy.

Here's my recipe for landing a good publicist:

1. Consider publicists who come highly recommended.

2. Be prepared to spend $9,000 to $15,000 for three months of a publicist's time.

3.  Audition a potential publicist. What is her track record? Has she handled books like yours before? What was her level of success with these books?

4.  Ask for references and check them.

5.  Find out what her main marketing focus is and determine if this is compatible with your abilities and availability.

Once you hire a book publicist, expect to be extremely busy promoting your book for a year or more.

John Kremer lists over 125 book publicist and PR agency recommendations at his Web site: www.bookmarket.com/101pr.htm

## Sample Marketing Strategies
From my book proposal for this book.

### Marketing Strategies
I am already in promotion mode when it comes to my writing/publishing-related books. I will continue on the course I have set, which includes promoting this book through the SPAWN Web site and newsletter and in my numerous email communications with SPAWN members and visitors to the site. I will continue to write articles for various writing-related magazines, newsletters and Web sites such as *Writer's Digest Magazine, Freelance Writer's Report, Canadian Author, Absolute Write, Writing-World, Writer's Weekly, NAWW newsletter, Writing for Dollars, Spannet, PMA Independent, Writer's Connection, Working Writer Newsletter, Writer's Journal, Writer's Review* and others.

To discover the magnitude of promo I've done for my other writing books, do a Google search. Even doing a refined search—using quotation marks around my book,*Over 75 Good Ideas for Promoting Your Book*—you'll get over 3,000 hits and over one million when typing in my name.

I will arrange for book reviews on writing-related sites as well as in magazines and newsletters. I've had approximately 100 reviews for my writing books in recent years.

I also promote my writing books through speaking engagements. In February of this year, I spoke at the Much Ado About Books event in Jacksonville, FL (including audiences of about 200 school children and 150 adults) and at the National Association of Women Writers conference in Texas (one hundred women writers). I am scheduled to speak in October at the Meet Me In St. Louis Book Festival and the Central Coast Book Festival in San Luis Obispo, CA in September.

I was invited to speak at the Toastmasters International convention this month in Reno, however, I had to cancel due to a broken foot. I also canceled an invitation to speak in New York for the Society for Professional Journalists because of the injury. I'm on their agenda for 2005.

I have applied for speaking opportunities in 2005 at book festivals and writers' conferences next year in Las Vegas, Phoenix, Flagstaff, Illinois, Wisconsin, Virginia, Florida, San Diego and Los Angeles.

Through SPAWN, we frequently rent booths at book festivals, where I typically sell numbers of my writing/ publishing-related books. We generally secure booths at the Santa Barbara Book Festival, Los Angeles Times Festival of Books, Austin (TX) Book Festival and the Central Coast Book Festival. In 2004/2005 we will also have booths in Florida, Arlington, St. Louis and, hopefully, those listed above (Las Vegas, Phoenix, Flagstaff, etc).

I have a Web site through which I promote my books at matilijapress.com

I am also available for any tours or speaking engagements that you might arrange.

When you're writing the promotions section for your book proposal, be realistic. Be bold, be creative and be clever. It is your job to convince the publisher that you can manage the promotion of your book every bit as successfully as you can the writing of it.

If you need more help coming up with specific promotional ideas that are within your comfort zone, you can jump to Chapters Eleven-Thirteen.

## Recommended Reading:
*1001 Ways to Market Your Books* by John Kremer (Open Horizons, 5th edition, 2000).

*The Post-Publication Book Proposal*, an article written by Patricia Fry for the many authors who skipped the book proposal process BEFORE they wrote their book. Order this free, one-of-a-kind article via email: plfry620@yahoo.com. (Put "Post-Publication Book Proposal" in the subject line.)

# Chapter Seven

## OKAY,

# NOW ORGANIZE

## YOUR BOOK

### The Chapter Outline

One major reason for writing a book proposal for a nonfiction book is to find out if you actually have a book at all. The chapter outline or chapter-by-chapter summaries will tell the tale. It will also become your guide for writing the book.

Why does a writer need to follow a guide? While a fiction story can develop almost as if by magic, a nonfiction book generally takes some manipulation to make it work. Many authors have difficulty putting the material for their nonfiction book in a logical order. In fiction, you are concerned with telling a good story in an interesting way. Nonfiction is successful when the material is worthwhile, thorough and easy to understand and use.

Organizing a nonfiction book can challenge even the most methodical and orderly writer. It helps if you can break your book down into subjects, themes, steps or techniques—each representing a chapter. Avoid presenting too many ideas at once as this can be confusing. Perhaps the following will help:

1. Design a table of contents for your book, but don't become too attached to it. It might have many incarnations before it is set. Some authors write possible chapter titles on index cards because they are easy to shuffle and shift. Divide a book on

dog training into eight or ten steps, for example. A book on herb gardening might be separated into seasons, regions or plant types. A memoir would probably be divided into historical time periods, one's age or significant life events.

2. Separate and file the material you've gathered. Whether you're writing a novel, a children's story or a nonfiction book, you've probably gathered a variety of facts, figures and anecdotes. You've collected thoughts jotted on paper napkins, information printed from the Internet, magazine articles, lists of resources and newspaper clippings. You've earmarked certain books that you want to use in your research. Much of this is probably held in one or two file folders and several additional stacks and piles. When you are ready to start writing, separate this material into subtopics or chapters and place it in appropriate file folders.

3. Evaluate each folder. Are they relatively equal in size? Consider splitting large file folders into two chapters. For this book, my chapter on book proposals grew to such proportions that I split it into four. My file relating to agents was skimpy and I combined it with the chapter on approaching publishers.

4. Arrange your file folders (or chapters) in logical order. Be sure to make corresponding alterations to your table of contents.

5. Write your chapter outline. Give each chapter a title. For a nonfiction book, you may also want to create subheads based on the type of material you'll include in each chapter. Let's refer again to the book on how to photograph your pets. Your chapter on kitten photography might include subheads such as, *Choose an Appropriate Background, Working With What's at Hand, The Close-up Shot, Capturing Kittens at Play* and *Kitten Photography Challenges.*

## A Word About Chapter Titles

Have fun choosing intriguing chapter titles for a fiction book. For nonfiction, think service. Be practical. Devise titles and headings that are functional, not frilly. Help the reader to navigate easily through the information and steps you've laid out. Logical organization and succinct titles are two excellent methods of doing this.

This is not to say that you can't have fun with chapter titles. A little humor and some interesting innuendoes help to lighten up an informational book.

Another note about chapters for fiction: It's not actually necessary to use chapter titles; in fact it's probably best not to when you have over twenty-five or thirty chapters.

## Techniques for Creating Your Chapter Outline

This is your moment of truth. It's time to show the potential publisher that you actually have a book. If you cannot list at least five or six (or twelve to sixteen) stand-alone chapters and describe them, you probably don't have a book at all.

Your chapter outline (or summary) will help the publisher understand the flow of your proposed book. It will tell him whether your book has substance and relevance and whether you have the writing skill to carry off this project.

Writing a chapter outline can be overwhelming for the beginner as well as the seasoned author. While some of my own books just sort of fall together naturally, others cause me a great deal of frustration when it comes to the task of organizing. I've been known to spend several days enmeshed in the material I've gathered for a book, trying to create a logical order.

Balance your chapters. If the publisher wants 40,000 words, that's 160 typed, double-spaced pages. You might plan to break your book down into ten chapters of sixteen pages each. Don't worry if you have one very important, very short chapter and one or two that are longer.

It's not necessary to stress over this. It just makes a nicer presentation when chapters are broken down into similar size bites.

The point of a chapter outline is to summarize the purpose of each chapter and reveal how you will accomplish the goals you've set forth. How will you communicate your message, for example?

Lately, during my presentations, audience members will challenge me with regard to the term *chapter outline*. When I tell them that a chapter outline involves summaries—a sort of mini-synopsis for each chapter—they respond with, "But that isn't an outline." That's right. The outline typically used in research projects lists main topics, subtopics and sub-sub topics in a sort of bare bones form. That isn't what we want here. This portion of the book proposal might more accurately be called the chapter-by-chapter summary.

**Additional Tips For Creating Chapter-by-Chapter Summaries**

- ✎ Evaluate other books on your subject as well as some outside the subject. What do you like/dislike about the way these books are arranged? Which aspects would you like to copy and which ones will you reject?

- ✎ Try viewing your chapter outline as a synopsis in another form. In fact, your well-written synopsis, with a beginning, middle and end, will be a useful guide in organizing your chapter outline.

- ✎ I look at each chapter as an article. I ask myself, what is the purpose of this chapter? What will it teach? What information should it include? How will it inspire? What encouragement will it provide? Why is it important? In your chapter outline, simply summarize the purpose and point of each chapter and reveal how you will accomplish the goals you've set forth.

*The Ojai Valley: An Illustrated History* was my most difficult organizational challenge. I wondered, should I have a separate section for profiles of early pioneers or weave their stories throughout the book? Would I organize chapters chronologically or by subject?

I experimented a little and eventually made my decision. I started the book with a chronological overview of the geology of the valley and the early native American cultures here. Then I followed by reporting on major activities in chronological order (Mission Period, Rancho Period, early oil exploration here and the establishment of the village). Each chapter, thereafter, focused on topics: the first churches in the valley, the history of early schools, the railroad to Ojai, the early newspapers and so forth. I wove profiles of early pioneers into appropriate chapters based primarily on when they arrived in the valley and their particular contributions as these related to historical events.

## Decisions, Decisions...

The chapter outline gives you a boost toward actually writing the book. But there are still many decisions to make. What style will you choose for your book? Will you start each chapter with a quote or a question? Will you end each chapter with recommended reading? What about subheads, bullets, boxes or graphs? Will you use some of these techniques to break up your text and make strong points? Whatever style or pattern you decide upon, carry it throughout the book.

There are several ways to use illustrations or photographs, for example. For my fatherhood book, I planned to include a photograph of a father and child at the beginning of each chapter. I wanted to heavily illustrate my Ojai Valley history book with old photographs. I decided to spread the photos throughout the book rather than putting them all in one section like some publishers do. To create a more balanced appearance, I chose approximately ten photos for each chapter. I positioned the photos appropriately throughout the book (a picture of the first Presbyterian Church near the text describing the church, for example). I also tried to intersperse photographs evenly throughout the book. You will see photos at least every two or three pages.

Will you have a resource list, bibliography and/or index? Describe your ideas for these in your chapter outline. I recommend an index for most nonfiction books. It is an important tool for researchers.

My Ojai history book is a very substantial book with an enormous amount of data, facts and information. Someone wanting to look up his family name can do so by referring to the index. If a reader wants to know something about early architects in the valley, he can look up architects in the index. Those who want to read the story of our oldest private boarding school, need merely refer to the index. This book, by the way, has over thirty pages of index entries. That's one reason why it is so valuable to local Chamber of Commerce personnel, librarians, city hall workers and museum docents. In fact, if I hadn't gone to the trouble of creating an index for the Ojai history book, I might have missed out on a lot of sales to libraries, researchers and those who use the book as a reference.

Your suggested enhancements are just ideas which a potential publisher may or may not embrace. But I believe that most publishers appreciate receiving a well thought out proposal that helps them to envision the completed project.

**Describe Your Chapters**

Once you have identified your chapters, describe them. Write a brief (100-400 words) overview of each chapter. Write more text where the material is complex, but avoid padding or rambling just to fill space. I see two common problems among my book proposal clients and students. Some of them overstate their point and purpose in their chapter outline and others withhold information. Avoid redundancy, but don't play coy with the publisher, either. Give him what he needs in order to appropriately evaluate your project.

Write your chapter outline in the same style as you plan for your book. Include examples and anecdotes. Where important, give statistics and share quotes. Some professionals suggest writing a chapter outline in the third person as you are describing each chapter to the publisher. Others agree that first person is okay.

## Sample Chapter Outline

For my book, *Write On! Journal-keeping for Teens.*

# Part I: <u>THE BASICS OF JOURNALING</u>

**Chapter 1: What is a Journal and Why Should I Keep One?** This chapter will describe the purpose and benefits of keeping a personal daily journal. A journal can be a trusted friend to whom teens or a pre-teens can safely share their most private thoughts and feelings. And when they do, they'll begin to better understand those thoughts and feelings and him or herself.

It's hard to be a pre-teen or teen today. Teens feel misunderstood. There's a lot that they don't understand. They should know that this is also true in adulthood. This chapter will explain how journaling can help teens discover the answers to their questions, guide them in solving problems and even help them to work through serious personal dilemmas. Through regular journal-keeping, teens can overcome fears, learn to identify and manage their grief and anger and heal heart pain. They'll learn to get along better with others and gain the tools to recognize true friendships and to strengthen them. Journal-keeping opens the door to a deeper understanding of oneself and the world. And understanding always leads to greater personal joy and happiness. The practice of journaling, then, is a beautiful gift a teen can give to him or herself.

**Chapter 2: How to Choose Your Very Own, Very Special Journal Book**. This chapter includes tips for selecting a ready-made journal book as well as instructions for making one. Through guided self-evaluation, the teen will discover his journal book preference. While some teens enjoy keeping their secret thoughts in a beautifully-bound journal, others can't bring themselves to write on the pages of such a fine book. Some people are more comfortable writing in a stenographer's tablet, legal pad, composition book or three-ring binder.

I'll recommend that the teen be practical: choose a journal with plenty of space on the pages. Lined pages are useful. The pages in a spiral-bound book or tablet lay flat and are easier to write on than those in a perfect-bound book. A small journal is more portable—easier to carry. If someone is a prolific writer, however, or she writes big, she'd probably rather have a larger book. Also discussed in this chapter will be pros, cons and how-tos of computer journaling.

**Chapter 3: Your Journaling Routine: Finding the Time and Space**. This chapter addresses that one most difficult issue we all face when introducing something new into our busy lives: change. The teen will most likely ask, "How will I find the time to keep a journal? What will I have to give up in order to start the habit of journaling?" I'll include tips such as, finish your homework right after school and treat yourself to a thirty minute journaling session after dinner each night instead of watching television. Get up fifteen minutes earlier in the morning and write while everyone else is still sleeping. Learn to recognize opportunities to write in your journal.

This chapter will teach teens the basics of scheduling and prioritizing as well as how to be flexible—skills they'll need in order to get along well in school, college, the workplace and life.

As to the questions, "Where will I find the privacy to write in my journal whenever I want to?" This can be a problem for young people who share a bedroom with siblings, for example. Here's where flexibility comes in. I'll suggest that they wait until their sisters or brothers are involved in a television program, are doing their homework or have gone to soccer practice—when they have their room all to themselves. I'll suggest that they ask Mom if they can use the desk in her bedroom for a few minutes every day. On a nice day, they can go outside on the patio to write or under a tree in the garden or a nearby park. If a teen's siblings depend on him for their entertainment and won't leave him alone to journal in peace, he might encourage the child to start a journal and spend time journaling quietly together. A teen can strike a bargain with a sibling. She might say, "We'll bake cookies together when I finish here if you'll just leave me alone for fifteen minutes."

I'll advise kids: If finding time and space to journal seems to be a monumental problem in your household, use the journaling technique in Chapter 7 (Journaling as a Problem-Solving Tool) to resolve it. Journaling every day is best, but a habit of three times a week or even once a week is better than not journaling at all.

**Chapter 4: Get Ready, Get Set, Write!** There's nothing more frustrating than opening your journal book for the first time, eager to start filling the pages and you can't think of anything to write. This is what most young people and adults experience the first few times they sit down to journal.

This chapter offers exercises and assignments to help teens get started. I'll suggest that they just start. A teen might address his journal by writing, "Hello, journal" or "Dear Diary." Maybe he'd like to give his journal a name. I suggest that a teen describe the room she's in, write about the weather, tell about her day at school. I'll advise that teens just write what comes to mind, "I'm sitting here under the oak tree in the backyard trying to think of something to write in my new journal. I hope my sister doesn't come to get me for dinner before I think of something to write…" I call this rambling. Sometimes rambling leads to real journal material—something a teen wants to document, resolve or understand.

When the teen is ready, he can begin to write about something that's troubling him, worrying him, making him feel said, angry or happy. Writing will come easier some days than others. Some days a journal entry may take up several pages and other times the child will do well to write one sentence.

Many people find that on days when words don't come easily, it's because there is something on their mind—something, perhaps, they don't want to talk about. One 12-year old girl sat down every day for three days with her journal and wrote nothing. All she could think about was the fight she had with her best friend, Laura. Finally, she decided to write about the fight. She described what happened and wrote about how she was feeling inside. Not only did she begin to feel better after writing about it, she could see the problem more clearly. Later that day, she figured out how to resolve the issue and soon she and Laura were best friends again.

There are no rules to keeping a journal. This book will offer suggestions, however, based on what has worked for other teens.

# Part II: <u>JOURNAL-KEEPING IN REAL LIFE</u>

### Chapter 5: Learning About Yourself or Who Am I?
This chapter explains how the teen can use journaling to get to know him or herself better because you cannot improve if you don't recognize your faults and shortcomings and you won't excel if you don't know where your strengths are.

Through exercises and sample journal entries, the teen will learn how to become acquainted with who she is so she can take an active part in who she will become.

We are all changed by time and experiences. Those who have found the secret to true happiness, have found joy within themselves. This is only possible when you know yourself well and journaling is an important means to that end.

By writing honestly about one's feelings, fears, beliefs and impressions—things that they may not normally take the time to examine—a teen is creating the opportunity to develop into the person he or she wants to become—preferably somebody whom they admire and trust.

**Chapter 6: Document the Events of Your Life.** Life is a series of events and we don't always know which ones are significant to our growth. It's fun and enlightening to document life events, such as the day the teen's drawing took second place in the junior division at the county fair, when his brother fixed his bicycle and asked for nothing in return or the time his dad took him shopping for a new pair of ice skates. Although events such as these may not seem hugely important, something in the experience may have provided an insight or lesson that will help the teen to understand himself, someone else or a situation in the future.

I'll suggest that the teen start her journal by telling her life story— documenting everything she can remember about her childhood. Within those early years is sometimes woven a string that emerges in a pattern that will help a youngster to overcome or understand something that's going on in his or her life now.

Fourteen-year-old Angela didn't get along very well with her 10-year-old brother. They fought about everything. When she began to write her life story, she could see that she and her brother had been at odds ever since her mother resumed her career. Of course, Angela put most of the blame on him.

She began documenting the details of their arguments. She also noted times when they did get along. What Angela discovered was that she had the power to create fights or peace.

When the two of them got along, it was because Angela took the time to acknowledge him, listen to him or play with him. When fights occurred, it was when Angela pushed him away. What Angela realized was that with both of their parents working all day, she had become her brother's security blanket and when she ignored or rejected him, he felt angry and hurt and he would lash out at her. She, in turn, would react to his behavior and soon they were fighting.

## Chapter 7: Understanding Others or Why Are They Like That?

A key to understanding and accepting ourselves is understanding and accepting others. This chapter will focus on a child's or teen's relationships with parents, siblings, extended family members, friends and even passing acquaintances. Here, the teen will learn some of the principles of getting along in a world where everything isn't always all right and where everything doesn't always go his way. One way to get along without compromising one's values is through deeper understanding of self and others. I'll demonstrate journaling techniques that will help youngsters examine problem issues and difficult situations that involve others. These techniques will help them to find answers to such questions as, "Why did he do that?" "Why doesn't she seem to understand?" "Why does he hate me?" Journal-keeping can help kids resolve issues by changing their mind. Rarely do we have control over a situation that involves someone else. When a teen can't change the circumstances, however, she can change how she relates to another person and how this person affects her.

**Chapter 8: Journal to Solve Problems.** When a teen is unsure about how to handle a situation or confused about how to approach something, journaling comes to the rescue. I'll share exercises and examples demonstrating how to use journal-keeping to make difficult decisions about which girl to ask to the prom, for example, whether the teen should go out for cheerleading or track or whether it's in a student's best interest to attend a particular party.

This chapter will guide kids in turning to their journal when life is confusing or they have a specific problem and teach them how to resolve the problem through journaling.

**Chapter 9: Your Journal: Healing for Hurt Feelings.** This chapter is the essence of what journaling is about—healing emotional pain. Whether a teen is suffering guilt, anger and fear after his parents' divorce or devastation and loss after the breakup of a friendship, courtship or death of a loved one, for example, regular and honest journaling is key.

If they're grieving a major loss in their life, they're not alone. Divorce is rampant among adults. Twenty-three million children went to bed last night without their fathers in the home. Millions more feel abandoned by parents who choose drugs and alcohol over responsible parenting or who work away from home most of their waking hours.

Even those youngsters with caring parents are bombarded every day by negative choices. Negative peer pressure is at an all-time high and even kids from ideal home situations are put in temptation's way. It's not an easy time to be an adolescent, but I will demonstrate how journaling can help heal grief and guide the teen in making the right choices, particularly in these challenging times.

## Part III: <u>JOURNALING AS A LEARNING TOOL</u>

**Chapter 10: Journal Your Way to Better Grades.** Often the reason a student does poorly in school is lack of organization and the ability to prioritize. Through journaling, these attributes/skills can be practiced and honed. This chapter will demonstrate how through example and simple exercises.

I'll address the student's cognitive skills. When a student leaves school at the end of the day without a clear understanding of the class assignment, he is not going to get very far in completing that assignment. I'll teach kids how to gain greater clarity by writing down things they know and the things they don't know about the assignment and processing this information so the assignment becomes more clear.

**Chapter 11: Improve Your Writing Skills Through Journaling.** Journaling is writing and practice makes perfect, so it follows that if a child or teen writes in his journal regularly, he is practicing writing skills. As a writer with 27 years professional experience, I will offer exercises to help the teen improve her writing skills.

**Chapter 12: The Creative Journal**. A journal can be a book of poetry, creative prose or a collection of short stories. It can be a continuing life story. A child's journal pages might have drawings that reflect her thoughts. Some teens put their whole journal in picture form while others enhance their entries with drawings or sketches. Kids need to know that their journal is theirs to do with as they please. There is no right or wrong way to keep a journal. This chapter will encourage creativity and give examples children and teens may want to explore.

**Chapter 13: Just Look at Me Now.** In the chapter, I will recommend that kids read their journal entries every few months or so to evaluate their personal growth. There's nothing that can boost one's confidence quite like seeing evidence that they're learning and growing in ways that are meaningful to them.

I'll help readers to recognize the signs of growth as these can be overlooked at first glance.

### Tips for Sending a Proposal Package to the Publisher

Generally, you're going to start the process of approaching a publisher by sending a query letter. Once the proposal is requested, send it per the specific requirements that publisher has outlined in his submission guidelines or letter of request. Some publishers want to see sample chapters as part of the proposal. Others won't ask to see sample chapters until after reviewing the proposal.

Send your proposal package by mail unless a publisher requests it sent by email. And then follow the publisher's guidelines. Do they want to receive it as an attachment or in the body of an email? For additional details on how to prepare your proposal package, refer to Chapter Four.

This is the end of our lesson on how to write a book proposal. Once you have completed your chapter outline, it is time to start approaching agents and/or publishers.

But first, consider hiring an editor who has had experience with book proposals in your subject or genre. This is a good insurance policy, and generally, well worth the $300-$1,000.

## Recommended Reading

*How to Write a Successful Book Proposal in 8 Days or Less*, by Patricia Fry (Matilija Press, print edition, 2005).

# Chapter Eight

## HOW TO APPROACH AND
## WORK WITH AGENTS
## AND PUBLISHERS

Most authors, at some point in their careers, wonder, "Should I get an agent?" The answer to this question depends on a couple of factors. If you want to be published by one of the mega-publishers, you will probably need an agent. If your project appeals only to small publishers, you may not need one. In fact, some small- to medium-size publishers prefer working with authors who do not have outside representation.

Random House, Simon and Schuster, St. Martin's Press and Grand Central Publishing (formerly Warner Books) make it a policy to reject a submission unless it comes through an agent. Of course, humans make policies and they can change policies. You could be the lucky one who lands a contract by slipping one over the transom at Grand Central, Morrow or Ballentine.

In fact, according to one source, just eighty percent of books accepted by major publishing houses are represented by agents. So, while I won't discourage you from trying to infiltrate the system by sending an unagented submission to a major publisher, I urge you to arm yourself with enough information so that you are operating within the realm of reality. Before venturing off into the unknown and crossing over long-standing barriers, at least do so with your eyes wide open.

Be realistic. Is your book actually one that would interest a publisher at a large publishing house? Few of them would take a risk on a first novel. You might consider building a reputation and a following before approaching Simon and Schuster. A book on bird-watching in the Ozarks or creative window dressings for a child's room probably wouldn't appeal to a major publisher. They wouldn't be interested in your memoir, either, unless, perhaps, you are someone of celebrity status.

## What Does an Agent Do for You?

An agent might help you to fine-tune your proposal or manuscript before sending it to a publisher. When it's ready, she will show it around to suitable publishers—especially those with whom she has worked before. She'll give a sales pitch. She'll follow up with a publisher, when necessary. And she'll bring you any contract that is offered. She'll also advise you in negotiating a better deal—a larger advance, perhaps, and a higher royalty percentage.

Agents sometimes run in the same circles as publishers and can get inside information. An agent might know what type of manuscript a particular publisher is currently seeking. One author I know received a tip from her agent. She said that a certain major publisher was in the market for a book on a particular topic. The author quickly put together a proposal and promptly landed a contract.

An agent might elicit a bidding war in an attempt to get the author more money. She may show your manuscript to two or three publishers. If they're all interested in it, she may challenge each of them to up their ante.

An agent can sometimes get your manuscript read faster than when you submit one on your own. Some acquisitions editors prefer working with qualified agents as opposed to less savvy authors.

A good agent will make sure that your royalty checks arrive on time. After all, she has a vested interest. Your agent doesn't get paid until you land a publishing contract. Along with a percentage of your royalties, she may also receive a portion of the advance she negotiates for you and a percentage of any escalators that might come your way.

Have you heard of an escalator? This is a bonus that an author gets from his publisher should his book receive accelerated recognition. The royalty percentage might rise (or escalate) once sales have reached a certain agreed upon level, for example. An agent can negotiate for escalators as part of the publishing contract.

> If you choose not to use an agent, I recommend that you hire an intellectual properties or literary attorney to look over any publishing contract you might receive.

Before choosing an agent, understand that they don't all come with the same knowledge and values. While many agents are legitimate and have had years of experience working within the publishing industry, there are plenty of newcomers trying to ride the wave of opportunity at the expense of hopeful authors.

An agent typically signs with you for a year or two. This can create a rough road ahead if the agent is a poor one. It can tie you up for months and keep you from pitching your own manuscript.

A bad agent can be worse than having no agent at all. Here are some warning signs indicating that you may have contacted the wrong agent:

- She asks for money up front, usually in the form of a reading fee. Many agents will request a minimal amount to handle copies and postage. That's okay. It's when they ask for a substantial reading fee or an advance against royalties that you should start to see red flags.

- He suggests that you turn your manuscript over to a particular book doctor or editor before he will start working with you. It's not uncommon for an agent to suggest that you hire an editor. Nor is it unusual for him to make recommendations. But if he gives you just one or two leads, he may be running a scam. Sometimes, people calling themselves agents are just operating editorial services. They don't have any actual experience as an agent.

- He is unwilling to give references. Legitimate agents are pleased to share their successes. If the agent has never signed an author within the category of publisher you hope to land, this may not be the right agent for you. It's important that you find out what types of manuscripts he or she has placed and with whom. I suggest talking to some of the authors he represents to learn if this agent is professional and effective.

- She goes for long periods without communicating and will not respond to your letters, email or phone calls.

I've had trouble landing an agent over the years. Generally, agents will tell me, "It sounds as though you're doing alright without an agent." And let's be real. Most of the books I write aren't exactly bestseller material. I'm a *give me the facts, ma'am* sort of author with targeted how-to books. Finally, however, I found an agent who was eager to represent my fatherhood and fathering book. I sent her my proposal package and $20 for copy and mailing expenses. I also gave her a list of the publishers I'd already approached with this manuscript.

I received one additional letter from her in which she asked for another $20. I sent it and then there was nothing. Months later, I tried to contact her. She did not respond to my letters. When I called her number, I was told that her phone had been disconnected. I waited to hear from her. Finally, a year had gone by—our agreement had come to an end. All I needed was her accounting of the publishers she had approached with my manuscript and her professional recommendations.

I sent another letter—still no response. Finally, I sent her quite a brusque letter demanding the return of my manuscript along with her update. She eventually responded using my self-addressed-stamped envelope curtly stating that she had already returned the manuscript some time ago, period. That was it.

Of course, I never received the manuscript or any other material from her. My guess is that either she got caught up in a personal crisis and didn't have the energy to appropriately handle her business partnerships or she was operating a scam.

That was my sad experience with an agent. I've heard several similar stories—and many much worse. Some opportunists who masquerade as agents, con unsuspecting authors out of hundreds or thousands of dollars. It would behoove you to thoroughly check out any agency you are considering before signing with them. It could take time to find the right agent. But it is important that you choose one who is legitimate, with whom you are compatible and who believes in your project. Locate agents through the following channels:

- Access the Association of Authors' Representatives (AAR) database at aar-online.org. All 382 literary agents on this list have gone through a stringent screening process. All come recommended. Before signing with an agent, make sure that he or she is a member of this prestigious organization.

- Visit the Agent Research and Evaluation Company's free access agent database at agentresearch.com. Here, you'll get agent names and contact information. For a $210 fee, they'll offer a more detailed search involving five agents of your choice. They will provide a new agent list for $75.00.

- Join the National Writers Union (NWU) and access their database of recommended agents. Go to nwu.org for more information.

- Find agents listed in Writer's Digest's *Guide to Literary Agents* and *Literary Market Place.*

- Consider an agent who is recommended by another author who has a book similar to yours.

- Find agents listed in recently published books similar to yours. An author will often mention his agent on the Acknowledgements Page.

- Meet agents at writers' conferences.

## Tips for Choosing and Working With An Agent

Most agents, like publishers, specialize. Match your project to their expertise. Peter Rubie, at the Peter Rubie Literary Agency in New York, represents a variety of fiction and nonfiction books for adults, but you would not approach him with your children's picture book. Jennifer Jackson of Donald Maass Literary Agency is seeking good fiction, horror, science fiction, fantasy and thrillers for adults only. Catt Le Baigue of the Heacock Agency in Los Angeles is always on the lookout for excellent children's books, children's picture books and young adult fiction.

Beware of the newbie or wannabe masquerading as a literary agent. There is no licensing of agents, thus no industry standards. I am not an agent. Some of my clients, however, have asked me to act as their agent. I will go through the paces of finding potential publishers for a client's book in the same way that I seek out publishers for my own works, but not as a literary agent. In fact, once a publisher expresses an interest in a client's manuscript, I'm out of the picture. I leave contract negotiations to my client, his intellectual properties attorney and the publisher.

Many authorities recommend soliciting an agent before you begin showing your manuscript around. An agent will reject manuscripts that have already been submitted to the prime publishers.

On the other hand, sometimes it pays to distribute your proposal to a few publishers before contacting an agent. If you get positive feedback from a couple of publishers, you may have a greater chance of engaging the services of an agent. Tell the agent, for example, "ABC Publishing has asked to see my sample chapters. Would you represent this project for me?"

You approach an agent in much the same way you do a publisher—with a query letter and/or a book proposal representing your current project. Of course, read the agent's submission guidelines for authors and comply. Generally, you will send a query letter to appropriate agents once your book proposal is completed. If yours is a novel, you might wait until the book is finished. Send the same query letter you would send to a publisher, only address it to the agent and refer to your desire for representation rather than publishing.

As with any query letter, keep it brief, professional and easy to read. The job of a query letter is to pique the agent's interest. If you adequately do this, she or he will ask to see your proposal and/or manuscript.

Working with an agent is similar to working with a publisher. You should strive for mutual respect and an air of professionalism. Avoid calling every time a question occurs to you. When you do call, be prepared. Gather your thoughts before dialing and use the time with the agent efficiently. When you receive a contract, read through the entire contract, make notes and then schedule a call to discuss all of your questions and concerns at once.

I want you to stand up for yourself, too. If you feel that something is remiss, request an explanation. If you don't understand the contract terminology, insist upon clarity.

## How to Find a Publisher on Your Own
Can you find a publisher on your own? Absolutely. In fact, some publishers prefer negotiating without the interference of an agent.

You already have an A, B and C list of publishers (see Chapter Two). You know which publishers you want to target. You have their submission guidelines. You understand which publishers prefer to receive your query letter, which want the book proposal and which want to receive your complete manuscript first.

### Prepare, Prepare and Then Prepare Some More
A publisher is a publisher is a publisher. Right? After working with publishers for thirty years and getting to know many of them through my affiliation with SPAWN and other writing/publishing organizations,

I'd say, only to an extent are publishers the same. Of course, publishers are people and you certainly have a variety of personalities represented within this industry. You've already read about the rules and procedures related to the process of contacting a publisher. And you know that there are varying degrees and levels of protocol requirements among publishers.

Some publishers will return unsolicited materials unopened. Don't even waste your money on postage. Others may look at your submission but, without name recognition or agent representation, reject it. Still others welcome solicited and unsolicited submissions and, in fact, prefer working with authors directly.

If you've submitted your manuscript to ten, twenty or even fifty publishers without success, you may feel as though publishers, today, are not accepting anything from anyone. One publisher told me recently, however, that smaller publishers are looking for authors who will write outside the New York box. They want fresh voices that have something new to say. But first you must know what that is. This is where the submission guidelines come in.

Once you've decided which publishers to contact, solicit the most recent copies of their submission guidelines. (See tips for locating and studying submission guidelines in Chapter Two.)

## Give 'Em What They Want

If the publisher asks for a query letter, send only a query letter. It is presumptuous, unfair and unprofessional to send an entire manuscript along with copies of commendations, a resume and your photograph when the publisher just wants to see a simple, yet polished query letter.

I often work with new and some experienced authors. One author, a few years ago, sent me large box unsolicited. I didn't know the package was coming until he contacted me via email to ask if I'd received it. He told me that he had sent me the only copy of his hand-written 500-page manuscript along with original drawings. He asked me to look it over and tell him how to find a publisher for it. Of course, he wanted me to provide this service out of the kindness of my heart. (Sigh.)

The problem was, I had not received the package. I went to my downtown mailbox and then to the post office in desperate search of this package. It took a few days, but I finally located it. And it was a wonder because the author had omitted part of my address. There was no return address on the outside of the box and no return postage inside. I shipped the manuscript back to him, immediately, at my expense with a stern warning to never EVER send out the only copy of a manuscript to anyone. I also advised him to send his manuscript to someone only upon agreement.

I didn't even mention the importance of using a return address on an irreplaceable package. Someone who doesn't know this shouldn't be allowed to go to the post office alone.

I can tell you from vast experience, that publishers do not always return even solicited manuscripts which include adequate postage for the return trip. But still I urge you to comply and conform to each publisher's requests. Your chances of being treated as a professional are greater if you do. Reject this advice and you lessen the likelihood of being published.

I would not fault you for including a clip of an article you've written on the subject of your proposed book, even though the publisher has asked for just a query letter. Go ahead and tuck in one example of the artwork you plan for the book—this might actually help sway the publisher toward requesting the complete manuscript. Just don't inundate or overwhelm him with reams of paper when all he asked for was a query letter. Put your energy, instead, into writing an excellent query letter.

You might hear something different from an author who has made it. But then, this author is in a completely different category than you are. I sat on a panel with a well-known romance writer a few years ago.

She told the audience of sixty-five writers that a query letter wasn't necessary. She advised, "I would send the complete manuscript, no matter what the publisher has asked for." Well this might be true for this bestselling author. Her publisher contacts her when he wants another manuscript. She doesn't have a clue as to the process the rest of us go through.

## The Query Letter Explained

You've seen the term *query letter* approximately two dozen times so far in this book. Expect to see it several more times. Why? Because this is one of the most important elements to the publishing maze. As I said in Chapter Two, a query letter is your first chance to make an excellent impression.

Most agents and publishers request a query letter as a first step in approaching them. I recommend waiting to write the query letter until the book proposal is completed. By then, you'll have a clear idea of the scope and focus of your book. Believe me, a book idea can change right before your eyes once you've been forced to examine it through the process of writing a book proposal.

### The Format

Type the query on your letterhead. Make sure that your letterhead is up-to-date. Do not use an old version where you have to pencil in your Web site address or cross out your old email address and write in the new one. Technology is such that creating letterhead on your home computer is easy and inexpensive. There's no need to give less than a perfect presentation.

Adhere to the requirements of most publishers. That is, single-space your letter with an extra line space between paragraphs. Do not indent. Use 1-1½ inch margins. Keep your query letter to one page, if possible—no more than two pages.

Type the date toward the top of the page on the far left side. Leave one line space and type the name of the acquisitions editor (or agent), then the publishing company (or agency) name and then the complete mailing address.

If the publisher prefers an email query, type the letter in your word processing program without the address block. You can also omit the date as it will appear automatically on your email. Do, however, include your full name, address and phone number at the bottom of the letter. Make it easy for the publisher to respond in the way that makes him or her most comfortable. When the letter is finished, do a spell-check and copy and paste the letter into the body of an email. Publishers and agents, like everyone else, are hesitant to open unsolicited attachments.

## Your Subject Line
Before you click "send" make sure that your subject line message appropriately reflects the content of your email. Think about what will trigger a publisher's or editor's interest. What will entice him or her to open your email? One possibility is name recognition. Does the publisher or editor know you? Is he or she expecting your query? If so, type in, "Requested Query from Jeffery Sampson." If not, you might type, "Query: Children's Book." Or "Query: Successful Hawaiian Luaus," for example. For additional information about how to more effectively use the subject line in your email communication, read the article, *What's in Your Subject Line* at www.spawn.org/internet/whatsinsubjectline.htm.

## Making Contact
Avoid, if you can, addressing your query letter to "Editor" or "Publisher." Study a recent edition of the submission guidelines and/or the editorial pages at the publisher's Web site to locate the name of the acquisitions editor. If you're concerned that the information you have is out of date, call the publishing house and ask the receptionist for the name of the current acquisitions editor.

Make sure you are addressing the appropriate editor. Larger publishing companies often assign certain topics/genres to different editors. Some companies have as many as eight or ten editors, each representing different types of manuscripts. If your proposed book is a young adult novel, make sure you address the acquisitions editor who handles young adult novels.

There have been times when I thought I had the name of the current editor, only to have my query letter returned with a note stating, "This editor no longer works here." Now, why they didn't pass my submission along to the new editor, I don't know. My point is that you can't always rely on the universe (or a publishing house staff) to give you a helping hand or a leg up. Take charge.

While we're on the subject of being proactive, I'd like to caution you against using a submissions service that charges authors a fee for contacting editors and publishers. These services cannot be any more effective than you and are probably less so. I highly recommend that you do your own legwork and headwork when it comes to pitching your manuscript. If you're already working with an editor whom you can trust, and you'd like to hire him or her to handle the submission process for you, I have no quarrel with that. But I still prefer that an author strive toward heavy personal involvement throughout the submission process and beyond.

Address the appropriate editor as Mr. or Ms. If she has a Mrs. before her name, of course, refer to her as Mrs. Johnson. Do not address an editor or a publisher by his or her first name in your salutation until and unless he or she signs a letter to you using just a first name. I generally allow the publisher to establish the level of formality in a relationship. If he sends me a letter signed, John, I address him as John in my next email. If he addresses me as Ms. Fry and signs his letter, John Maxim, I'll probably address him as Mr. Maxim.

Sometimes the editor has a generic name such as Pat, Dana or Marty. When I can't define gender, I typically use both the first and last names: *Dear Pat Spencer* or *Dear Dana Gross*. Do NOT address your query letter, *Dear Sir*. Not only does this demonstrate that you haven't done your homework, it can be insulting to the recipient if she is a woman.

Women run SPAWN. Virginia is our executive director, I, Patricia, am the working president. Wendy is our newsletter editor. Anyone who visits the SPAWN Web site can readily see that this organization happens to be female powered. This is not by design, but it is obvious. Yet, I still receive emails through the SPAWN site addressed, "Dear Sir." Do you think that these people are going to get the same quality of attention and regard from me as someone who addresses an email *Dear Patricia* or *Dear Ms. Fry*? Not even!

Okay, so we have the protocol out of the way. Now let's explore what goes into a successful query letter.

## The Basics of a Successful Query Letter

Your magnificent query letter must:

1. Contain an intriguing beginning or a hook—something that catches the agent's, publisher's or editor's attention. Don't fret over this—just come up with something that creates enough interest so the editor will keep reading. Don't try to be too cute or clever; you might come across as trite.

2. Identify this as a query letter and ask for what you want. Sometimes we become so involved in choosing the perfect words that we forget to focus on clarity. State or indicate early on that this is a query letter. Say, for example, "The book I propose is..." or "Please consider my book, *Beyond the Rainbow*, for publication."

3. Describe your project succinctly and briefly explain (based on information from your book proposal) the need and/or desire for a book such as this.

4. Mention the highlights of your project and any special aspects.

5. Name a few of your experts. (You might want to include a separate list of experts, if it is extensive and impressive.)

6.  Share something about yourself—your background in the subject of your book and as a writer. I sometimes include a separate page listing my published books or titles of any articles I've had published on the topic of this particular book.

7.  Let the publisher know that you have a book proposal ready to send or a completed manuscript. I know, I told you to forget about the manuscript until after you've completed the proposal. But there will come a point when you have completed the manuscript and you'll want to mention that to the publishers you contact.

## Should You Send Simultaneous Submissions?

It is perfectly okay to send out query letters to numbers of publishers at once. Some publishers even sanction sending a book proposal to more than one publisher at a time. I usually send my initial query letter to my first choice of publishers only. If he or she isn't interested in my project, I start sending out simultaneous query submissions.

Do not, however, send your manuscript to more than one publisher simultaneously. An exception to this rule is when a publisher holds your manuscript for a long time without responding. If you can't elicit a response from XYZ Publishing after a reasonable waiting period, write or call and let that publisher know that you will be sending the manuscript to another publisher who has requested it. And then tell the new publisher that the manuscript is also being considered by XYZ Publishing House.

## How Long Should You Wait For a Response?

What is a reasonable waiting period? My rule of thumb for a requested manuscript is two to four weeks past the projected response time for that particular publisher. Most publishers state in their submission guidelines when you can expect a response to a query, a book proposal and a manuscript. FYI, the average response time for a query letter is one to two months; for a proposal, it's around two months, and three months for a manuscript. Unless otherwise stated by the publisher, use these standards.

Sometimes, you'll contact the publisher only to learn that he has misplaced your submission or he claims he did not receive it. Don't throw yourself in front of a bus. Often, perceived disasters such as this can work in your favor. Think about it, suddenly your project becomes a priority for that publisher. Re-submit it at his request and he will go out of his way to look at it.

A publisher might admit that he received your package, but he just hasn't had time to review it. There's still hope. Or he will tell you that it is being circulated among his editorial staff. This is a good thing. When a publisher responds promptly, it is often with a rejection. Publishers at most larger houses will distribute what they view as more promising proposals or manuscripts among the editorial and marketing staff and this always takes time.

Some editors have become uncommonly lax about responding to query letters, book proposals and even manuscripts. I hear more and more authors complaining that their carefully designed letter or package did not elicit a response at all. I'm told that one reason is youth. Apparently, there are a lot of young editors working for publishers—young people who have never been on the creative side of the keyboard. They don't understand what it's like trying to carve a business out of the writing profession and they don't comprehend the part they play in our success or failure. Some don't seem to appreciate the part we play in their success or failure, either.

Some observers say that the younger editors simply don't know what an SASE (self-addressed-stamped envelope) is. So why doesn't someone educate them? When they disregard our query, proposal or manuscript, they're holding up our forward motion. No, I don't think they're ignorant. I maintain that their indifference is a sign of the times. The trend is toward disrespect. You see it on the freeway and on the city bus, why not in business?

If I haven't said it before, let me go on record now: authorship is not for the weak, desperate or faint of heart. There is nothing glamorous about rejection. There is nothing nurturing in neglect and abuse. If you're in this business long enough, you will experience all of the above and it ain't a pretty sight.

If you think that writing is a lonely activity, just wait until you enter into the competitive field of publishing. You'll be ignored, shined on, dissed, talked down to and even treated rudely. You'll sometimes feel like a second-class citizen. To get along, an author must be humble, patient, persistent and always professional. Drinking a couple of beers at the end of a difficult day doesn't hurt, either.

## Surefire Ways to Get Your Query Letter Rejected

Here's a list of mistakes to avoid when developing and submitting your query letter.

1: Do not send your query letter to the wrong publisher. Christine Holbert is founder and director of Lost Horse Press. She publishes fiction only. She says, "A writer needs to do a bit of investigative work before submitting a query or a manuscript to a publisher; find out what the publisher's vision is and what the previously published titles of that particular publishing house are. I receive hundreds of manuscripts of inappropriate genre that are a waste of my time and the author's effort."

2: Don't tell the publisher his business. In other words, don't say, "You've really got to add this book to your list if you hope to make a success of your publishing company." Or "This book will make you rich."

3: Do not threaten the publisher. It will do you no good to say, "If you don't buy my book, I will kill myself." Or "You're missing the book of the century if you pass on this one."

4: Don't claim that your book contains no mistakes. Have you ever read a book that doesn't have a mistake? I don't think it is humanly (or even mechanically) possible to produce a book without a mistake. And from what I'm told by publishers, many authors who claim to have hired professional editors for their books, have been taken for a ride. So make sure you hire a reputable editor before submitting your book proposal or manuscript. Make sure that it is the best that it can be and avoid making wild claims as to the pureness of your project. Let the publisher be the judge.

5: Don't try to convince a publisher to accept your book by saying that your family and friends love it. This is a blatant red flag sign of an amateur.

6: Don't tell the publisher that everyone will buy your book. A publisher will be more impressed by an author who has done his homework and is quite clear as to who his audience is.

7: Do not state that this is the only book you'll ever write. Publishers prefer working with authors who are likely to produce more than one good book. If your book is successful and you are a pleasure to work with, the publisher would just as soon accept another book from you than from someone he doesn't know.

8: Don't reveal that you've been working on the book for twenty-five years. There is nothing impressive in the fact that you have not been able to complete a twelve-month project in over two decades.

9: Do not try to bribe the publisher. Unless you can offer him a large sum of money or a free vacation in Tahiti, don't bother to entice his favor through bribery.

10: Avoid sending a query letter with spelling and grammatical errors.

## Keep Current
Things change rather frequently in the publishing industry. Because of this, I suggest that you do not rely on submission guidelines that are more than six months old. In fact, I suggest writing the date on copies of submission guidelines as you receive them.

As editor of the *SPAWN Market Update,* I'm constantly researching and noting changes within the publishing industry. I can tell you that it is not uncommon for a publishing company to grow out of its quarters and move, hire and fire editors or experience a shift in publishing focus. Demonstrate your level of professionalism by keeping a close check on changes within the publishing companies of your choice.

Fairview Press, for example, a division of Fairview Health Services, which is affiliated with the University of Minnesota, founded Deaconess Press in 1989. They originally published only chemical dependency and recover materials. Then they expanded their list to include psychology, self-help, humor, reference, inspiration, sociology, parenting, child care, general health and children's books. In recent years, the press has decided to focus on two main categories—health/medicine and aging/end of life/death and dying/grief.

Treble Heart Books was established in 2001. Last year, they had three divisions: Treble Heart (romance, paranormal, metaphysical, science fiction, etc.); Mountain View (inspirational and Christian books) and Sundowners, which publishes Westerns. Their newest division at this printing is WhoooDoo Mysteries. And they say they will add more divisions in the future. If you were to obtain their submission guidelines now and refer to them in a year or two, you might miss the fact that they have added a genre that you could write for.

## Sample Query Letters

January 27, 2004

Editor's Name
Big Name Publishing House
Address
City, State, Zip

Dear Ms. Name:

Fathering is finally fashionable. But because their role models are outdated, countless men are struggling in this capacity. Today, fatherhood doesn't necessarily imply a wage-earning married man who lives with the mother of his children. The concept of dear old dad has taken on new dimensions, thus creating greater challenges for men who want to fulfill even the basic requirements of being someone's dad.

The latest U.S. Census Bureau figures reveal that over 2.75 million children are in the custody of their fathers. The number of primary care-taking fathers is on the rise as well. In 1991, there were 1.4 million dads caring for their pre-school age children while their wives worked. And there's a sharp increase in men involved in raising their stepchildren.

At the other end of the spectrum are estranged dads who pay child-support for the privilege of spending every other weekend with their kids—a hard pill to swallow and a difficult part to play even for the most confident, devoted father. Too many of these men become walk-away fathers, leaving too many of our children sadly and dangerously deficient in the *dad* department.

The book I propose is called ***Fatherhood and Fathering: The Ultimate Guide for Today's Dad.*** It promises to offer information, education, support, guidance and resources for every dad, with emphasis on the growing number of unconventional fathering styles. It includes a fascinating history of fatherhood in this country and reports on the current trends representing fatherhood today, the struggles and obstacles fathers face and how fathers are coping in the new millennium.

This book explores fatherlessness in America and the damage this epidemic is creating. It outlines the steps our government, the court system, the corporate sector and advocacy groups are taking to eliminate this blight on the future of our youth, thus our country.

This extensively researched volume includes dozens of statistics depicting the state of and the effects of fatherhood as we know it today. There are over 100 individual stories and case histories to which the readers can relate and vital contributions, tips and guidance from nearly 85 experts and professionals in the area of fatherhood and fatherlessness.

Our children have been telling us for a long time through their actions that they are not being nurtured. They do not feel loved. This is evidenced by increased gang involvement, teen pregnancy, suicide and rampant drug and alcohol use. This book is a wake-up call for parents, educators and others involved in the welfare and well-being of our kids.

I have been writing for publication for over 30 years. My articles have appeared in *The World and I* (articles related to the emotional healing of our children and the state of today's educational system), *Los Angeles Times, Teaching Tolerance, Writer's Digest, Catholic Digest, Kiwanis Magazine* (an article on teaching children the work ethic), *Living With Teens, Living With Children, Christian Parenting Today, L. A. Parent, Prime Times* and many, many others.

I have 19 books to my credit including *Creative Grandparenting Across the Miles, Ideas for Sharing Love, Faith and Family Traditions* (Liguori Publications,1996) and *Youth Mentoring; Your Gift to the Next Generation* (Liguori Publications, 2004).

***Fatherhood and Fathering, The Ultimate Guide for Today's Dad*** is complete. I can send the manuscript or the book proposal. Let me know which you prefer.

Sincerely,
Patricia L. Fry

I mentioned earlier the value of a *hook* to catch the editor's attention. A stronger lead for this query letter might be, "The fastest growing crime in America today is children killing children. Fatherlessness is a major factor in this horrendous trend."

Here's another query letter that captured the interest of a publisher.

August 22, 2004

Editor's Name
Publisher
Address
City, State Zip

Dear Ms. Name:

### Re: Catscapades, Tales of Ordinary and Extraordinary Cats.

Gift books are big business and cats are more popular than ever. Combine the two and you have a book that will leap off the shelves into the welcoming hands of readers everywhere.

The book I propose is a collection of true cat stories. These stories, taken from my own 50-years' experience with cats and those experiences of others, will entertain, teach, fascinate, enchant, surprise and delight readers.

I'll share the story of Max, the once feral kitten who, with lots of love and support, is now the purrrrfect lap cat. Max is probably the most creative cat I've ever seen. There are a hundred stories to tell about his daily antics. He greets me at the door looking for a toy treat when I return from the grocery store. He will gingerly take a miniature rose from a vase and float it in his own water dish. He'll hide a toy under a throw rug or pillow and act surprised when he finds it a few seconds later. And he comes to me when I call him.

I'll tell stories of on-hands healing successes and communication between myself and some of my cats. I used "mind talk" to coax a reluctant calico named Daisy, into the cat carrier once. After rescuing Maggie from the humane society, she was diagnosed with a serious ailment that would surely kill her unborn kittens. Shortly after using a hands-on healing technique, Maggie gave birth to three healthy, robust kittens. Not only did she take excellent care of her own kittens, she also took on an abandoned newborn kitten.

I've had some unusual experiences with cats: my Persian, Crystal, swallowed a needle. Molly almost lost her tongue when she found a sardine can in the trash and tried to lick it clean. One of our cats disappeared and returned about a year later with a newborn kitten. What's unusual about that? Nothing, except that we'd had this female cat spayed.

Another mother cat went into attack mode when one of her kittens was injured. She wouldn't let anyone near the kitten except me and she gave me free rein to care for the comatose kitten. Surprisingly, even this story has a happy ending. I'd also like to include stories about how we named some of our cats. We find it works best to let the cat name him or herself and this concept has resulted in some interesting situations.

I'll include stories of abandoned and even abused cats that now live in workplace environments. There are nearly 300 known "shopcats" in the U.S. today and over 400 library cats. Dewey Readmore Books, an orange tabby kitten, was found one frosty morning in Iowa under a pile of heavy books in the book drop at the local library. He now works at the library as official greeter.

Among other stories I'll tell, is the one about Cassidy, who inspired the woman who found him abandoned to start an organization to protect animals from abuse.

I envision this book being about 5" x 6 ½" with 175 – 200 pages. The stories will number around 20 or 25 and encompass anywhere from two to ten pages each.

I've been writing for publication for 30 years. I write articles for magazines full time, having contributed to *Cats, Cat Fancy, I Love Cats, ASPCA Animal Watch, Pet Age, Western Horse, Horse Illustrated, The World and I, Kiwanis Magazine, American Health for Women, Writer's Digest, Freelance Writer's Report, Writer's Journal, Canadian Author, Catholic Digest* and many, many others.

I'm also the author of 19 books ranging in topic from horse care to local history to writing and book promotion. My newest book, on youth mentoring, debuted this year (Liguori Publications).

Please let me know if you'd like to see the book proposal for

***Catscapades, Tales of Ordinary and Extraordinary Cats.***

Sincerely,
Patricia L. Fry
www.matilijapress.com (for more about me)

Waiting is hard to do. But it helps if you don't make your book project your only focus. While the publisher is reviewing your query letter, you can be working on Chapter One. Consider writing an article on the subject of your manuscript while waiting for a publisher's response. Not only will this fill your time, but, if accepted, it would also show a prospective publisher that there's an interest in your topic.

In the meantime, keep excellent records. Don't rely on memory. Know exactly when you sent a query or a proposal and to whom. Log each response and each tracer letter sent. Effective record-keeping isn't just a convenience, it's a necessity. (Read more about bookkeeping systems in Chapter Fourteen.)

## A Word About Rejection

We write, we get edited and we sometimes get rejected. There is no such thing as a writer's life without editing or without rejection and criticism.

Robert Olmsted, publisher at Dan River Press told me once, "The average writer thinks because he/she writes brilliantly, that publishing should follow. Not real. Publishing is a commercial activity engaged in for profit. Writing is art. If you are asking a publisher to invest in your art, give the publisher a reason and he will. All rejections happen because the publisher has other options on which he believes he can make more money."

What if you get that dreaded rejection letter? Here's a reality check. Publishers don't know everything. And they don't always recognize a *Wow* project when they see it. Some tremendously successful books were rejected many times before they were discovered. The first in the series of *Chicken Soup* books was reportedly rejected by 140 publishers before Health Communications agreed to publish it. Since then, there have been more than fifty-six million copies of the thirty Chicken Soup titles sold.

James Redfield's *Celestine Prophecy* was rejected by several publishers before Redfield decided to self-publish. He sold so many copies on his own, that Warner Books (now Grand Central Publishing) agreed to publish it. The book has sold millions of copies, since.

While I want you to focus on the positive and believe in your project, I also stress the importance of realistic evaluation. Keep an eye on trends. Make it your business to know what is selling and what is not. Get into the minds and hearts of readers. Avoid being so emotionally attached to your project that you become blind to reality.

A gentleman came to me a couple of years ago and requested that I review his manuscript. He was showing it around to publishers and wanted to know why he was continually being rejected. He told me that his book was designed to help parents work more successfully with their autistic children. In reality, it read more like a personal journal or letters to grandma. There was no self-help element to this book. If the author had written a book proposal, he would have been forced to more succinctly assess the direction of the book he planned. Unbeknownst to this author, he was targeting the wrong publishers and misrepresenting his project. When I pointed this out to him, however, he adamantly defended his manuscript and refused to consider making any changes.

The same author contacted me recently to ask if I would help him with a rewrite. He finally got a reality check after being rejected by dozens more publishers. Some of them even gave him advice. Two publishers suggested that he write a book proposal and one of them went on to point out that his book was not a self-help book, as he claimed, but more of an essay or a memoir. The publisher said, "I believe that a book such as you describe is publishable, but yours, the way it is written, doesn't quite fit the bill."

It's rare that a publisher will take the time to offer commentary. When it happens, it behooves an author to pay attention. Consider the suggestion or advice, do further research, cut through the emotional crap and make an educated decision.

## What Happens When You're Issued a Contract?

Not all correspondence from a publisher comes in the form of a rejection letter. There's always the chance that you will eventually receive a contract. When this happens, I urge you to read it carefully and thoroughly and then hire an intellectual properties or literary attorney to review it. He or she may point out areas that you'll want to discuss with the publisher. He might advise you to negotiate higher royalties or a better percentage for book club sales.

Yes, most contracts are negotiable—at least aspects of them are. I've even had publishers ask me what royalty percentage or advance I want.

Some publishers will offer to purchase your manuscript outright. Probably two-thirds of those I researched for this chapter had the outright purchase option. What can you get for a manuscript? Publishers offer anywhere from $600 to around $20,000, with $2,000 to $5,000 being most common.

Royalties are generally paid quarterly, but there are exceptions to this rule, too. Read your contract carefully. Are you getting royalties on the retail or the wholesale price? About half of those publishers I researched pay on the retail price.

In May of 2007, I did a survey of thirty-five publishers and came up with twenty-four combinations of royalty percentages offered by these publishers. For print books, the percentages range from two to five percent on up to ten to twenty percent with every combination imaginable in between. One publisher offers five to twelve percent, another seven to ten percent. There were publishers giving a straight ten percent, a straight fifteen percent or six to fifteen percent. Still the average royalty percentage you'll find among traditional publishers is between ten and twelve percent. For electronic books (ebooks), royalties are in the twenty-five to fifty percent range.

Not all publishers will pay an advance. In fact, advances run from 0 to $50,000. The majority of publishers offer $1,000 advance in two equal payments: $500 at the time the contract is signed and $500 upon satisfactory completion of a manuscript. The advance is deducted from future royalties.

There are many new twists in the publishing arena. Some publishers today ask prospective authors to solicit funds among the corporate sector in order to finance their project. If you can't land a publishing contract the traditional way, you might consider asking for some sort of financial support. Of course, the business owner will want something in return—either in the form of royalties, or an advertisement on the inside cover of your book. This may seem like an unusual idea, but if you can come into a publishing agreement with a chunk of money, just think of the difference it could make.

A contract is generally issued before the book is written. In this case, the author is given a deadline on which to complete the book.

Sometimes a hopeful author will be asked to write a book or several chapters on speculation (or spec). This means that the publisher wants you to produce something tangible and to his liking before he issues a contract.

Several years ago, a publisher expressed an interest in my book on successful solitary living. He wanted me to shift the focus of the book, however, and he assigned me an editor. For several weeks, I worked with the editor, making all of the changes she suggested. But each time I did a rewrite based on her specifications, she would change those specs and I found myself rewriting what I had just rewritten. I began to feel as though someone was playing an evil joke on me and I eventually gave it up. Frankly, I think the editor was twisted.

As authors, we have to decide how much we are willing to bend in order to satisfy a certain publisher. Do you really want to rewrite your young adult novel for an adult audience? Are you willing to alter the true story of your grandfather's war experience so that it reads like fiction? While I encourage hopeful authors to make the decisions necessary to get published, I also caution you against selling your soul.

## How to Work Successfully With a Publisher

When you enter into a contract with a publisher, he has certain obligations and so do you. Your responsibilities go beyond the parameters of the contract. It is to your benefit to develop a good working relationship with your publisher for the life of your contract. For example:

- Give the publisher your best effort. Hire an editor before sending your manuscript to a publisher. Shortchanging your publisher in this area means shortchanging yourself.

- Respect the publisher's time and space. How? Respond with just the information requested and send just the materials required. Do not inundate the publisher with frequent phone calls. Don't send the first twelve drafts of your manuscript unless, of course, he or she asks for them.

- Keep your word. The publisher is counting on you to meet agreed-upon deadlines and to follow through with promotion.

- Keep an open line of communication. Stay in touch regarding deadlines. If something changes and you can't meet a deadline, communicate that.

- Expect to do a rewrite. The publisher may or may not ask you to rewrite parts of your book. Most likely, he will send you an edited version of your manuscript for your approval. Study the edits carefully to make sure that the meaning of your message or story has not been altered.

- Be prepared to hand over control. A publisher may change the title that you have become so attached to. He may ask you to reorganize your chapters. Of course, you can question his judgment and negotiate for what you want, if it means a lot to you. But realize that the publisher probably has more experience with matters of book publishing than you do.

## After the Book is Published

Once the book is published and you're holding it in your hands, go ahead and celebrate. Let the bubbly flow. Dance around the office/block/town showing off the fruits of your labor.

Okay, that's enough dancing and drinking. It's time to enter promotion mode.

You've already outlined much of your promotional agenda in your book proposal. Now contact the marketing director that the publisher has assigned and begin discussing the company's promotional plan. Ask how you can help. Send him a list of potential reviewers and potential bulk buyers of your title. For my book on youth mentoring, my list included all forty-five organizations and agencies noted in my resource list and about thirty magazines.

Keep the publisher informed as to your promotional progress. Let him know when you've had an article published, you've appeared on a radio program or the book has been reviewed. Send copies of articles and reviews to the publisher.

## Recommended Reading

*Jeff Herman's Guide to Book Editors, Publishers and Literary Agents, 2005: Who They Are! What They Want? How to Win Them Over* by Jeff Herman (Harper Collins, 2005).

# Chapter Nine

## GET READY
## GET SET
# WRITE

This is what you've been waiting for—the opportunity to write your wonderful book. You've established that there is a market for it. You've decided on a publisher. You've sent out at least one query letter. And you've developed a chapter outline. It's finally time to shift into writer mode. But first let's do a little detective work.

## Read What You Write

Before launching into your manuscript, I want you to read books similar to the one you plan to write. Familiarize yourself with the tone, format and style of books in your genre. Read a variety of authors. If yours is a young adult novel, study half dozen or so young adult novels. Pay attention to the language. What drives these stories? Identify the elements of the most successful books in this category and apply some of them to yours. I'm not suggesting that you copy these books, but use them as guides in organizing and writing yours.

Maybe you're writing a how-to book. Not everyone can write directions or a series of steps with clarity. Read instructional books on many topics. Notice how they are organized. What techniques seem to work and which ones don't? Do you prefer books with lots of shaded boxes and bulleted lists to break up the monotony of text? Perhaps you like how-to books sprinkled with humor. What type of illustrations are appropriate for a book on your topic?

Different genres require different approaches. And some genres have pretty specific requirements. Children's literature is one of them.

If you are writing a children's book, you particularly want to read books at that age level. Note the language used in books for that age group. How many pages do these books run? What is the typical word count per page?

## How to Get Beyond Overwhelm

The thought of writing a sixteen- or even eight-chapter book can be intimidating. I often feel overwhelmed when confronted by a large writing project. You should have seen me when it was time to start this book. I sharpened pencils until they were nubs. I straightened my desk over and again. I separated small paperclips from large ones and tested the strength of the rubber bands in my desk drawer. It's way easier to procrastinate than to dive in and start writing. But it's certainly not very productive.

Writers, listen up! Shut down that computer solitaire game. Stop checking your email. Turn off your phone ringer. And start writing.

If you feel a bit intimidated when faced with a large writing project, just knock it down to size. Perspective is everything. Rather than looking at the book as a whole, focus on one chapter at a time. And, you don't even have to start at the beginning.

Start with the chapter that you feel would be easiest to write—the one containing the material or theme you're most familiar with.

I generally begin with the introduction because it helps me to focus on the point of the book. It reveals the purpose of the book and sets the stage for what's to come. Some authors write their introduction last on the theory that you can't properly introduce your book until you've written it.

If you're still having trouble getting started, consider writing a short piece or two for a local newspaper or a national magazine. This is a great method of building up your confidence while honing your organizational and writing skills. This is also an excellent way to test consumer interest in your topic and to establish credibility in your field and as a writer. (Read more about writing and submitting articles in Chapter Thirteen.)

Psychologically, writing an article or a stand-alone chapter is less overwhelming than the thought of writing a 60,000-word book. If you are comfortable writing a 2,000 – 4,500-word article, you should have no problem writing a chapter. Just look at your book as a series of articles or stories—each with a beginning, middle and end.

Of course, you have your book proposal as a guide to organizing and writing your nonfiction book. But don't be surprised if things change. Follow your original outline only for as long as it makes sense. If you see a good reason to change, by all means, do so.

## How to Manage the Mountain of Material

There are a variety of ways to handle material while preparing a book. I file research material in file folders and store them in a large Stor-All box in hanging file folders throughout the duration of the writing process. Some authors type everything that comes across their desk into the computer immediately. Others use index cards to organize topics or a storyline. One writer I know pastes pages from her current book-in-progress all over her office walls. She likes having a constant visual of the project.

The right way to proceed with a book project is the one that works best for you. And this might change from book to book. Having said that, I'd like to share some of the techniques that work for me and other authors I've polled.

By now you've probably written the first draft of your introduction. If not, here's a tip: Start with the description of the introduction from your chapter outline. Remember, the chapter outline is part of your book proposal. This description may, in fact, become your first few paragraphs. Bring material from your synopsis into the introduction, as well.

I generally spend some time perfecting the introduction because it sets the tone for the rest of the book. And then I move on to Chapter One. I start each chapter using the material from the corresponding chapters in my well-written chapter outline (or chapter-by-chapter summaries). Next, I open the file folder devoted to each chapter in sequence and type in the additional information, facts and statistics.

Don't give too much thought to style and grammar, yet. This is not the time to fret over sentence structure and punctuation. Just write. Document your ideas and thoughts along with the information you've collected. You can organize, fact-check and edit later.

While you're compiling and writing during the first go-around, note any additional information you might need for that chapter and where it should be inserted. I type notes within the text in parenthesis using all caps and/or color. I might type, for example, (EXPAND THIS THOUGHT) or (LOCATE ADDITIONAL RESOURCES).

You can either work through the entire book chapter by chapter using this method or you can fine tune each chapter before moving on to the next. Because chapters sometimes change right before your eyes, I suggest the former. Here's basically how I work:

1. I type all relevant information I've gathered into the pages representing each chapter.

2. At the same time, I type any commentary that comes to mind.

3. I print out these pages and go through them making sure that the material is logically positioned.

4. I cut and paste information, quotes, narratives, etc. that seem out of place.

You should be able to look at each chapter of a nonfiction book as a complete mini-book or an article with a beginning, middle and end. Each chapter should make a point and serve a purpose.

As an example, for this chapter, I decided that I needed an introduction, tips for getting started writing a book, ideas for organizing your material, research techniques, interview tips, ideas for disciplining yourself to write, a section on editing, a bit about how to finish a book and something about taking criticism. I started working on this chapter by listing each of these section ideas and numbering them.

I then assigned corresponding numbers to each piece of material that I had accumulated for this chapter. By this time, I had all of the material typed into the computer. Using the cut and paste feature, I moved each piece of the information, quotes, etc., into the appropriate section within this chapter. Then I began to organize each section and tie the material together with my commentary.

**What About Fiction?**
When writing a story, chapters may not be evident at first. It could take some contemplation and practice to learn where to make chapter breaks. Some breaks will be obvious, others will not. I like to see novelists start each chapter with a hook to pique the reader's interest and end it with a cliff hanger or at least an unanswered question to keep them reading. Chapters may be determined by a timeline, the introduction of characters or location or the natural progression of events and occurrences.

## Hone Your Research Skills
Just as there are varying ways to write and organize a book, the process of conducting research and interviews can differ. Some writers complete the research and interviews before starting to write. Others research as they move from chapter to chapter. For most nonfiction authors, research is an ongoing process.

Research is necessary for most nonfiction books and many fiction books. Even if you are an expert in your field, you'll want to bring in current information, statistics and, perhaps, the opinions and experiences of others. If you're writing about something outside your realm of expertise, you'll be required to do more in-depth research.

Even though writing and publishing are my professions, I did an enormous amount of research in order to write this book.

When I revised it for the second edition, I conducted research again. Things are ever-changing in the publishing industry and I wanted to make sure to bring you the most up-to-date information.

I find that people either love research or they hate it. Those who hate it or aren't accustomed to it are often intimidated by it.

A man once asked me what kind of work I do. I told him that I'm a writer and he asked what I write. I explained that I write on a variety of subjects, including parenting, business issues, writing, publishing, public speaking and book promotion. He looked at me and, in all seriousness, said, "Wow, you must be the most intelligent woman I have ever met."

Obviously, this gentleman doesn't understand the concept of research. The fact is that, if you're a good researcher, you can actually write a book on a subject you know nothing about. You may be interested in writing an informational book on Alzheimer's disease or building a sod house, but you have no practical experience. Perhaps you want to write a novel reflecting the pre-depression era in New York City, but you're only 45 years old and didn't experience it. Does this mean that you cannot write a book on these topics? Absolutely not. It just means that you will need to do a lot of research.

Most authors have a comfort zone when it comes to research. I'd like to encourage you to step outside that zone in order to provide your readers with the most complete information or the most exact historical accounts. Your reputation as an author and as an expert in your field depends on your accuracy. And you owe it to your readership to be precise.

**Start With Books**
Study books from your home library. If you're interested in the subject or genre that you'll be writing about, you probably have books to

prove it. For nonfiction, gather ideas, information, statistics and resources. Note the experts that were quoted and referenced. Contact some of them for fresh quotes and additional information.

Note the title, author, publisher, copyright date and the type of material you found in each book in case you want to reference this material again. You may also consider including this book in your bibliography and/or your resource list. Some publishers will request this sort of information for fact-checking purposes.

For fiction, notice the writing style, the way authors handle dialogue and what makes the stories intriguing, interesting or suspenseful. Why do these stories work? Practice these techniques.

**Visit the Public Library**
The public library is still a great place to conduct research. While you don't find many new books in libraries, these days, you're likely to locate some good sources for historical and statistical information.

Use reference books on your topic, the period or the geographic location of your proposed story. Search out statistical data in appropriate reference materials. Locate current articles on the subject or location of your story through the *Reader's Guide to Periodical Literature*. This series of books lists articles by subject and the magazines in which the articles appear. Use old newspapers on microfiche for factual data on once current events, the political climate back then, the cost of living in earlier times and even the weather conditions during a certain time period.

There's more to a library than is immediately obvious, which is why I recommend that you seek help with your research. Make friends with the librarian. She/he can open up new worlds of awareness for you.

**Step Into the Bookstore**
You can purchase books to use in your research from brick and mortar bookstores as well as online. There are many online bookstores today that sell new books at discounted prices. Start at amazon.com. Scroll

down on the page where the book appears and you'll usually find some discount options. Or do a Google search to find a discount bookstore to your liking. Use keywords "discounted books" or "discount books" or "cheap books."

## A Note About Plagiarism

I'm not suggesting that you plagiarize (copy copyrighted materials). Research means gathering and verifying information, facts and statistics. It means locating expert sources for your book. If you wish to use a substantial passage from a published book, you must get permission.

Write or email the publisher and request written permission to use a specific passage or quote. I typically provide the publisher with the exact quote I want to use, information about how I'll use it and a permission form to be signed. Sometimes there's a fee for such permission. And sometimes the information is worth the fee. I've never had a publisher ask for more than $100 for a paragraph or two.

Always give full credit for any material used. Just because you pay for it doesn't mean that you own it. In fact, most publishers and authors will specify that you have paid for or have been given permission for one-time use of the material, only.

If you want to use a statistic or just briefly paraphrase a quote or a concept, you may not need permission. But always give written credit to the author or researcher.

## Pursue Computer Research

As writers, we have unlimited research resources at our fingertips. All we have to do is enter the information highway. Yet, still many people don't know how to find the onramp.

I often reply to writers' questions. And generally, I must do some research in order to respond accurately—research that the individual could have done him/herself. Someone might ask me to define *creative nonfiction* or *chick lit*. They may want to know, what is a reasonable fee for a good editor? I don't always have a definitive answer at the ready, so I launch into research.

If the topic is one I've covered in my own writing/publishing-related books or in an issue of the *SPAWN Market Update*, I generally start my research there. Next, I might refer to some of the many reference books I have in my home office. To learn the going rate for editors, I will probably turn first to the "How Much Should I Charge?" pages in *Writer's Market*. When these resources are tapped out, I launch an Internet search.

## Google
I start with everyone's favorite search engine, *Google*. I type in the subject and away I go. In the case of chick lit, I might type in *chick lit* or *chick lit definition*.

Sometimes you find the answer to your question quickly and other times it takes a while. But the process can be rather interesting. I often discover unexpected information and data whenever I'm doing a search.

If you stumble across something interesting and pertinent to your project, print it out and/or bookmark the site for later reference. Perhaps you're looking for information or statistics related to uniforms worn by a certain regiment in the Civil War. While searching, you discover a page describing plants and trees that grow in the region of certain battles—information you will need in a later chapter of your historical novel. Print out that page or bookmark it so you can reference it later. A good researcher builds and maintains his own directory of significant sites. Collect those that relate to your current project.

## Tips for Using Web Sites
Not all Web sites are straightforward and easy to use. In fact, some present quite a challenge. If you want to know more about the site and the people behind it, click on "About Us." This is also where you will sometimes find their contact information. The first place to look for contact information, however, is "Contact Us."

When you find a good site on your topic, study the articles and interviews posted there and check out the links they recommend. Some links will prove to be great resources for additional information.

**Message Boards**

I like to visit message boards and forums related to my book topic. It's a good way to meet people to interview for a book project. When I was in research mode for the long-distance grandparenting book, I found several grandparents at family message boards who had some great ideas to share. These folks loved participating in my book and most of them purchased copies. I found people with unique pork roasting tips and recipes for my book, *The Mainland Luau* through cooking and barbecuing message boards.

To locate message boards on your topic, at Google, or the search engine of your choice, type in "message board" plus your topic or topic plus "message board." It works either way. For example, "message board Alzheimer's," "message board photography" or "pet message board."

## Interview Techniques

If you hope to add interest and credibility to your book, you will probably want to tap into the opinions and expertise of others. Let's say that you're writing about obesity in children. After you've given your views and you've reported on current findings, enhance your book by interviewing people in the know. Talk to the directors of innovative fitness programs in schools throughout the U.S., parents of obese children and a couple of doctors who specialize in childhood obesity. You may be surprised at how the scope of your project will change when you start pulling in expert perspectives and quotes.

If you're timid about approaching experts or have trouble asking the right questions, here are some tips to help you conduct more successful interviews. First, let me say that some of my favorite people to interview are high profile professionals. I find most busy professional people to be more easily accessible, eager to be interviewed and cognizant of my time constraints.

1: **Locate experts**. Start a search for professionals and other individuals who can add credibility and anecdotes to your book. I always try to interview people from throughout the U.S. and sometimes the world for a more diverse representation. There are many ways to find experts—here are a few:

- Study books on your topic.

- Engage a search engine to locate experts on the Internet. Use your topic or the name of the individual as the keyword.

- Find specialists listed in online and print articles related to your topic.

- Search university staff Web pages to find a qualified authority.

- Visit organization pages to locate an appropriate professional.

- Discover author experts at amazon.com.

- Locate nonprofessional experts through message boards. (See above.)

- Peruse sites dedicated to expert sources such as: Expertcentral.com and Expertclick.com.

2: **Learn something about the interviewee.** Before contacting an individual for an interview, find out something about him. Study articles in which this person is quoted. If she's an author, read her bio on the book cover or on her page at amazon.com. If he's a business owner, professor, organization leader or a politician, call his office and request an information packet.

3: **Write a list of questions**. I try to come up with less than ten specific questions. Four or five of those will usually require some discussion. Ask open-ended questions. Instead of, "Are you looking forward to retirement?" ask, "What will you miss most about working?" Instead of, "Were you sad when your kids all went away to college? ask, "How did you feel when you watched your last child leave for college?" I always like to ask almost everyone I interview, "What would you advise others in this situation?" For example, "What would you advise those who want to retire early?" or "What would you like to say to someone who plans to live for a year on a remote island?"

4: **Make contact**. Call or email the interviewee and briefly introduce yourself. Explain a little about your project. If you have a publisher lined up, be sure to say so. Ask him or her if you can call within the next few days and conduct a telephone interview.

Sometimes the interviewee will suggest that you do the interview on the spot, so be prepared with your questions.

I bought a mechanism at Radio Shack with which I can record telephone conversations. I always ask permission to record. It's the law. If the individual hesitates, I explain that I want to be sure to quote him accurately.

If the subject wants to schedule the interview for another day, I let him know how much time I'll need—generally fifteen to twenty minutes. Before setting an appointment, find out which time zone he's in. And offer to email him the questions ahead of time so he can prepare.

5: **Suggest an email interview**. This has become my favorite way to conduct interviews. There is no transcribing involved. And most people are willing to participate in an email interview because they can think about their responses and write them out at their leisure. There are still people who prefer speaking by phone, however. And there are some valid reasons for avoiding an email interview:

- You get a greater sense of personality when you conduct an interview in person or by phone.

- Some people will procrastinate right past your deadline, if left to respond to questions via email.

- You usually have to send some follow-up questions for clarity and depth.

6: **Ask for clarity**. It is easy for words and phrases to be misconstrued. When you aren't sure about something the interviewee says or writes, ask for clarification. Don't take anything for granted when you're quoting someone, especially when the subject matter is outside your realm of expertise.

7: **Encourage anecdotes**. Text is more interesting and points can be made more effectively when using anecdotes. When an individual spews an interesting statement or makes a provocative point, ask for examples. An artist might say, "I really prefer working outdoors." This is charming, but wouldn't it be even more charming if she painted a word picture? You might say, "Give me an example of pursuing your art out of doors." Follow up with something like, "And how does it make you feel to sit at your easel on that knoll overlooking the meadow?" "How does this site make a difference in the results of your art?" Can you see the colorful possibilities?

8: **Confirm personal information**. Always verify the spelling of the interviewee's name. Ask how he would like to be credited. An author may want his latest book mentioned. A public relations agent will ask you to include her business name. A professor might prefer having his college affiliation mentioned.

9: **Ask for more**. Before leaving an interview, always request more information. Say, "Can you recommend any additional material that might help me with this project?" or "Is there anyone else whom I should speak to on this subject?"

10: **Send a copy of the quoted passages to the participant**. Once you have finished writing, send a copy of the sections where you mention or quote this individual and ask for permission to use it in your book.

It is a good idea to save all interview tapes and transcripts in case there is ever a question about something that was said. Your publisher may request your tapes before proceeding with the project, particularly if it involves a sensitive topic.

Note the interviewees' contact information so you can let them know when the book is ready for purchase. I generally give one copy of the completed book to individuals who participated in a major way, along with an order form for additional copies. I send flyers and order forms to those I may have just mentioned in the book.

## How to Discipline Yourself to Write

Writing habits vary from writer to writer. While one author can only sit at a desk and concentrate for an hour at a time, others regularly put in sixteen-hour days. Most hopeful authors have one thing in common. They must make some sacrifices in order to pursue their craft.

> Excuses do nothing more than keep you from living your dreams and meeting your goals.

Disciplining oneself to write can be a very real challenge. For me, at this stage in my career, finding time *away* from work is a problem. I have to use tricks and rewards to get myself out of the office. Writing is my life and I schedule other activities, such as yard work, housecleaning, walking, socializing, grocery shopping, etc. around my work. In fact, I delegate and hire people to do more and more tasks for me. This may also be your challenge some day. But for now, if you're struggling with the issue of finding or making time to write, consider the following:

- How much TV do you watch?

- What time do you get up in the morning/go to bed at night?

- How many hours do you work at your job each week?

- How much time do you waste in a day?

Are there areas of your life where you could make changes and free up more time to write?

Let's say that you gave up two hours of TV watching each evening, stayed up an hour later, stopped working overtime, exercised in the morning before work instead of on weekends and stopped meeting friends at the club on Saturday nights for drinks. What difference would this make in your life? I see a potential of twenty-five hours per week freed up for writing. Can you commit to that?

Reevaluate your priorities. Just this weekend, a woman attending one of my workshops asked how one finds the time to write when he or she absolutely has no extra time. She said that she never watches TV, so that isn't a problem. I suggested that she reevaluate her current lifestyle choices. Everything we do in a day is by choice. In order to fit in an additional activity, such as writing, it may be necessary to make new choices. It's called *prioritizing*.

We typically do the things that we consider most important. If you have young children at home and a job, those are your priorities. Maybe you are also highly involved in your church, you teach adult education classes two evenings a week, you belong to a club that meets once a month and you spend Saturdays cleaning and gardening. If you want to add writing to your busy schedule, you'll probably have to drop or cut back on one or two other activities. Pay someone to clean your house, for example. Or step down as editor for your church bulletin. If you aren't willing to make this sort of sacrifice, you probably aren't ready to start writing.

If you are rather impulsive, it may behoove you to become more organized. You may be wasting hours without realizing it. Keep track of your daily activities this week. Once you get a sense of exactly how you spend your time, you'll most likely discover minutes and even hours in your days that can compute into writing time.

If you can't quit your day job and/or you have a busy, hectic schedule, learn how to write in small pockets of time. I used to carry a notepad everywhere I went. You can carry a notebook computer. Jot down a few notes while waiting in the doctor's office with your child. Write a paragraph during your son's soccer practice. Flesh out a character during your lunch break at work.

## Avoid the Writing Course Excuse

There are numerous ways to procrastinate and taking writing courses is a popular one. I've met people who have taken writing classes and attended writing conferences for years. They claim that they want to write a book, but they never put pen to paper or fingers to keyboard. They are always too busy working up to it.

Don't get me wrong. I whole-heartedly believe in taking writing classes, belonging to writers' groups and attending conferences. These activities are inspiring for writers. They provide great opportunities to hone writing skills. Also, many successful collaborations result from networking opportunities such as these. I can't tell you how many members have come together for purposes of mutual benefit since SPAWN's inception.

Two years ago in the SPAWN booth at the Los Angeles Times Festival of Books, member, Ray, was asking me numerous questions about how to sell his book as a screenplay. About that time, member, Joseph, who happens to be a successful screenplay writer, stopped by. I offered the two gentlemen chairs in the back of the booth where they could discuss this in relative privacy. Ray walked away with quite a bit of new information and felt ready to test the screenwriting waters. (Note: This year, in the SPAWN booth at the LA Times Book Festival, Ray showed me the award he won with his new screenplay.)

I met Vanessa through her cousin, Joanna, who first visited the SPAWN booth at the San Luis Obispo Book Festival some years ago. Joanna said that her cousin was an artist. When I decided to self-publish *Young Writer's Handbook*, I emailed Vanessa who, by then, was a SPAWN member, and asked her if she would design the cover.

Several months ago, SPAWN member Laura contacted me asking if I knew a good artist for her children's book, I quickly recommended Vanessa. As it turns out, the two women live thousands of miles from me, but just a few miles from one another. Here's an excerpt from the email I received from Laura a few weeks ago. "I want to thank you so much for recommending Vanessa. I have been looking for an artist for a long time. Her style and personality are just what I was looking for. She even has the same passion I do about seeing the work come to life."

Yes, writers' groups and conferences definitely serve a purpose. It's important to get a sense of the industry, to learn skills, to network and to take steps toward bolstering your confidence level. But there comes a time when you must fish or cut bait.

If you have been taking writing courses or participating in conferences for more than a year, but you aren't doing any writing, you may not be helping yourself as much as you are simply procrastinating. About fifteen years ago, I met a woman at a writers' group meeting. She was in the final stages of writing a book. I saw her periodically after that at writers' conferences and book festivals. She even contacted me from time to time for advice on different aspects of her project. She was always in the final stages of writing this book.

I ran into her again just last summer and asked how her book was coming. She said, "Well it should be finished soon. By the way, are you going to the Santa Barbara Writer's Conference? I want to take it there and see if I can get it reviewed." Fifteen years later, she is still procrastinating.

## Do You Need an Editor?
In a word, YES. Most professional writers are naturally good with words, but few are English majors. Many of us have areas of grammar, punctuation, composition and style that give us fits. And surprisingly, some people, who just love to write, just plain stink at it. I think that excellent writing is a mix of talent and skill. And I believe that we never stop learning. A writer must stay constantly in student mode. We must be observant, inquisitive and always willing and eager to learn.

I hear inexperienced authors state, "My manuscript is almost ready— it needs a little editing—but I'm going to send it to the publisher, anyway.

If he wants it, he'll edit it, right?" Not likely. Send a manuscript that is less than your best and it will probably be rejected.

Once a publisher accepts a manuscript, however, yes, he will have his editors tighten it up. They might change your title, throw out what you thought was the best part and completely revamp your favorite chapter. Or they might just do some light editing. But a publisher does not want to receive your unedited manuscript. He wants to see your completed, polished, already edited best effort.

NEVER, NEVER send something that is less than your very best. If this means hiring an editor, then do it. Even an experienced writer will turn his manuscript over to an editor before sending it off to a publisher.

Why does every writer need an editor?

- When you become too close to your work, you tend to overlook things that could actually make or break your manuscript. There may be problems that either you haven't noticed or you feel you've fixed with some clever technique.

- A writer sometimes becomes attached to phrases that add nothing to his story or, in fact, that detract from it. A good editor can help save you from yourself.

- You may have a style of writing that isn't exactly easy to read or to comprehend. You understand what you're saying because you wrote it and because you have read it many times. It makes complete sense to you. But it may still be unclear to readers.

## Tips For Choosing an Editor

Authors frequently ask me for guidelines to use when auditioning editors. First, you should determine whether you need a copy editor or line editor. A copy editor edits for spelling, grammar and punctuation errors. I recommend that most authors hire a line or content editor— someone who edits for clarity and flow as well as grammatical errors. When choosing an editor, here's what I suggest:

- Consider an editor who has been recommended.

- Read something she or he has edited.

- Find out the editor's track record. Has the work she edited been published?

- Ask the editor to demonstrate his or her editing style on a few pages of your project.

- Choose an editor who has some experience editing books like yours.

- If the editor knows something about the topic of your book, all the better.

Expect to pay a copy editor around $30-$40 an hour. A content or line editor will require $50 or more per hour.

There are things that you can do before hiring an editor. Read your manuscript as if you are someone from outer space. Does it still make absolute sense to you or are there areas that need more explanation or that could be simplified?

Use spell-check.

One of the biggest problems I see with hopeful authors is a tendency toward muddy writing. My main work as an editor is cleaning up the mud—helping the author to clarify his/her material. Here's an example of what I call muddy writing:

> "This gives the information I found through my own extensive research and my observations involving young children as they pursued various media over an extensive period of time."

Instead, I suggested that my client try this:

> "This book is the result of five year's research which includes my observations involving the artistic pursuits of a dozen youngsters."

Here's another example:

> "Jeremy hoped beyond all hope for the potential success that would be his as he jumped into the air reaching for the glory of all players who dream of ultimately catching a ball like this."

Why not simply say this, instead:

> "Jeremy sprang into action hoping to make the greatest catch of the season."

The second most common thing I do as an editor is to eliminate words.

Example:

> "On that particular day—a Wednesday—John decided to walk over to the corner store."

Why not this:

> "On Wednesday, John walked to the corner store."

Remember, one of the most famous succinct, strong sentences ever written was "Jesus wept."

## Introduction to Self-Editing

I suppose it is impossible to know when our writing stinks. With training and practice, however, I think we can definitely learn. I know where my strengths and my weaknesses lie. I have been a "give me the facts, ma'am" type nonfiction writer for so many years that I've lost any natural ability to spew lovely prose. I'm working on a book of cat stories as we speak, and feel myself stretching like Gumby trying to give each tale a storytelling quality.

The best way to perfect your writing skills is to read and to write. But don't just read the easy stuff. Challenge yourself with thought-provoking materials of excellent literary quality. And don't just write in the same lackadaisical manner

Use your best grammar and punctuation skills each and every time you write, whether it is an email to a friend or potentially the world's greatest novel. Once you decide to become a writer or an author, you owe it to our profession and to yourself to communicate as if you are an author. How often do you send out a quick email without using spell-check? Do you feel that most people are generally forgiving of spelling errors and grammatical oversights? I don't think so—not when you are trying to pass yourself off as a writer/author.

You wouldn't believe some of the mistakes in the emails I get from people claiming to be writers. Here are a couple of actual examples:

> "i am wrighting a book but i don't know ware to get it published after its done could you help me get my book pubished."

> "I would like you to look at my proposl but it is only half way complete and I have to finish it before you actuslly look at it. Or at leawst let me write a few chapters, I am almost done with one. Before you go ahead. Is thqt okay to wait until im done."

The next several pages are devoted to the most common errors I see in the course of my editorial work.

## New Punctuation

They say that there's nothing new under the sun, but I've learned a thing or two since the advent of the computer age. For example, did you know that the old rule you learned in typing class in the 50s, 60s, 70s and even the 80s—two spaces after a period—is passé? Now, the rule is one space after a period, colon, question mark, etc. Why? Because we used to prepare typed material for typesetters. Now, that we're using computers, we *are* typesetters. So, if you are using digital means to produce material, it is one-space after all punctuation.

The em dash is no longer left to dangle between words. It connects the two words. I notice that *The Associated Press Style and Libel Manual* (copyright 1992) suggests leaving a space on each side of the em dash—the long dash generally used within a sentence to initiate a change in thought or a pause. Here's an example of that style, [em dash — the long dash]. This seems to be the European style. Today in America, however, words are connected by the em dash—so named because it is traditionally the width of the letter m.

Perhaps you've been confused about the placement of punctuation with relationship to quotation marks. I was taught that commas, periods and so forth, go inside quotation marks. And then I began seeing them outside quotation marks more and more frequently. I learned recently that, with a few exceptions, punctuation inside quotation marks is correct here in the U.S. But, in other countries, commas, periods, question marks, etc., go outside quotation marks.

Those of us who cut our teeth on typewriters were taught to underline book titles and other words and phrases that needed to be italicized. You couldn't create italics when using a typewriter or when writing by hand. Underlining was a signal to the printer that a word should be put in italics. Now, if you use a computer, you can add italics yourself and you should. Underlining is no longer appropriate.

Many writers seem confused when it comes to using the cute little apostrophe. Use the apostrophe to denote possessive and plural possessive. "The boy's boat" indicates that the boat belongs to the boy. "The boys' boat" shows that two or more boys own the boat.

Use an apostrophe to show personal ownership, as well. For example, Patty's purse or Margaret's shawl. When the name ends in s, simply add the apostrophe to denote the possessive. For example, "Dennis' book," "Frances' guitar."

While it is correct to use an apostrophe when writing in single letters— he got all A's and B's or Mississippi sure has a lot of i's—it is incorrect to use an apostrophe when referring to a series of years. For example, 1920's is wrong. Write, 1920s, instead. Use an apostrophe in place of omitted numbers in the date. An example would be, "I remember the '50s like it was yesterday."

## Editing Tips

The following is a basic guide to editing. Unless you are an English professor, you may notice at least a couple of familiar errors that you make from time to time. These are all things that you really must be aware of when writing a book, article or anything else for publication. Be sure to:

- Write complete sentences.

- Eliminate unnecessary words. Instead of "Joanne spent every free minute during that particular time period practicing and reciting her most recent class assignment." Say, "Joanne studied diligently."

- Use simple terms and words. If you try too hard to impress your readers, you may succeed only in confusing them.

- Edit for words that are repeated/overused. Come up with several different words to use in place of something to which you'll be referring frequently throughout a paragraph. Instead of using the word *thought* fifty times in a chapter, substitute other words such as, idea, contemplation, notion, inspiration, concept, opinion and philosophy. If you're writing about a dog, call him by name, and use additional words such as, pet, pooch, the animal, the furry critter, canine and wooly guy instead of continually referring to him as *dog*.

- Vary sentences. Intermingle sentences of all sizes and many styles throughout your book to make it easier and more enjoyable to read. Imagine reading a book with sentences all containing just five words. It might read like this: "Jack went to the track. He spent over five dollars. He bet on the bay. He really hoped to win." Booooorrrring!!!

- Know when to end it. Some writers try to say too much in a single sentence. They use commas where they should put periods. If you create an extraordinarily long sentence, examine it and see if you can successfully break it into two or three sentences.

- Avoid over explaining. Practice clarity without getting too involved in complicated explanations. Tell your story and share facts using succinct sentences and descriptive words.

- Use the active rather than the passive voice. Instead of, "It was her choice to opt for the blue coat." Say, "She chose the blue coat." Instead of, "There were hundreds of birds flying in our direction." Try, "Hundreds of birds flew at us." One way to make sure you're not using the passive voice is to eliminate *it* and *there* at the beginning of sentences. Another indicator that you're using a passive instead of active voice is the word *by.*

  Passive: She was hit by the ball.
  Active: The ball came out of nowhere and hit her on the head.

- Be consistent. Keep to your choice of tense, for example. Don't change back and forth between past and present tense or first, second and third person. By the way, first person is *I,* second person is *you* and third person is *he, she, they.* Be consistent with commas, periods, indents and your choice of words. Will you use *Web site, website* or *Website*, for example? Which do you prefer, *ebook, eBook* or *e-book.* In situations where more than one usage is correct, make a choice and stick to it.

- Avoid clichés. I love clichés and I tend to overuse them in speech. I must consciously edit to eliminate them from my writing. A cliché is a trite, predictable and generally over-used saying such as: "You can bet your bottom dollar." "It's like throwing the baby out with the bath." "Better late than never."

"You can see the writing on the wall." Be creative—come up with new phrases to make your point.

- Avoid using what I call qualifiers. The words *very* and *really,* often weaken a perfectly good sentence. Instead of "Jacob had a very good time," try "Jacob had a great time." Rather than "I am really hungry" say, "I'm famished." Instead of, "It's a really very small cat," tell us how small.

- Catch spell-check errors—real words that can change the meaning of your sentence, but that are not picked up by spell-check. You might intend writing "no hurry," but accidentally type "now hurry." Big difference there. You might mean to type, "He does not wish to be disturbed" and write, instead, "He does now wish to be disturbed." Or you may want to say, "I don't eat worms." But you miss a word and it reads, "I eat worms." Other words that can trip you up are sign/sing, course/curse, plus/pus/pulse, about/abut, manger/manager, trick/thick, cove/cave. Don't get burned by your spell-check. Sometimes your computer will correct a word wrongly. You might want to write definitely. If you make a mistake while typing it, your computer may change it to defiantly. I just spotted a couple of spell-check mistakes in this manuscript. I meant to type willingness. I must have hit a wrong key and the computer spelled out wiliness, instead. In another instance, I meant to say that a colleague's sales soared and I (or my computer) inadvertently typed soured. Big difference.

- Use the right word. Some words sound alike or look alike, such as angle and angel, presumption and assumption, assure, and ensure, born and borne, breach and breech, appraise and apprise, breath and breathe, avenge and revenge.

- Watch out for redundant phrases or instances of unnecessary repetition. Here are a few: ISBN number, two twins, widow woman, unmarried old maid, autobiography of my life, unexpected surprise.

## Use Words Correctly

Understand the differences between common words that are similar and always use them correctly. Here are a few words that can be troublesome.

Whose and who's:

> *Who's* is a contraction for *who is*. "Who's coming to dinner?"
> *Whose* is the possessive. "Whose horse won the race?"

Who and that:

> Too often, we hear newscasters and others refer to a person as *that* instead of *who*.
>
> You would say, "It was the storm that did the damage." And "But, Lila is the woman who saved the day."

Then and than:

> *Then* means at that time—"He was younger, then."
> *Than* is used in comparisons—"Sharon is taller than Sam."

Your and you're:

> *Your* means this belongs to you and *you're* is a contraction for you are.

There, their and they're:

> *There* denotes a place. "Set the plant over there."
> *Their* is the possessive of belonging to them. "It's their blanket."
> *They're* is a contraction for they are. "They're coming home today."

To, too, two:

> *To* indicates motion or action as in "I gave the blanket to him." Or "He is going to jail."
> *Too* means also, in addition to or in excess. For example, "He wants a blanket, too." "I think he is too greedy."
> *Two* refers to the number 2.

By, bye, buy:

> *By* is used in numerous ways. Here are a few examples: "The blanket is in the chair by the fireplace." "That book was written by Jonathan Robles." "I'd like to drive by that place again." "He should be finished by now."
>
> *Bye* is short for good bye.
>
> *Buy* means to purchase. "She said she would buy him a new blanket."

It, its, it's:

> *It* refers to an object.
>
> *Its* is the possessive form of it. "The tree lost its leaves." "The ant made its way along the cabinet."
>
> *It's* is the contraction of it is or it has. "It's hot today." "It's never been hotter."

A and an:

> There seems to be a lot of confusion about using the word *an* before a word beginning with an H. The rule relates not to the letter itself, but to the sound of the letter. If the H is silent as in the words, honor, hour and heir, *an* is correct. If the word has a hard H sound, such as in hammer, horse, heaven or head, use the word *a* before it.

Examples of H words used with *a*:

> "Let's go to the library and check out a history book."
>
> "I'd love to ride a horse."
>
> "You have to wear a helmet if you plan to ride your bike."

Examples of H words used with *an*:

> "You must wait for an hour after eating before you can go swimming."
>
> "I am an heir to a small fortune."
>
> "I'm going to ask for an hourly wage."

There is no excuse for turning out a manuscript riddled with poor grammar and spelling errors. If in doubt, refer to an online grammar site or a trusted style manual. I keep two style manuals on my desk and I refer to them anytime I have a question or need verification. See the Resource List in Chapter Sixteen for grammar sites, reference books and other helps.

**Edit, Edit, Edit**
Once you've finished editing your manuscript, start looking at it from different angles. Here's what I suggest:

- Print out the manuscript and put it in a three-ring binder.

- Proof it again and again, if necessary.

- Check facts and statistics.

- Make sure that the font, headings, subheadings and so forth conform in size and style throughout.

- Make sure that chapter titles and headings correspond with the table of contents.

- Start making a list of the words you plan to include in your index.

- Ask appropriate experts if you can send a chapter or two for them to review for accuracy.

## Let's Become Familiar With the Parts of a Book
What will you include in your book? There's the text, of course. This comprises the story, information, instructions and other material you've written and compiled for your readership. What else does your book need?

### Fiction
A novel or children's book generally needs only a copyright page, title page, table of contents and the story. You could also include a dedication page and acknowledgements page if you want to. Some authors of fantasies, science fiction and so forth, might include a chart listing characters. If this is one of a trilogy, provide information about the other two stories. You can also add an about the author page, testimonials page or any other inclusions you desire. It's your book, after all.

**Nonfiction**

A nonfiction book—that is a biography, how-to, self-help or history, for example—needs a copyright page, title page, table of contents, text and an index. Depending on the subject matter and scope of the book, you might also decide to include a dedication page, about the author page, acknowledgements page, testimonials page, preface, foreword, introduction, glossary, and/or bibliography.

Here are your options and a description of each:

# FRONT MATTER

**Title Page**

This is the first page that appears in your book. It is a right-facing page and generally includes the book title, subtitle, author's name, the publishing company name and contact information.

**Copyright Page**

This is usually a left-facing page where you post your copyright information, Publishers Cataloguing-in-Publication (PCIP) information and ISBN (part of the PCIP block). You can also list your cover design and book design persons here, if you like.

**Dedication Page**

Here, you might want to acknowledge someone special in your life—a parent, spouse, child, friend, mentor… Generally, this is someone whom you'd like to thank for standing by you while you toiled on this tome, who gave you the inspiration to write it or who helped you to gain the skills to write it.

**Table of Contents**

A table of contents is your chapter outline designed for the reader's convenience. Start the table of contents on a right-facing page. Make it as detailed or as simple as you wish. Of course, you will list each chapter by name and give the starting page number. I usually list the subheads for my nonfiction books, as well. You can include page numbers for subheads or not. A table of contents for fiction generally includes just chapter titles and the starting page number for each.

## Foreword

A foreword is written by someone other than the author—an expert in the area of your book topic, perhaps or another author.

## About the Author

Most readers are interested in who you are. Whether they're about to purchase or read a novel or a how-to book, they want to know who wrote it and what qualifies that person to write it. I believe that something about the author should be included in every book. But it doesn't have to be a long resume in the front matter of the book. It can be a blurb on the back cover with your photograph or an afterthought on the last page of the book.

## Acknowledgements Page

Here is where you thank everyone who helped with your book. In my Ojai history book, I have an acknowledgements page that includes over 100 names. You can thank your mentor, your page and cover designers, the folks who provided information for the book, your editor, your agent and even your cat, if you wish.

## Testimonials Page

By the time you are ready to reprint your book, you've probably accumulated many book reviews and testimonials. Consider publishing some of them in the front matter. You'll notice that I've included a Testimonials Page in this second edition.

## Preface

A preface generally contains a message from the author—what compelled him/her to write the book, how the research was conducted, etc.

## Introduction

An introduction can be useful for nonfiction works. An introduction is generally written by the author.

## Disclaimer

You might want to add a disclaimer to your book. Most authors who do this, place the disclaimer just before the first chapter begins. You might state in your "Yoga for Beginners" book that, while the yoga moves you suggest are safe for a healthy person, you recommend that each individual do the exercises only with a physician's approval.

You may notice that I included a disclaimer in this book letting readers know that it does not come with a guarantee of publication for every reader. It is a book of information, tips and useful skill-building techniques, but not every hopeful author will become rich and famous as a result of this book.

Note: Every expert I consulted about the front matter listed these pages in a different order. Some suggested that an author could also include an errata, frontispiece, list of tables, list of projects, list of abbreviations and list of contributors to the front matter. As you will notice, I included a list of my additional books in my front matter for this book.

I recommend consulting books similar to the one you are producing and choose the front matter additions and order that is logical, practical and appealing for your particular book.

# BACK MATTER
## Afterword or Epilogue
This material follows the main text and includes the author's final statement or conclusion.

## Appendixes
An appendix might comprise additional explanations for aspects of a book. This is where you put material that you don't want to include in the text because it is cumbersome or it bogs down the story or the flow of the text. You might want to simply mention in the text that Jesse James was accused of stealing a horse. You can tell the rest of the story in an appendix, if you wish.

One of my clients is self-publishing a book featuring the story of her daughter's successes despite struggles with a lifelong fatal illness. This author has ended the book quite appropriately, yet she wants to add comments that some of her daughter's friends made after she died. The author planned to tack them on at the end of the story. I suggested that she create an appendix in the back matter for these comments and letters. This way, the book ends as it should and readers won't be confused by the additional material. If they want to access it, it is in the appendix for their perusal.

## Glossary

A glossary defines any industry-sensitive words the author uses throughout a book. Even though the uncommon words may have been defined within the text, a glossary provides a handy guide for folks who desire additional explanation or who want a quick reference to the words.

Sometimes authors of fantasies provide guides identifying meanings of the words they've made up for their stories.

## Bibliography

Generally this is a list of the books and other material you used in your research for a nonfiction book. A bibliography is helpful for students and others who need additional information on the topic.

## Subject Index

An effective subject index helps readers to quickly locate information contained in your book. I recommend studying indexes in other nonfiction books to help you design yours.

I reviewed a book on the business of writing by a fellow author a few weeks ago. I gave the book an excellent review, but I had to take a half-star away for the sloppy job on the index. He listed words such as, art, talent, tricks, education, and even phrases like, "what if I don't make it?" and "talents, hearts and minds." Some words weren't even in alphabetical order. I found "acquired mastery," "intelligence," and "abilities" listed under T. I guess he hired someone to do the indexing and got in a hurry and didn't proof it.

## Other Matter

You might want to include a page listing photo credits or an advertisement for your services. It's all okay. If you are self-publishing, you are in charge. You can even sell advertising space in your book in order to finance publication, if you so desire. I know authors who have done this quite successfully.

## How to Finish a Book

Finishing a book is sometimes hard to do. Authors often fall so completely in love with their project that they look for any excuse to continue. By now, you've established a routine of writing that you enjoy. It's hard to think about giving it up. But, if you expect to see this book in print, you will have to finally end it.

How do you know when your book is finished? As a rule of thumb, if you can read all the way through your manuscript without making a change or bogging down in places—when you can feel good about it from start to finish—then you are ready to end it and turn it over to a good editor.

### How Long Does it Take to Write a Book?

I spent five years researching and writing the 360-page comprehensive history of the Ojai Valley, California. I was also busy planning weddings for my daughters and welcoming grandbabies in the meantime. Likewise, I spent five years researching and writing the history of a local 80-year-old private school. This was a commissioned project and I worked on it just thirty hours per month. In 1986, I wrote a 200-page book in eight months while working a full-time job. And I wrote a sixteen-chapter book in three weeks once at the request of a client.

Generally, a book will take between three months to a year from the glimmer of the idea to the last page of the book. This depends on the amount of research necessary, the size of the book and the time you spend writing.

Surveys show that a typical nonfiction book takes 725 hours to write or 90 eight-hour days. That's approximately eighteen work weeks or four and a half months.

### Counting Words

Determining word count is another question that will come up as you're working on your book. How does one determine word count and compute typewritten pages to finished book pages? While some people will advise against relying on your computer word count program for accuracy, I always use mine. What other measurement do you have that even comes close?

A double-spaced manuscript page with 1 ¼ to 1 ½ inch margins typed using 12-point Times New Roman contains approximately 250 words. There are around 300 words on a typical printed book page. So for a 200-page book or approximately 61,000 words, you'll need to produce around 244 manuscript pages.

## Criticism—Take it Like a Wo/Man

When you become a published author, no longer are you able to keep a low profile. The days of sitting quietly in your private space and relishing every word you pen may be over. Once you bring your writing to the surface—actually begin the process of publishing it—you are opening yourself up to opinion. Some of those opinions are positive and will feed your writer's soul. Others may come in the form of criticism. Showing your work to a publisher may be your first experience with both positive and negative feedback.

A publisher might suggest that you do more research, for example. That could hurt, especially if you feel that you've spent more than ample time studying your topic. She might tell you that your concept has been done hundreds of times and is old hat. "Ouch!!" And you thought you had a fresh idea. He might say that your manuscript needs editing.

Rather than arguing with a publisher, just take it. Do not say anything that you might later regret. If you think about it for a while, you may realize that the publisher is right. Once you have a good cry, punch the wall a few times and eat a barrel of your favorite comfort food, spend some time pursuing the possibilities presented by this experienced professional. He may be wrong. On the other hand, he may have just given you the key to success.

## Recommended Reading:

*Grammar Traps* by Stephen Dolainski (Paragraph Publishing, 2004).

# Chapter Ten

## THE

# SELF-PUBLISHING

## OPTION

Self-publishing is another publishing option and one that countless authors choose. While today's technology makes it easier to produce your own books, it is still fairly costly and it's a lot of work. Self-publishing should not be taken on purely as a means to boost one's ego.

To be successful, you must enter into the world of self-publishing with a viable project, an open mind, creative ideas, lots of energy, a bank roll and a willingness to work hard. Authorship is a business. But when you are also the publisher, your business responsibilities multiply as do your opportunities for success. A large part of your job as a publisher is to choose projects with potential. (More about this in Chapter Five.)

> Publishing is not an extension of your writing.

## Why Self-Publish?

There are a variety of reasons why people choose to self-publish. Some authors love having total control over their projects. Others need to get a book out quickly. Some people simply dislike the politics and discrimination they feel is apparent in the publishing industry.

One woman I know self-published because she was fed up with the system. She told me that two years of sending query letters to large and small publishers was enough for her. She said, "I just got tired of their huffy-puffy power trips and game-playing with small writers. I decided to take control." She adds, "I don't regret my decision. Having control over my story has been very nice."

Some of us self-publish because it is more lucrative. Sure, you must foot the bill to publish your own book, but you get to keep all of the profits. When you go with a traditional royalty publisher, your take is fifteen to eighteen percent—sometimes it's as low as five percent.

Let's say that your self-published book sells for $22.00. The costs for your first run come to around $3.00 per book. If you sell only 500 copies on your own, you've earned a profit of $9,500. If you're collecting even fifteen percent royalties on the retail price from a publisher for this book and together you sell as many as 1,500 copies, your profits are under $5,000.

If you work harder and sell 1,500 copies through your own publishing company, you've earned yourself $28,500. Self-publishing is beginning to look rather attractive, isn't it?

## Is Self-Publishing for You?

Self-publishing can be daunting. It's easy to be overwhelmed in the process of setting up a publishing company, writing a book and taking care of the business aspects of producing that book. And then there's promotion.

Publishing is not for the faint of heart, the short-sighted or the introvert. It's a commitment that demands courage, risk-taking, planning, energy, creativity and assertiveness. Before entering into the realm of self-publishing, consider the following:

- Is there an audience for your book?

- Are you willing to take the steps necessary to establish and operate a publishing business?

- Do you have the funds available to pour into your publishing project?

- Do you have room to store boxes and boxes of books?

- Do you have the time and inclination to promote your book?

I know hundreds of authors who have self-published their books. Some produced books while working full-time jobs. Others have one book that they self-published and are marketing until their stock runs out. But most of them have set up publishing companies in order to produce numerous books.

I'm often asked, during self-publishing workshops, which I prefer— going with a traditional publisher or self-publishing? Truth? I like the ease of having a traditional publisher handle the business end of the project and pay quarterly royalties. I like not being responsible for storing the books. Since I'm still involved in promoting the books, even with a publisher, however, I actually prefer self-publishing. I'd rather be in control of the project. When I self-publish, I choose the title and the cover design. I decide which chapters stay and which ones go. I set the price. But this also means that I have total responsibility for producing, promoting and distributing the book.

Certainly, self-publishing is not for everyone. I know elderly and ill people who want their memoirs published, but who do not relish the hassle of self-publishing—setting up a company; finding a cover designer, printer and distributor; promoting the book; taking orders and shipping books.

Someone with a full-time career and who writes a book as a sideline, probably doesn't want to get involved with operating a publishing business.

Anyone on a small income will find it difficult to finance a self-publishing venture.

I often coach authors in starting their own publishing companies and have observed about a fifty percent success ratio. Those who succeed have built a business around their project and they take that business seriously. They have reasonable expectations. They also have goals and they evaluate their goals regularly. They give their projects their full attention. If they lack skills in a particular area, they hire someone to take up the slack.

I don't do page layout, so I hire a designer to perform that task. I find shipping and handling large mailings rather mundane and time-consuming. I hire my grandchildren to help with these projects and we do them outside of regular business hours.

Self-publishing can be a prelude to traditional publishing success. I have had three of my self-published books picked up by traditional royalty publishers. You might be surprised to know that Richard Paul Evans self-published *The Christmas Box* because he couldn't find a publisher. Some say that he sent his manuscript to only six publishers before deciding to publish the book himself. Simon and Schuster eventually paid Evans a hefty advance and they took over publishing this *New York Times* bestselling book.

Other famous self-published authors include Elizabeth Barrett Browning, Robert Bly, Zane Grey and Ernest Hemmingway.

If you're not sure that you can handle or would enjoy the task of becoming a publisher, run a test product. Write a book or a booklet with which you can test the waters. Produce the book on your home computer and have a local business center copy and bind the book. Most business centers have the capacity to fold and saddle stitch (staple) a book or finish it with plastic comb binding. Or use a POD printing company (not a POD publisher) to produce your book in small quantities for consumer testing. While most will print as few as one book, I suggest a print run of at least 100.

## Exploring the Pros and Cons of Self-Publishing

What is a *pro* to one author, quite frankly, may be a *con* to another. Before deciding to self-publish, take into account your talents, skills and abilities. It's important that you know the limitations, benefits, responsibilities and costs of self-publishing.

According to first-time publisher Norma, "The process of self-publishing a book involves two tasks. First you give birth to the book, which is the easier part. If you're smart, you'll choose a subject that people want to know more about or that is in. The second and hardest part of publishing is the busy work that follows the writing—finding an editor, setting aside enough money to avoid debt in case book sales are sluggish, getting printer bids, designing the cover. The worst part of this business for the creative, right-brained types is marketing/promotion. Here you must become a pushy alien person making phone calls, writing letters and surfing the Internet all the while in this ego-shattering rejection process trying not to become a sherry-guzzling, bewildered basket case."

Let's review the benefits of self-publishing:

- You'll definitely see your book in print.

- You can have a finished product within weeks instead of months.

- You have the potential to make more money.

- You have all of the control.

- There are tax breaks to owning your own business.

- You are the best possible marketing agent for your project.

- Your book will sell for as long as you are willing to promote it.

What about the downside to self-publishing?

- Marketing a book is a fulltime job.

- Self-publishing is costly.

- There's a lot of decision-making involved.

- Promoting a book is hundreds of times more difficult and time-consuming than writing it.

- Your book will keep selling for as long as you are willing to promote it.

## Self-Publishing Basics

If you're still interested in self-publishing, here are some of your options: You can have your book printed through a traditional printing company, take it to a print-on-demand (POD) company, print and bind it at home or produce an ebook.

The most cost-effective way to produce a quality print book is through a traditional printing company that uses the old ink-on-paper method. But the total cost may be more because you have to order books in larger quantities. There are often wide differences in quality and price among printers. Ask half dozen or so printers for price quotes, samples of their work and references.

Printing will be your largest production expense. Expect to pay anywhere from $1,500 to $20,000 for 1,000 to 5,000 copies of your book (depending on page number, quality of paper and cover stock, number and type of illustrations, amount of color used, binding style and so forth).

### Request for Price Quote

When requesting a price quote from printers, make sure that you are comparing oranges to oranges. In other words, send the same information and specs to each printer that you contact. Tell the printer your estimated number of pages. Don't worry if this changes with time. You may decide later to add a fifteen-page index. Your primary concern now is to get a ballpark idea of the cost you're facing, to compare costs between printers and to examine some of their samples so you can decide which company you ultimately want to work with. When the book is finished, you will request an exact quote for your project.

Here's a guide for creating your own Request for Price Quote:

- Provide your book title, publishing company and author's name.

- Ask for quotes on two or three quantities, generally 1000, 3000, and 5000.

- Give your projected number of pages.

- What size book do you want? (Give the dimensions and indicate whether it is formatted in portrait or landscape.)

- Give the number and type of illustrations.

- What weight paper and cover stock do you want?

- Will it be a paperback or hardcover?

- Choose ink colors (inside and out). Your choices are 1, 2, 3 or 4 colors. You might want a 4-color (full color) cover with black ink only for inside text.

- What binding do you prefer? (Hardcover or perfect bound, for example.)

Some self-publishers forego the hassle of dealing with outside print companies by producing their books in-house. Anyone with a home computer and printer has the capacity to manufacture a book. You can even bind and trim it yourself using a saddle stapler and commercial cutter or a plastic comb binding machine.

For smaller books, booklets and pamphlets, it may be cheaper to let a local business center print, saddle stitch, fold and trim your books. We just had 100 copies of a seventy-page book produced at a local business center for $2.15 per book.

## Design Your Book

Even if you are not technologically or creatively equipped to design your own book cover, it will behoove you to take some responsibility in the process. The cover is highly important. Study the design of popular books in your genre. What makes these books stand out? Learn from the experts. Spend time at your local bookstore. Look at the books on the bestseller list. While in the bookstore, watch to see which books are being handled. What is it about the cover that attracts people?

Self-publishing guru Dan Poynter has compiled statistics that say, a bookstore browser typically spends eight seconds looking at your front cover and fifteen seconds on the back cover. That's how long book buyers generally take to decide whether or not to purchase a book.

I've watched thousands of book browsers at dozens of book festivals over the years and what Poynter says is true. I also notice that some books attract people and others do not. If a cover isn't interesting or attractive and the title isn't catchy or intriguing, the book is bypassed time and time again. People don't even bother to pick the book up.

Style and color are important factors in a good cover design. But so is ease of readability. A title should be easy to read at some distance. Unless you are Danielle Steele or James Patterson, the author's name is relatively insignificant. For the title, use bold lettering in an easy-to-read font and a color that makes the title stand out.

In most cases, you're going to hire someone to design your cover and you can expect to pay anywhere from $450 to $3,000—an expense that could make or break your book. Before hiring a cover designer, check his track record. Has he designed books before or is his expertise in another area of graphic work?

A designer may want to read a portion of your book to get an idea for a cover design. You've been working intimately with this book for several months and probably have some ideas of your own. Share these ideas with your designer. Many a collaboration between author and artist has resulted in dynamite book covers.

You might also need to hire someone to design the interior of your book. Before hiring a page layout and design expert, study books similar to yours and determine the style you prefer. Will you produce a rather straightforward book using all text? Perhaps you'll want a lot of boxes, shading and bullets to break up the text. What font size and style do you prefer? Where do you want your page numbers—top? Bottom? Center? Right? Left? I saw a book recently with page numbers placed boldly in the outside margins of each page. Will you include a quote or drawing at the beginning of each chapter or a recommendation at the end?

Choose your font. Traditionally, books are printed in Times New Roman or another font that is equally easy to read.

Your cover design person and your page layout person should have the expertise to work with the printer in transferring your files appropriately. This may sound elementary, but many a book has been destroyed by miscommunication at this crucial point. Many sloppily designed POD published books are the result of inexperienced page designers who didn't know how to accurately prepare files for the printer. A good printer will catch potential problems and work with your designer until there is a suitable resolution. But don't count on this. Always hedge your bet by working with experts.

Locate a page layout person and a cover designer (usually two different people) by talking to other independent publishers and authors. Ask for recommendations. When you find books in your home library or at the bookstore that you particularly like, check the copyright page or acknowledgements page for the name of the companies or individuals who designed them. You'll find numerous layout and design people listed on the Internet, advertised in writing/publishing magazines and newsletters and even in your local Yellow Pages. Certainly, many of them are talented and reliable. To find out which ones are, ask for references and samples of their work. Use the SPAWN Member Directory to locate graphic designers (spawn.org).

Hire someone who is accustomed to producing books such as yours. A designer who has only designed brochures for corporations, might not understand the mechanics and psychology of producing a book cover. If your page layout person hasn't worked with a saddle-stitched (stapled) book before, she might not know that she has to use a technique called *creeping* to keep text from being buried in the center fold.

### Be Prepared for Promotion

A major part of self-publishing is promotion. A successful self-publisher must have a business head, ongoing enthusiasm for his project and a bent for promotion. Some experts say that you should set aside as much money for marketing the book as you paid to have it produced. But, there are also countless ways to promote your book for little or nothing other than your time.

Don't expect to produce a book, do a blast of marketing during the first few months and then just sit back and collect money for evermore. Your book can live for as long as you are willing to promote it. Once you stop promoting, it will likely die.

How do you plan to market your book? Don't assume that Barnes and Noble and Borders will clamor to get copies of your book to stock by the caseload. It's more and more difficult for an independent publisher to get shelf space in the big bookstores. One way to get the attention of these mega-bookstores is to publicize your book widely and strongly enough that customers start asking for it by name.

If you did the appropriate research before writing and publishing your book, you are prepared for the task of promotion. When you are prepared, willing and able to aggressively promote your book, you will most likely succeed.

I was able to pay back a family loan for my first self-publishing venture within four months after the book came out because of aggressive marketing. When I reprinted that book fifteen years later, I paid the printing costs with prepublication orders before the book was even delivered. How? I did a mailing to my mailing list. (See promotional ideas in Chapters Eleven through Thirteen.)

A publisher must wear many hats. He or she is responsible for specific tasks and the steps can be confusing. Here is a clear, concise guide that you will find most helpful for your current and future projects.

## Your Time-Line for Producing a Book

### Before Writing Your Book

1: **Write a book proposal.** While a book proposal is generally thought of as your foot-in-the door to a publisher, there is an even greater purpose. As I pointed out in Chapter Four, a book proposal will tell you if you even have a book at all and, more importantly, an audience. Before sinking your life savings and a year or more of your life into this project, make sure you actually have something worth publishing.

2: **Determine if publishing is for you.** Talk to others who have self-published to find out what it entails. Read about self-publishing. I recommend *The Self-Publishing Manual* by Dan Poynter. Review pages 195-200 of this book. Study how a book is marketed. Preparing the book for market is a huge job, but promoting your book is ongoing. The amount of time you put into marketing will relate directly to how successful your book will become.

### While Writing Your Book

3: **Name your publishing company**. Be careful about using a name that reflects the nature of your book. You may decide to publish books in different genres/subjects in the years ahead.

4: **Apply for a Fictitious Business Name**. The form is available through your County Clerk. Have two or three names in mind in case your first choice is taken.

5: **Establish a business address**. If you're working out of your home, consider signing up for a post office box or one at a business center to use for business correspondence. If you get some major publicity, you don't want the world to know where you live.

6: **Order business stationery and mailing labels**. Keep it businesslike and simple.

7: **Open a business checking account**. You will soon be receiving checks to your publishing company—you'd better have a place to deposit them. It's wise to use this account for paying bills related to your business, too.

8: **Request a block of International Standard Book Numbers (ISBN).** Assign one number to each title you publish. This number identifies your publishing company and the book and is necessary for books sold in the retail market. R.R. Bowker is the U.S. agency for distributing ISBN. You cannot purchase just one number. You will probably want to start with a block of ten numbers; however, you can also order blocks of one hundred or one thousand. The cost, as of this printing, is $225 for ten plus processing. (Add $100 or more for a fast turnaround.) For more information and to purchase your ISBN printout, visit www.isbn.org. Contact the Agency by phone: 877-310-7333 or email: isbn-san@bowker.com.

9: **Fill out an Advance Book Information (ABI) form**. About six months before your book is finished, fill out the form at bowkerlink.com. This insures that your book will be listed in *Books in Print*, one of the industry's most important directories. There is no charge for the form or for the listing. *Books in Print* is the directory or database that bookstores use to locate ordering information for your book when customers ask for it by name. According to R.R. Bowker, *Books in Print* data is used in major and independent bookstores and chains as well as libraries to locate books. So you definitely want to be listed and it's free.

Note: I had difficulty filling out this form online and having it accepted by the Bowker Web site. So I have begun printing it out, filling it out and mailing it to RR Bowker Data Collection Center, 630 Central Ave., NJ 07974. You can call 888-269-5372 for help.

10: **Request Copyright forms**. Contact the U.S. Copyright Office at Library of Congress, 101 Independence Ave., SE, Washington, DC

20559-6000 or loc.gov/copyright. While it is okay to apply for a copyright before your book is completed, I generally wait until after I've finished the book. On July 1, 2006, the filing fee rose to $45. Now they also offer a reduced fee of $35 for those who file electronically.

11: **Contact your State Board of Equalization** and request a resale permit. See the state government pages in your telephone directory.

**When You're Almost Finished Writing the Book** (About three months before completion)
12: **Assign an ISBN to your book**. (See above.)

13: **Commission someone to design your cover**. Since a good cover design can sell books, it follows that it can turn the heads of reviewers as well. You may want to have your cover design set before you send prepublication review copies. Perhaps your designer could print out a few copies of the cover to use in binding your review galleys or just enclose a sample of the cover with your manuscript. An excellent cover could make the difference between a review and no review.

To locate a good cover designer, contact authors and small publishers to find out who designed covers for their most successful books. Locate graphic artists and illustrators through an organization such as SPAWN, (spawn.org) the Yellow Pages or a local arts directory.

**While Editing Your Book** (About one month before the book is completed.)
14: **Search for a printer.** Send a *Request for Price Quote* to a half dozen printers. (See instructions for preparing a Request for Price Quote above.) Find printers listed in your local Yellow Pages, in *Literary Market Place* (in the reference section at your library) and ask for recommendations from other small publishers. See the list of recommended printers at Spawn.org/printers.htm. I've also included some in the extensive Resource List in Chapter Sixteen.

15: **Send prepublication review copies.** While some experts are now suggesting that the small publisher doesn't have a chance for a review by the important prepublication reviewers, others recommend submitting your galley proof. If you get a review, this could jumpstart your book sales in a big way.

Some prepublication reviewers are opening up review possibilities for self-published and POD published authors FOR A FEE. I know self-published authors who have had marvelous reviews in these major review publications without paying a fee, however.

Prepublication reviews appear in magazines that are read by the book industry: bookstore and library buyers. And these particular reviewers want to see the book before it's published. While you can send your manuscript, you'll make a better presentation if you have it bound as a book—create a galley proof.

Enclose a cover letter with your book that includes the title, author's name, publication date, ISBN, name of publishing company, price and contact information. If you have a distributor or wholesaler lined up, list their contact information, as well. Generally, however, you don't approach distributors and wholesalers until you have a book to show them.

Here's a partial list of prepublication reviewers. For information about general reviewers for published books see Chapter Eleven.

Publisher's Weekly
360 Park Ave., S.
New York, NY 11010-1710
Publishersweekly.com for submission guidelines

Library Journal
(same as Publisher's Weekly)
Libraryjournal.com

American Library Association Booklist
50 Huron St.
Chicago, IL 60611
Ala.org.

Kirkus Reviews
770 Broadway
New York , NY 10003-9597
kirkusrev@kirkusreviews.com

*Kirkus Review* has been doing prepublication book reviews for over seventy years. They are finally offering their review services to self-published, e-published and print-on-demand published authors through a new program called Kirkus Discoveries. No, they are not opening their hearts and minds, they are standing in the long line of folks who are holding out their hands in hopes of getting some of your earnings. They charge $350 to review your book. Yikes! To learn more, visit their Web site at: kirkusreviews.com/kirkusreviews/discoveries/index.jsp or go to KirkusReviews.com and click on Kirkus Discoveries.

I've heard, from authors who have made the Kirkus Discoveries plunge, that this service is not worth the fee.

16: **Set your book price**. There are a couple of ways to figure your price. Some experts suggest pricing your book at an amount eight times the cost per book. This means that if the total cost of producing each book is $5.00, you should charge $40 for the book. If you produce an 80-page book for around $1.50, you must charge $12. This doesn't seem logical to me.

I recommend comparing the price of books similar to yours to help in determining your price.

17: **Order a bar code**. There are numerous companies that produce bar codes. I use Bar Code Graphics, Inc. barcode-us.com, sales@barcode.us.com. You will need an ISBN and the price of the book in order for the company to create your bar code. I generally pay around $30 for a bar code.

18: **Order your Publisher's Cataloguing in Publication information (PCIP)**. This information, which will be printed on your Copyright Page, is important for library use. Contact Quality Books at 800-323-4241 or visit their Web site at quality-books.com. Your cost depends on how quickly you need the PCIP information. Or use the Donohue Group, Inc. They have a quicker turnaround time and a cheaper price. They also issue bar codes. Call 860-683-1647 or visit their Web site at dginc.com

## When the Manuscript is Finished
19: **Choose a printing method and a printer**. Find out how they want you to deliver the book and cover design. (If you have hired experts to help with these aspects of your book, they should be well-qualified to work with your choice of printers.)

20: **Prepare the book for the printer.**

## While the Book is at the Printer (approximately two to six weeks prior to publication)
21: **Solicit prepublication orders**. Send announcements to your mailing list, which should include everyone who has expressed an interest in your book, as well as friends, family, neighbors, co-workers and acquaintances. Tell those to whom you plan to give complimentary copies that they have one coming and that if they'd like to order additional copies, they may do so.

Mail notices to local libraries, bookstores and anyone else who may be interested in the topic. Promote a book on pet photography to pet stores, photography and camera shops, photographers, camera clubs, animal trainers and veterinarians. A book on childhood obesity might be promoted to doctors, family therapists, schools and parents' groups.

Make it easy for people to order books and you will receive orders. By this I mean design an easy-to-use form. Allow payment by check or credit card and consider offering a discount for orders placed by a certain date.

Don't cash checks until the books have been delivered/shipped.

22: **Fill out and send the copyright form.** There's a $45 filing fee ($35 if you file online).

**23: Create a list of post-publication reviewers.** This might include book reviewers for magazines, newsletters and Web sites on the topic of your book, as well as general book reviewers. (Check out the collection of ideas in Chapter Eleven.)

**24: List those to whom you wish to send complimentary copies.** This might include those involved in helping to create the book: cover designer, typesetter and anyone else who contributed in a major way.

Address mailers for key book reviewers and in preparation for your first shipment.

**25: Start planning your promotional program.** (Read Chapters Eleven through Thirteen.)

### After Publication
**26: Ship and deliver review copies, complimentary copies and prepublication orders.**

**27: Send two copies of the book to the Copyright Office** (address on Copyright form)

**28: Send three copies of the book to the Library of Congress** (address on Copyright form)

**29: Send one copy of the book to Quality Books.** Ask them to consider your book as a distributor to the library market. (1003 W. Pines Road, Oregon, IL 61061-9680)

**30: Fill out paperwork for the State Board of Equalization.**

**31: Apply for a business license.** Check into your city/county requirements for the necessity of a business license. I must purchase a county business license and one for the city since I live (work) in the county and sell books through bookstores in the city.

32: **Contact distributors and wholesalers**. Find listings in *Literary Market Place*. (Read about working with wholesalers and distributors in Chapter Eleven.)

33: **Put your promotional plan into action**. (Refer to Chapters Eleven through Thirteen.)

## Recommended Reading:

*The Self-Publishing Manual* by Dan Poynter (Para Publishing, 15th printing, revised, 2006).

# Chapter Eleven

# BOOK PROMOTION BASICS

## FOR THE BOLD AND THE BASHFUL

I feel it is my duty to discuss the nature of book promotion: the realities regarding the competition, the sad truth about bookstores as an outlet for your books and the necessity to be creative when promoting your book. I won't lie about the energy, time and, in some cases, money, it can take to make a book successful.

**News Flash**: People will not swarm to purchase your book just because it exists. In most cases, it takes a lot of thought, preparation, planning, work and compromise in order to break even, let alone profit as an author. And the work is ongoing for as long as you want that book to sell. Just as you were consumed with the process of writing the book, now you will need to totally immerse yourself in the process of promoting it.

Writers are notoriously reclusive. Most of us work in solitary confinement and we like it that way. When we become authors, we hope to see our books hit the bestseller list, but we'd rather not get involved with making that happen—unless it is to share the limelight with Oprah or Montel. What we want is to continue writing, right?

Unfortunately, this concept is not realistic. In order to entice readers for your book, you must promote it. And this is true whether you are self-published, have a traditional publisher or have gone the POD "self-publishing" route.

Sure, you can hire a publicist to jumpstart your book sales. But even this won't absolve you from the promotional process. Debbie Puente solicited the assistance of a publicist to boost sales for her little gift book, *Elegantly Easy Crème Brulee and Other Custard Desserts*. First, let me say that this author has the marketing gene. Upon publication of her book, she launched a promotional campaign and sold thousands upon thousands of copies of her book on her own. When she felt as though she'd run out of ideas and connections, she hired a publicist. But she still didn't get any rest. She says, "I've never been so busy." If you hire a good publicist, be prepared to travel all over the country making personal appearances, possibly even giving radio and TV interviews.

Most publishers today do little or nothing to promote your book. They rely on the author to get the word out and to make those sales. And who better to promote than the author? You know your book better than anyone else does and you care about it more. Promotion is a whole different activity than writing, however.

Children's book author, Sandra Cropsey said, "Had anyone explained to me the ins and outs, the ups and downs of marketing, I'm not sure I would have ever published. Marketing is so far removed from the experience of writing that it is like this constant stranger who speaks a different language with which I am neither equipped nor have the ability or even the desire to understand. If someone would lock me in a room, tie me to a chair and maybe threaten me with bodily harm, I might be enticed to market. Most days, however, I would prefer to just have my teeth ground down. Success for me will be selling all the books and repaying the loans."

## Set Reasonable Goals and Keep Raising the Bar
No matter how distasteful the concept of promotion seems to you, if you want to sell books, it's necessary. The greater understanding you have of this process before you become a published author, the better.

I had an interesting email conversation with a relatively new author last year. He said that he has sold "only" 50,000 copies of his book. I told him that was a very good number. He said, "Not according to my expectations." We talked about expectations earlier in this book. I warned you against having unreasonable expectations, but encouraged you to have meaningful goals. This author reminded me that there is sometimes a fine line between unreasonable expectations and lofty goals.

Lofty goals become unreasonable expectations when one is ill-informed and ill-prepared. In order to meet goals, one must recognize potential obstacles and be willing to work around them. He must become aware of the opportunities and take advantage of them.

Publisher/author, Elizabeth Burton says, "I see far too many aspiring writers with unrealistic expectations who simply won't accept that they aren't going to become the next Stephen King or Annie Proulx the minute their book comes out. So after the first five or ten times they try to promote to a bookstore and get turned down, they give up instead of looking for alternatives."

The only way that anyone can fail is to quit. So how did this young man sell 50,000 books? He had an article published in *Playboy Magazine* (3,200,000 circulation) and this led to an interview on a prestigious TV show. He said that now sales are strictly word of mouth and he spends most of his time working on his next book. Must be nice, eh?

This could be you. All it takes is a well-written book on a timely topic for which there is a large audience and your ability and willingness to vigorously promote to that audience. Before ever writing the book, you should be thinking about promotion.

One author told me recently, "My expectations were definitely not met because I failed so miserably in the marketing of the book. I was just unable to find a way to reach the audience that I needed to target and then I ran out of funds to have the book included in the mass mailing offered by PMA. There are thousands of people out there who would benefit from this book if only they knew about it."

I'm pretty sure that the mass mailing would not have pulled this author out of the quagmire. The "masses" were not her audience. Hers was a book useful only to a small segment of people utilizing a specific type of medical procedure. Her audience would be found through physicians' offices, medical centers, hospital gift shops, pharmacies, medical/health magazines and Web sites and targeted mailing lists.

So how does one approach the sometimes daunting task of promotion? In a nutshell, set reachable goals. When you meet a goal, consider yourself successful and set a new one.

## What You Must Do To Promote

Build promotion into your book. As I suggested in Chapter Six, involve a lot of people in your book, connect it to an organization or industry that might help with the promotion and sales and make sure that the book has everything it needs in order to be sold through traditional means.

An author came to me a few years ago asking for help promoting his book. He was frustrated because he couldn't get it into bookstores and other retail outlets. I agreed to take a look at his book and discovered several problems right away. First, his subject matter was not conducive to a mainstream audience, so traditional bookstores were probably not his venue. He had self-published this book and had not bothered to identify it via an ISBN. The book did not have a bar code nor did he get the Library of Congress block.

All I could suggest to this man was that he promote and sell his book via the Internet and maybe through catalog sales and back-of-the-room sales at civic group meetings.

He had another option. He could order an ISBN and have a bar code printed on stickers to be placed on each book. He still may not be invited to sell his book through bookstores. But, if he had the opportunity, he would be prepared.

### Books in Print

Make sure that your book is listed in *Books in Print*. Your traditional royalty publisher will arrange for this. If you are working with a new publisher, remind him to take this important step. If you are self-publishing, it is your responsibility to fill out the Advance Book Information Form (ABI). If you go through a POD "self-publishing" house, be certain that they are taking care of this detail for you. If not, you get the forms and do it. (Refer to Chapter Ten.)

*Books in Print* is the primary resource list of books published in the U.S. Bookstores use this system to locate books requested by customers. If you are not listed in *Books in Print,* you could be missing out on sales.

If you fill the form out yourself, you most likely will get a call or an email from the Bowker Company asking you to pay for an annotated listing. When they contacted me, I thought they were suggesting that I start paying for what has always been a free listing in *Books in Print.* But I soon realized that the voice on the other end of the phone belonged to a salesman who was asking me to spring for a paid ad. I have received that call a couple of times since and always politely turn them down. Actually, I wasn't so polite the last time that salesman called because he was a little pushy and I was heavily concentrating on a project. I hear from colleagues who have purchased these ads, that they aren't worth the asking price. At this point, I'm going to go on record as saying that the original free listing in *Books in Print* is generally all you need.

## Bookstore Sales

Up until 1996, the books I published through Matilija Press were of local interest only. And then I produced two books that I wanted to sell nation-wide. Because I was still ignorant about the way books move through the system, I envisioned them being sold primarily through bookstores. I saw plenty of ethnic cookbooks, party books and New Age books shelved at every bookstore I visited. Why not mine? And so my main promotional effort to jumpstart sales for *The Mainland Luau* and *Quest for Truth* was a large mailing to bookstores.

I had promo pieces created from extra book covers, bought a mailing list featuring hundreds of bookstores and invited my pre-teen grandchildren to help me prepare the mailing. I spent over $400 on this promotional activity and not one sale resulted. Not even one.

It might also help you to know that even established publishers have trouble getting their books on bookstore shelves. There are just too many books. And as with everyone else in business, the dollar rules the bookstore owners' and managers' decisions. The books that are selling get space; those that aren't, are returned. Also, it is my understanding that large book publishers get preferential treatment because they purchase shelf space in major bookstores.

This is not to discourage you from ever entering a bookstore with your book. On the contrary, I have enjoyed many sales through bookstores. How? I visit independent bookstores and pitch my book locally and while traveling. When I plan to be interviewed for a radio show or make an appearance at a conference in another city, I alert a couple of independent bookstores in that area. The bookstore managers will typically order a few copies of the book in preparation for any resulting sales. If the books sell, they order more. It is up to me to keep customers coming in, so my next logical step is to send press releases to the local newspapers and write articles for their regional publications.

I frequently receive purchase orders from bookstores nationwide when customers order copies of my books. These customers might have seen one of my writing books mentioned in my bio at the end of an article published in *Writer's Digest Magazine*, noticed my grandparenting book in the library or learned about my metaphysical book from a colleague who heard me speak at a conference.

The primary way to get into bookstores is through your track record. You must do something to generate sales: Send press releases, do speaking engagements, write articles, do radio shows and solicit book reviews, for example. The key is to get word out about your book.

When customers keep asking for the book, bookstores will start carrying it. I have also done well selling books through specialty bookstores.

Did you know that there are bookstores that specialize in books related to cats, cooking, metaphysics/spirituality, ethnic topics, women's issues, children, art, science, home and garden, travel, photography and mysteries, for example? Pandora's Books in Los Angeles, Vision Quest in Arizona and Mystical World in New Jersey all focus on spiritual and metaphysical books. Books for Cooks in Maryland specializes just in cookbooks. Jennie's Garden Books in British Columbia sells only books related to gardens and gardening.

Standard bookstores are generally the first and sometimes the only place most new authors think of for selling their books. But it may be the last place you'll want to pursue. Why? The reality is that bookstores account for less than fifty percent of book sales each year.

Even if you do get your book on the shelf, it doesn't guarantee sales. And without sales, your book won't last long there.

I called Ingram recently to get bookstore sales figures for well-known books in the writing/publishing field. I was surprised to learn that the non-bookstore sales for my writing books are actually higher, in most cases, than bookstore sales for my colleagues' books.

Check your competition's bookstore sales by calling 615-213-6803. Have the ISBN ready.

Here's a reality check. According to the Book Industry Study Group (BSIG), in 2004 there were 1.2 million titles in print. That year, there were 665 million books sold. Only one percent of all titles represent sales of one million copies or more. And just 1.9 percent of the books in print racked up sales of from 5,000 to 49,000 copies.

What was the largest segment of sales statistics? Believe it or not, in 2004, a whopping seventy-six percent of books sold less than one-hundred copies. In other words, only ten titles sold over a million copies and 948,000 of them sold under one hundred.

Additionally, you should know that the largest bookstores carry less than thirteen percent of America's book titles at ony one time. That's around 150,000 titles out of the 1.2 million in print.

Do you really want your book in bookstores among the thousands and thousands of others? If so, here's an opportunity:

Last year, I stumbled across a page at barnesandnobleinc.com telling authors how to get our books into their stores. According to this announcement, they review more than 100,000 submissions from publishers of all types and sizes each year. They say that most of these books are actually added to their database and a few are ordered for their warehouse. When they accept a title, it is then available for sale on their Web site and to fill orders placed by any of their stores. The book you're holding in your hands, was accepted for this program. Learn more about this opportunity at barnesandnobleinc.com. Click on "For Authors." Go to the bottom of this page and click on "Getting your book in Barnes and Noble."

> The Small Press Department
> Barnes and Noble
> 122 Fifth Ave
> New York, NY 10011

Borders Books has a similar service for independent publishers. You can even go to their site and find out if your book is in their system. If your book is listed in *Books in Print*, it should be in their system.

What does it mean to be in their system? When someone comes in and asks for your book and it is listed in their database, they can order it for the customer. Check on your book title by going to, bordersstores.com/index.jsp. Those of you without Internet access can step into (or call) any Borders Bookstore and inquire as to whether your book is in their database. I just checked and this book is there. In fact they list eighteen of my books, even those that are out of print.

New Vendor Acquisitions
Borders Group, Inc.
100 Phoenix Dr.
Ann Arbor, MI 48108

For additional information about submitting your book for consideration, visit bordersgroupinc.com/artists/publishers.htm.

According to the folks at Borders, having your books with one of their distributors or wholesalers increases your opportunities with them. They use Ingram, Baker and Taylor, Biblio Book Distribution, Partners Book Distributing and Bookazine. (Contact information in Chapter Sixteen.)

These companies will consider books based on salability, which means, a book with all of the appropriate amenities on a topic that people are actually interested in.

## How To Work With a Bookstore

Bookstores purchase books from publishers in one of two ways. Generally they issue a purchase order (PO) for one book and you ship the book along with an invoice for the amount less the bookstore discount (usually forty percent), plus shipping. It is not unusual to receive payment as many as ninety-days or even 120 days later. I've had problems with some bookstores paying me at all. My few business losses have not come from individual customers, but mainly bookstores. More and more bookstore owners are issuing a credit card number so you can charge for the book prior to shipping. This works for me.

Some independent publishers I know adjust their bookseller discount according to the quantity ordered. They might give thirty-five percent for sales under twenty books and forty percent for sales of twenty to 100 copies.

Sometimes, you can negotiate a consignment agreement with a bookstore. The bookstore orders several copies of your book to carry in the store. You invoice them at the time of delivery/shipment and they pay you either by the end of that month or once the books have been sold. If a bookseller that I'm dealing with has a habit of paying late, I will collect for the previous shipment of books before delivering/shipping more.

I also offer booksellers a return policy. I tell them that if the books don't sell, I'll pick up those that are still in good shape and refund their money (or deduct what they owe me). This gives the bookseller more incentive to carry the books—no risk involved. If I do my job as promoter, there is no risk to me, either.

While I was in the process of revising this book, I asked colleagues, clients and customers what they would like to see added. One independent publisher said that she'd like to see more written about bookstore consignment agreements. Both this publisher and I have seen bookstores close and the proprietors disappear into thin air with supplies of our books. There's also the situation where you deliver a dozen books and the bookseller claims you left only ten. I don't know how one could prevent this from happening, other than to stay in close and constant contact with booksellers, which I recommend, in any case.

Use duplicate invoices each and every time you deliver or ship books to booksellers. I also recommend devising a consignment agreement. In the first edition of this book, I provided a Web site where you could access a variety of forms for authors and publishers. I see that this site no longer exists. But here's a book that might be useful to independent publishers: Tad Crawford's *Business and Legal Forms for Authors and Self-Publishers* (Allworth Press, 2005).

## Exposure Versus Sales
### Book Signings

While I recommend book signings, I have to warn you that this probably isn't the best way for the average author to sell a lot of books. First of all, you don't have a name that will draw a crowd. Sure, your friends and relatives will come out to support you, but they've already bought your book or you've given them copies. Without celebrity status, it takes a provocative subject and/or a great deal of promotion to get more than a few token attendees at a book signing.

### How Exposure Works

Am I trying to discourage you? Not necessarily. But from the onset of planning a book signing, I want you to be thinking about something other than sales—think *exposure*. Marketing experts say that a customer needs to see something or hear about it a total of seven or eight times before he is likely to buy it. Without exposure, just think of the customers you would never get.

Book promotion takes repetition. I preach this constantly to SPAWN members and those who attend my workshops. I say, "Think exposure and the sales will come." I've seen far too many authors leave a signing or a book festival feeling extremely disappointed after having sold only a few books. I've also seen authors at these events chase away potential buyers by their attitude because they are so upset about lack of sales. It's too bad when an author is so attached to big sales that he misses opportunities to create bridges to future sales.

Promotion is not necessarily sales, but it is the public relations essential toward growing sales.

Think about it, if you're a mystery buff and you hear about a mystery by a new author, you may not respond because, after all, you don't know this author. You hear the book mentioned again on the radio. You sort of half listen, but still don't rush out to buy it. Later, a friend tells you that he has read the book—hmmm, you begin to get interested. You notice the book while shopping for a Fathers Day gift and still don't buy it. Finally you see it listed on a mystery book Web site and you decide to order it. Don't say that you haven't done this. We all have. The point is, when you think *marketing*, avoid focusing only on sales. Consider exposure, as well.

A SPAWN member learned a good lesson last year. She sent me a notice announcing publication of the second edition of her book. I sent her a check for the book in the next day's mail. Later, she emailed me to say that she was a little surprised to receive my order. She told me that she almost skipped my name in the mailing since she knew that I was already familiar with her book. She had discussed the book with me a time or two via email and I'd seen it at a book festival.

What she didn't know was that, when I first saw the book, it sparked an interest. Each time I heard about it, I thought, "Someday, I'm going to buy a copy of that book." And when she contacted me recently about the revision, the time was right.

The author learned, that day, to never second-guess a potential customer. You may feel as though you're bugging people with your promo material, when actually you may be just reminding them of something they intend doing anyway.

Promote to those folks who have already bought copies of your book. My customers sometimes buy additional copies of my books as gifts. I've had customers come back for another copy after losing theirs in a move or loaning it to someone who didn't return it. The fastest and most surefire way to have a book fail is to stop promoting it.

Even though book signings generally don't generate a lot of sales, I recommend that you do some. As I said, it is great exposure and, who knows, you might get lucky. One of my clients sold fifty copies of his true crime book at a local signing. He drew about 150 people to the small independent bookstore that evening. How did he do this? He followed the guidelines outlined below:

## Book Signing Tips For Authors

1: Don't wait for an invitation. Take the initiative and approach the managers of businesses related to your book topic and local bookstores. Offer to give a presentation or to sign books for their customers. The latest thing for authors is book signings at coffee shops and wine bars.

If the subject of your book lends itself to demonstrations, plan one for this event. When Debbie Puente signs her book, *Elegantly Easy Crème Brulee and Other Custard Desserts*, attendees are usually treated to a demonstration and a sample. Teddy Colbert, the author of *The Living Wreath*, often shares her expertise in making succulent wreaths when she signs copies of her book at nurseries and garden shops.

**2 ½ weeks before the event:**
2: Send press releases with a photograph of yourself and/or your book cover to all newspapers within a forty-mile radius. Relate the particulars of the planned event and include a description of the book and your bio. Give your phone number. An editor may want to contact you for more information. (Learn how to write a press release in Chapter Twelve.)

3: Make calls and send postcards and emails inviting friends, acquaintances, business associates and others to your signing. Post flyers on bulletin boards where you work and in public places. Have notices placed in appropriate company and club newsletters.

**10 days in advance of the event:**
4: Find out if the store plans to design posters and flyers to advertise your signing. If not, do this yourself and deliver them to the store a week in advance of the event. Ask the manager to include a flyer with each purchase during that week. Offer to design a store display of your books.

**One week in advance of the event**:

5: Know ahead of time what to expect: Will you have a microphone? Lectern? Table at which to sit for signing? Or will you have to arrange for these things?

6: Make sure the store has enough books in stock. If you must depend on your publisher or POD "self-publisher" to ship books for the signing, request books several weeks in advance of the event. I've known many an author who sat at his or her signing table with only one or two books to show and nothing to sign and sell. It is important that you stay in contact with your publishing house representative until the books are actually shipped. And then maintain a close connection to the bookstore buyer making sure that he or she is aware when the package arrives. Sometimes the error occurs not with the publisher, but in the stockroom at the bookstore.

Keep a couple of boxes of books on hand at your home office in case someone at the publishing house or bookstore drops the ball.

**The day of the event**:

7: Dress to stand out in a crowd, but not so dramatically as to distract from your presentation. Dress so that you are approachable to the particular audience your book topic will attract, but still appear professional. A tasteful business suit works in most cases. Use color and accessories in relationship to the topic of your book. For a more serious book, you might wear a tailored blouse (for a woman) and a shirt and tie (for a man). For lighter subjects or genres, consider dressing in softer fabrics (for women) and an open-neck shirt (for men). If the theme of your book is aviation, go ahead and wear your WWII flight jacket. If yours is a dreamy romance, wear a pair of slacks or a skirt and a fitted tee shirt with the cover of your book screen-printed on the front. Let's say that you've written a children's book. Wear something colorful and fun or dress as a character from your story. For a cookbook, wear a fashionable, fun apron.

8: Be prompt. Arrive a little early so you can settle in.

9: Bring handouts—a bookmark featuring your book cover, a related article or a sample chapter, for example. When I sign my book, *Quest For Truth,* I hand out my article on meditation walking. When the event features *The Mainland Luau,* I give away a recipe. I always have a stack of appropriate articles for folks attending one of my talks about writing/publishing.

Provide a pertinent resource list or print a booklet of accompanying information, stories or poems, for example, to give to everyone who visits the bookstore the day of your signing.

10: Reach out to people. Hand copies of your book to folks in the audience or who visit your signing table. Someone is more apt to purchase something they've held in their hands. If you're sitting alone, walk around the store and strike up conversations with customers.

11: Ask the store manager to display your book at the register and tell customers that the author is signing this book in the back of the store.

12: Keep track of the number of books you autograph in case there is a discrepancy at the register.

**After the event:**
13: Send a note of thanks to the store manager and staff.

14: Attend other signings and note what works and what doesn't.

15: Arrange more book signings, presentations and demonstrations at bookstores and/or specialty stores. Consider a combined signing with another author—someone whose book complements your own, but doesn't compete with it. A book of animal-related poems and a novel about a dog might entice the same buyers. You could promote your book on writing thank you notes along with one featuring how to make paper products. Another compatible combination might be a book on marketing Web site businesses and one featuring how to gear up for a job in technology.

16: Realize that signings and presentations will rarely exceed your expectations and hardly ever meet your highest goals. But anytime you are given the opportunity for this sort of free publicity, you are making headway in your promotional effort.

Many authors sell books while traveling and some plan book tours. Clair Button currently works as a botanist in Oregon and is the author of *Cow Cookies*, a modern western mystery novel. He spends his vacations promoting his book. He says, "Before the trip, I attempt to find and evaluate whatever bookstores are in the towns we will visit. I let them know when I'll be passing through town and offer to meet with them to do a signing or a reading. I stop in and introduce myself and my book to the owner or book buyer. Each visit takes from ten to thirty minutes. I try to negotiate a discount sale or consignment. My goal is to sell them at least one book to evaluate."

If your book relates to business, a corporate leader may agree to sponsor your tour. A book for families of Alzheimer's patients might find a sponsor among appropriate organizations.

## Specialty Stores

Specialty stores are often overlooked as outlets for books. But think about how many stores carry books. Dan Poynter was among the first to point out to authors and independent publishers the concept of thinking beyond the bookstore. One of his first books was on parachuting. Like most of us, he expected to sell this book through bookstores. His diligence led him to discover, however, that a better place for that book was in stores that sell things related to parachutes and parachuting.

I know an author who sells her local hiking book through sporting goods stores. I've placed my luau book in several kitchen stores across the United States. A joke book related to cars might do well in automotive shops or parts stores. Pitch your book of hors d'oeuvres to wine bars and a book about knitting scarves to craft stores.

Choose your venue carefully. I've had a few retail agreements from hell. Several years ago, there was a popular yogurt shop downtown.

Knowing that they had a large volume of foot traffic, I asked if they would like to carry the Ojai Valley history book.

It wasn't long before the proprietor called asking me to replace a couple of books because his display copies were now soiled. It seems that even adults have no qualms about enjoying a good book while licking a dripping yogurt cone.

I suggested that we put just one book on display to be used and abused and store new books for purchase behind the counter. That wasn't completely satisfactory, either, because I didn't feel it was good business to have a less than perfect book on display.

Later, when major bookstores began serving fancy coffee, I wondered about their rate of returns because of sticky pages.

## Tips for Getting Book Reviews

Book reviews sell books. Most people, when they think of having their books reviewed, consider only the prestigious prepublication reviewers: *Kirkus Reviews, Library Journal, Publishers Weekly* and so forth. Rarely does a self-published or POD published book or even a book produced by a small traditional royalty publisher make one of these lists. This is primarily because of sheer volume. There are just a handful of these influential publications and over 290,000 new books coming out each year. The *Library Journal* staff reviews around 6,000 books annually and they receive as many as 40,000 submissions. The *Los Angeles Times* reviews just 1,500 new books per year.

Since they have to turn so many books away, major reviewers have made a policy against accepting POD published and self-published books.

I know one author who had her self-published book accepted for review by *Library Journal,* however, and sales soared. So while it is extremely difficult to land a review with these particular prepublication reviewers, it is certainly not impossible. You may just have the right book and present it at the right time. With a little luck sitting on your shoulder, a review could happen.

While you're waiting to find that four leaf clover, why not solicit the hundreds of other book reviewers who are willing and eager to share their opinion of your book? Who are these reviewers? They are editors of appropriately targeted magazines, newsletters and Web sites.

Book reviewers work in a couple of different ways. While most publications and Web sites that use book reviews actually have reviewers on staff, others will publish your review—a review that you submit. Of course you can pay someone to review your book and to write a review. But I would steer clear of agencies that charge large fees for review services. There are too many people jumping on the publishing bandwagon these days and charging for services that you don't need to pay for.

I sometimes ask colleagues to write reviews for me. When the review is published, they may even receive a paycheck from the magazine in the amount of anywhere from $50 to $200 or so. Mostly I submit my books for review by someone associated with the magazine, Web site or newsletter and that's what I urge you to do.

Before sending your book for review, make sure that your book topic is right for the publication. There are magazines, Web sites and newsletters representing practically every subject and concept on earth. And then there are sites and publications dedicated specifically to books. Your novel will probably have the best chance of being reviewed in the latter. Your children's book would surely be selected for review at any number of children-related Web sites and publications. *Christian Home and School Magazine* publishes reviews for children's books, for example. *BookPage* posts reviews of books for children. Have your fantasy or comic book reviewed at *Seized By the Tale* Web site.

A book review is an excellent way to promote your book for free. In fact, there are countless opportunities out there for getting your new and even your older books reviewed. It's just a matter of finding the right place.

My writing books have been reviewed in over 100 writing-related magazines, newsletters, Web sites and newspaper columns. *The*

*Mainland Luau* was reviewed in dozens of cooking/foods/Hawaiian magazines, newsletters and newspaper columns as well as on radio cooking shows and Web sites.

While some of the reviews were through invitation, most of them occurred because I was out there making it happen. I located appropriate reviewers, I contacted them and I followed up with them. How does an author go about finding reviewers for his/her book? Here are some guidelines:

1: Have clarity about your topic/genre. Let's say that your nonfiction book features techniques for dealing with depression. You could conceivably get this book reviewed in the health section of newspapers throughout the United States as well as Web sites, magazines and newsletters related to depression and other health issues. This is such a wide-spread topic that it would be appropriate for women's magazines as well as men's, teen, religious and many general magazines. Try soliciting rural magazines (pointing out the problems with depression for people who are isolated) or regional magazines (perhaps one of your major contributing professionals is affiliated with a university in Texas, you referenced a research agency in Virginia and you wrote of the difficulty with depression for folks living in New York City). Can you see the possibilities? You could solicit reviews in Texas-based, Virginia-based and New York-based magazines.

2: Research newspaper columns, magazines, Web sites and newsletters. You probably have a file full of resources. Use them, but also locate additional review possibilities. Do a Google search to find appropriate review opportunities. Refer to *Writer's Market* for magazine listings. Study *Gales Directory of Publications* for newsletters on your topic. (Locate Gales Directories in the reference section at your public library or online—probably for a fee.) You'll find directories of newspapers at newspaperlinks.com and newspapers.com. Use *Google Alert* to keep up with new review opportunities. *Google Alert* is a free service wherein you can sign up to receive the latest resources, news or information in your area of interest. Tell Google what topics you want to know about and they will keep you updated as to new Web postings.

This might include new magazines, newsletters and Web sites related to your topic or genre and/or news and information pertaining to your subject. google.com/alerts. (See additional resources in Chapter Sixteen.)

3: Introduce your book through a letter to the Webmaster, editor or columnist and offer to send a review copy. When you get the okay, send your book with a cover letter reminding the editor that he requested the book for review. Include copies of a few former reviews, your contact information and a press release. Unless there is a deadline or another reason for urgency, I always send review copies via media mail. The savings can be $1.00 or more per book. Be sure to log the books that you send for inventory and tracking purposes. (Read more about bookkeeping for the author in Chapter Fourteen.)

4: Follow up with an email, phone call or letter to make sure the book was received and to ask when the review is scheduled. You may have to follow up more than once. Unfortunately, not every reviewer who receives it will review your book. Even so, always remain professional and courteous.

5: Thank the reviewer once the review appears. Ask him or her to post the review at your amazon.com book page. (If your book is listed at amazon.com, readers and reviewers can easily post their reviews and comments there.)

If you dedicate just thirty days to soliciting book reviews—contacting a dozen editors/Webmasters each day—you could conceivably land as many as 200 reviews by the end of the month. How many sales would that generate? If your book is on amazon.com, if you have a Web site and if Baker and Taylor or Ingram is distributing your title, book sales could increase considerably. If even five people are inspired by each review to purchase your book, that's 1,000 books sold and anywhere from $2,000 to $10,000 or more in profits.

**Magazine Review Opportunities**
Here are a few magazines with book review columns: *The Iconoclast* editors review books in fiction and poetry genres. They want to receive

reviews of 250-500 words. But they may also agree to review your book and write the review themselves. Contact Phil Wagner at 1675 Amazon Rd. Mohegan Lake, NY 10547-1804.

*Bibliophilos* publishes 1,000-1,500-word reviews of books present or past. Request their guidelines by writing to: 200 Security Building, Fairmont, WV 26554. Contact Dr. Gerald J. Bobango.

*African Voices*. The book review editor is Debbie Officer at africanvoices@aol.com. Keep in mind when contacting this editor for a book review that your book must reflect the art, literature and history of people of color.

*Today's Christian Woman* publishes reviews. These are staff-written reviews on topics of interest to Christian women. Let Holly Robaina know about your book. Write to her at 465 Gundersen Dr., Carol Stream, IL 60188.

The editors at *January Magazine* review books of all types. They also publish stories about authors and others involved in the publishing process. Book topics of interest to the January Magazine staff range from children's to true crime and cookbooks to mystery. For more information about submitting your book for review contact Linda Richards at Linda@januarymagazine.com.

*Mothering Magazine* will publish reviews of books featuring the natural family—alternative sources to mainstream family living and health issues, for example. Contact Ashisha at POB 1690, Santa Fe. NM 87504.

*Grandparents Magazine* publishes book reviews of interest to our baby boomers and older generation. Learn more by writing to 281 Rosedale Ave., Wayne, PA 19087.

*The First Line* publishes reviews of books with an interesting first line. They don't pay much and their circulation is small, but if your book has an interesting first line, why not consider offering a book review to them? That's 250 more readers who will be aware of your great work. Contact David LaBounty, POB 250382, Plano, TX 75025-0382. Web site: thefirstline.com.

The editors at *Spirituality and Health Magazine* review books in the spiritual and health realm. Contact Frederic and Mary Ann Brussat at 75 Glen Road, Sandy Hook, CT 06482 or brussat@spiritualityhealth.com.

Ask for permission to send your historical novel to the *Historical Novel Society* for review in their magazine. Go to historicalnovelsociety.org/the-review.htm.

Get your romance novel reviewed in *Romantic Times Book Review*. Call 718-237-1097 ext. 23 or email Giselle@romantictimes.com.

James A. Cox at *Midwest Book Review* reviews a variety of types of books and gives primary consideration to small publishing companies and self-published authors. Contact Cox, 278 Orchard Dr., Oregon, WI 53575. midwestbookreview.com/get-rev.htm.

The editors at *InnerSelf Magazine* reviews books on many topics and in many genres. They have 26,000 circulation. Contact them at 965 Francis Street, Altomonte Springs, FL 32701. innerself.com.

## Don't Overlook the Library Market
Libraries purchase numbers of books every year. Contrary to what you may hear about your own community library system, libraries do have budgets. Even in lean economic times, they buy books. And if you can get them to purchase books from you, they will generally pay full price. Most libraries prefer to do business with library wholesalers, however. Why? Wholesalers give them a discount and, like bookstore managers, librarians find it easier and more cost-effective to work with a handful of wholesalers rather than hundreds of small publishers and authors.

Before signing with a library wholesaler, you might try to make some sales directly, especially if your book is suited to some of this nation's specialty libraries. If your book is historical in nature and/or profiles early pioneers, contact genealogy libraries such as the major one in Salt Lake City, Utah. There are also military libraries and those related to science, academics, aviation, architecture and law. There are over 15,000 public libraries in the United States alone. Add to that, school, university and specialty libraries and the number reaches over 100,000.

To locate libraries related to your topic, visit the Gale Group at galegroup.com. Inquire about their library lists for rent. Search libraries through Gale's print reference book in your local library. Or look at the American Library Association Directory at ala.org. Purchase a mailing list for libraries for anywhere from $59 to $199 at librarymarketinglist.com.

Get your book reviewed in magazines and ezines for librarians. Access a directory listing 150 such publications at: libdex.com/journals.html.

In the late 1980s, I personally contacted individual libraries nationwide with promo about my local history book and received numerous orders. Now, with the changing times, Baker and Taylor and Quality Books are handling my library sales. A couple of times each year, I will email press releases to appropriate libraries promoting certain books and asking them to contact Baker and Taylor, Quality Books or myself to place an order.

While libraries order almost year round, their main ordering periods are in late December and late June.

Make friends with local librarians by donating copies of your book. Offer to give readings at libraries. Donate a percentage of sales to the library fund. Libraries can be repeat customers. Books, especially paperbacks, take a beating when they're in the library system. The more they're circulated, the more wear and tear they endure. Librarians are eager to replace those books that get a lot of patron attention.

What type of books are libraries likely to reject? They typically turn away those with spiral, plastic comb or saddle-stitched binding. They also don't generally purchase workbooks. They require books with spines—it's best to have your title printed on the spine, as well. Libraries especially like reference books and those that are informative. Hardcover books last longer in library use. Books must have a Library of Congress Cataloguing-in-Publication block (your publisher provides this) or Publisher's Cataloguing-in-Publication block (provided by Quality Books or Donohue Group during the self-publishing process).

Librarians and bookstore managers also like to see a key on the upper left back cover indicating the type of book this is and the topic: reference/book publishing, writing/reference, history, autobiography, young adult fantasy, science fiction, parenting, etc.

Quality Books and Baker and Taylor are just two library wholesalers. Others include, Unique Books, Ambassador, Midwest and Brodart. There is a procedure to follow in being accepted by these wholesalers. Be sure to check their individual guidelines. (See list of library wholesalers in the Resources Guide, Chapter Sixteen.)

You generally pay a library wholesaler around fifty-five percent on sales. And you can expect to wait as long as ninety days for payment. Some wholesalers will make payments earlier if you give them a larger percentage.

## Working With Wholesalers and Distributors
At some point on your promotional path, you will wonder: What is a distributor? Do I need one? It is most common today for publishers to use wholesalers to fulfill orders to bookstores, libraries and other wholesale customers. And this is especially true for independent publishers. Bookstore managers, like librarians, prefer to order merchandise from a dozen or so distributors and wholesalers rather than hundreds of publishers.

Of course, if you can make the sale directly, you get to keep more of the profit. But you'll probably get more total sales if you partner with a wholesaler.

What's the difference between a wholesaler and a distributor? A wholesaler makes your book available to retail stores and libraries. There are two major wholesalers of books in the United States; Baker and Taylor and Ingram and about a dozen additional wholesalers that specialize.

Distributors, on the other hand, have sales reps out there showing your book around to booksellers. Most distributors either specialize in certain topics or genres or they are regional— they distribute books just in specific areas of the United States.

I've worked with about a dozen different distributors and most of my experiences were negative. I had a few very good distributors, however, who got out there and sold numbers of my books to booksellers. My best distributor was Bookline in Hawaii. They sold over 1,000 copies of *The Mainland Luau* in less than two years.

One of my distributors ordered a box of books. Within fifteen months or so, they went out of business. Only after months of pressure, did they finally return my books and most of them were damaged.

Currently, I have my self-published books listed with Baker and Taylor and Quality Books, which seems to be adequate for my titles. I also have all of my books listed with amazon.com and BarnesandNoble.com. While some self-published authors are reluctant to give up such a large percentage to wholesalers, distributors and online booksellers, I recommend that you do so in order to reach more customers. It is a stubborn, short-sighted author who keeps all of his eggs in one tiny basket.

**How to Work With a Distributor**
Many authors have been led to believe that a distributor is the answer to all of their promotional prayers. In today's fiercely competitive

publishing climate, a connection to a good distributor is definitely a plus, but it's only a piece of the promotional puzzle.

Choose one or more distributors related to the subject of your book. Then create a demand for your book and the distributors can more easily place it in bookstores and libraries.

A distributor wants to know your promotional plans. They like authors with more than one book in the pipeline. The reasons why they will reject your book are similar to the reasons a bookstore manager might give—it has the wrong binding, you have no promotional plans or the subject matter is inappropriate.

The Independent Book Publishers Association (PMA) has a free online directory of distributors and wholesalers. Go to pma-online.org/distribute.cfm. John Kremer lists a number of distributors at: bookmarket.com/distributors.htm. Dan Poynter offers distributor lists for sale at parapublishing.com. Here are a few distributors and wholesalers:

**General Distributors**
Independent Publishers Group, 814 N. Franklin St., Chicago, IL 60610. ipgbook.com.

Small Press Distribution, spdbooks.org.

**Regional Distributor**
Sunbelt Publications distributes books on California subjects, including regional travel and reference books, guidebooks and outdoor adventure books. Contact them at 1250 Fayette St., El Cajon, CA 92020 or sunbeltpub.com.

Washington Book Distributors serves D.C., Maryland and Virginia. washingtonbk.com.

**Specialty Distributors**
Rittenhouse Books distributes medical and healthcare books. Contact them at 511 Feheley Dr., King of Prussia, PA 19406. rittenhouse.com.

DeVorss and Company is a distributor for inspirational and new thought books. 552 Constitution Ave., Camarillo, CA 93012-8510. devorss.com.

Faith Works distributes Christian books. faithworksonline.com.

You can expect to give a wholesaler around fifty-five percent of the retail price of your book and distributors take anywhere from sixty-five to seventy percent.

## Amazon.com

In order to submit your titles for sale at amazon.com, go to amazon.com and scroll down to the bottom of the page. Click on "sell items." You'll see a list of over a dozen programs offered to authors. I suggest starting by including your book in the Advantage program. Choose "Advantage." The directions for signing up are there. Basically, you'll pay an annual membership fee of $29.95 no matter how many titles you list and fifty-five percent per book sold.

Amazon.com will order books via email. They ask you to send just the number they request and to include one copy of the purchase order with your shipment. In the Advantage program, amazon.com will order at least a few books to keep in stock.

If you have a link to amazon.com from your Web site, Amazon will pay you a referral fee for books ordered by customers who use that link. For additional information, go to amazon.com/advantage and click on "Associates Central."

Take advantage of some of the many advertising opportunities at Amazon. Ask book reviewers to post reviews of your book on your page at Amazon, for example. Encourage customers (and friends) to post comments.

## Fulfillment Services

If you expect a large quantity of orders and/or you don't want to handle order-taking and shipping yourself, you can employ a fulfillment company. Most companies offer a variety of services: shipping only, order-taking and shipping, an 800-number for you to use in promotion, etc.

There are many companies with a wide variety of offerings. Before signing up, find out if there is a set-up fee and how much it is. What is their order processing fee? Is there a minimum monthly order or a return processing fee? Do they charge to store your books? Also inquire about a credit card transaction fee and shopping cart services. Refer to *Literary Market Place* for listings of fulfillment companies. Listed below are a few of the many fulfillment companies that work with small presses:

Book Clearing House
www.bookch.com

Bookmasters
Contact Sherry Ringler
800-537-6721
www.bookmasters.com

Pathway Book Service
Contact Ernest Peter
800-345-6665
pbs@pathwaybook.com

www.pathwaybooks.com

## Recommended Reading
*Over 75 Good Ideas for Promoting Your Book* by Patricia Fry (Matilija Press, 1996).

# Chapter Twelve

# BOOK PROMOTION
## REACH OUT
## BEYOND THE BOOKSTORE

One of the biggest mistakes you can make as an author is expecting others to promote your book. It is your job to get the word out. No one knows your book as well as you do and no one loves it as much as you do. Not only are you the best one to promote your book, you are responsible for its success or failure.

While you may have an idea or two for promoting your book, I urge you to explore a variety of promotional activities. Pursue primary ones as well as some that may not seem so obvious. Chapters Twelve and Thirteen are designed to prime your promotions pump and fill your head with new ideas you can use.

I've learned that it's not a matter of *finding* the time to promote your book, it's a matter of *making* the time. Some experts suggest that you commit to at least four hours every week spent promoting or as John Kremer, author of *1001 Ways to Market Your Books* says, "Do five promotions each and every day."

Following, you'll find several promotional ideas that are recommended for most authors/independent publishers.

## Create Your Own Web Site
It's important to embrace the technology age. I know that some of you aren't quite there. Some don't want to go there. And others may

use a computer, but just haven't gotten around to delving into the world of Web sites and the Internet. It will behoove you, professionally, to take the plunge.

A Web site provides an amazing showcase for your book(s). It's a magnificent marketing tool. You can send potential customers to your very own Web site to get information about your book(s). Anyone who receives or picks up your letterhead, business card or brochure, will learn about your Web site. People that you don't even know will find their way to a well-publicized Web site. In fact, having a Web site is like owning your own bookstore.

But not every Web site is successful. Following are some ideas for building and maintaining one that is.

- Create a Web site that's easy to navigate. Your book should take center stage. Post an excellent picture of the book cover and a concise description. Give ordering information or provide clear links to the ordering page.

- Link your ordering page to amazon.com for added customer convenience.

- Make it easy for potential customers to reach you. Post your complete contact information at your Web site.

- Include your email link on every page in case a customer has a question.

- Use colors that are easy on the eyes. A black background with light red lettering or yellow lettering on a light background is hard to see.

- Avoid using a lot of animation and other distracting techniques as these things will cause your Web site to load much more slowly. Make visiting your Web site a pleasant experience or you're liable to lose customers.

242

- Visit several Web sites of different kinds to help you make the decisions related to yours. Do you want a link bar across the top, along the side or links listed at the bottom of the page, for example?

- Create a theme Web site. Along with your book descriptions, post articles related to your topic and link to appropriate sites. I've seen theme sites related to just about every subject imaginable: cats, specific breeds of dogs, cycling, traveling, World War I, architecture and depression, for example.

- Provide a sample chapter of your book for folks to read for free.

- Consider communicating with potential customers and others who are interested in your topic through a Web log or Blog. Your Webmaster can set up a blog for you. Or purchase appropriate software and do it yourself. Of course, I highly recommend that you talk to experts and check out comparison studies on blogging software before making a purchase. There are many and some of them are free. Here are a few that experts recommend: bBlog, Blosxom, Nucleus, Movable Type and WordPress.

## You Must Have a Merchant Account

Provide a merchant account so customers can use credit cards to purchase your books. I hesitated for a long time getting a merchant account. It just seemed too expensive. Finally I caved in and I'm glad that I did. I can take credit cards through my Web site as well as for books sold at book festivals and for client work. I've had my merchant account now for about three years and I've never had to pay the monthly fee out of pocket. Sure, the fee comes out of my profits, but I'm selling books that I may not have sold without the merchant account.

Check with your local banker about their merchant account fees. Most likely, you'll want to choose a merchant account company that specializes in Web site accounts such as Echo (Electronics Clearing House, Inc.) in Agoura Hills, California, Echo-inc.com; USA Merchant Account at usa-merchantaccount.com or Total Merchant Services, merchant-account-4u.com.

Make it easy for someone to buy your book. The fact is that everyone has his favorite way of purchasing books. While some prefer to pay by check, others will only make credit card purchases. Some customers love buying their books through Amazon and others will only purchase a book at a brick and mortar bookstore—even if it has to be ordered.

Many people use PayPal when making Internet purchases. You can hook your site up to PayPal, if you want. (PayPal.com)

It can cost anywhere from $200 to $4,000 to have a Web site designed. But you may be able to get one for free. Ask a Web design student to build one for you. That's how I got my Web site. A friend needed a project for her Web design class and I needed a Web site.

If you aren't interested in learning how to maintain your site, you will also need to hire someone reliable to update it and keep it operating smoothly. Make sure that this is someone who knows how to get you connected to the major search engines. This could be the same person who designed it or someone else. Expect to pay anywhere from $30 to $75 per hour for Web maintenance services.

Once you have a Web site, promote, promote, promote. Don't take the "build it and they will come" attitude. They will come only if you promote it.

We recently started a new column in *SPAWNews*, SPAWN's monthly newsletter which goes out to around 2,000 writers, authors, artists and independent publishers. We decided to feature a writer's Web site in each issue and we put out a call to members stating, "Let us feature YOUR site."

No one came forward. NO ONE!! I wondered, do any of our members have Web sites for their writing/publishing/graphics businesses? Aren't they selling books through Web sites? I went in search of members' sites.

My first stop was the SPAWN Member Directory. While virtually all members are listed there, few of them note a Web site. Was it that they didn't have Web sites or had they neglected to put their Web site address on their membership applications? I began emailing members to inquire. BINGO! All of the dozen or so members that I contacted said, "Yes, I have a Web site and I'd love to have it featured in *SPAWNews*."

So why didn't they bother to list their Web sites in the member directory? And why didn't they come forward to take advantage of this free and easy promotional opportunity? One can only speculate that they simply aren't paying attention.

Authors, stay alert. You never know when you're going to be presented with an opportunity to pitch your wonderful book.

## Your Book Trailer

The latest in book promotion is the trailer—a video advertisement for your book. If you're creative and technologically adept, write your own script and shoot your own trailer. If not, hire someone such as the folks at Circle of Seven Productions: cosproductions.com. They charge anywhere from $300 to $10,000 for a video depicting your book.

Use the trailer at your Web site, to entice browsers to buy your book. Show it during live presentations. And/or play it at My Space or You Tube. You might also arrange to have it shown at your local movie theater, on cable TV and at Web sites related to your genre/topic.

Simon and Schuster plans to launch Video Channel, a books video Web site sometime during 2007 or 2008.

## Blog For Exposure and Sales

As I mentioned in an earlier chapter, blogging is the rage. Webmasters and marketing agents everywhere are encouraging their clients to start blogs. But it isn't enough to just start one. In order for it to be effective, you have to use it. Here are my tips for maintaining an effective blog site:

- Add new blog entries regularly—at least twice a month.

- Provide something of value to your readers. Offer information, resources and your perspective on issues pertinent to your field, topic or genre.

- Note where you'll be speaking or signing next, online classes you'll be teaching and publications where your book has been reviewed, etc.

- Promote your book in each and every blog entry, even if it's just a brief reminder. Give ordering information.

- Encourage dialogue. If you decide to turn off the "comments" feature of your blog site (which I have done due to spam), give your email address in each entry.

- Advertise your blog. I send out emails to certain people in my address book about once a month, inviting them to visit my blog and view my latest entry. I also include my blog address on business cards, brochures, etc.

## Promote Through Fantastic Handouts

Always have something at the ready to hand out to individuals that you meet, to folks at book festivals and to send in the mail. I like to use the cover art of my book on a bookmark or post card-size promo piece with ordering information on the back. Choose a size that is convenient to mail and that fits easily into a pocket or purse.

Your handout should be every bit as professional and appealing as your book is. I've seen a wide variety of promotional pieces. While some seem like an afterthought, others are so attractive that I can't bring myself to discard them once I get home from an event and empty my pockets.

What is the function of a promotional piece? It's a reminder, it's a sales pitch and it provides ordering information. A good promotional piece should reflect the tone and appearance of your book.

Once, at a book festival, I found a lovely poetry book featuring photographs of charming kittens throughout. On the cover was a basketful of adorable kittens in full color. I wanted to remember this book and possibly order copies for holiday gifts. To my dismay, the promotional piece for this beautiful book consisted of a mimeographed flyer on solid pink copy paper. It even had a handwritten note at the bottom indicating a change of address. I took the handout, but didn't keep it. Nor did I order any of these books.

## Press Releases, Media Kits and Sales Sheets
### Press Release
A press release is a means of making an announcement or sharing information, generally through newspapers. You can send press releases to newspapers nationwide or just to those in a certain region. There are services that will send your press release for a fee. I generally advise authors against paying a service to handle tasks they can easily manage themselves.

I base this advice on my observations and reports from colleagues stating that most press release services don't actually do a targeted mailing (or emailing). They send generic press releases indiscriminately. Until recently, I'd never actually spoken to anyone who felt they gained anything from using one of these services. And then I began receiving conflicting information.

It seems that some authors are using press release services with some level of success. While a poor service can be next to worthless, a good one can be well worth the price. What you, as an author, want to strive for is a well-written, personal (non-generic) press release that is distributed to an appropriately targeted audience. If you are considering working with a press release service, make sure that you ask all of the right questions and get references. In most cases, the author should write his or her own press release, but don't circulate it until you've had a professional look at it.

Not every author can succinctly capture the essence of his or her book in a press release. It takes skill to create an effective promo piece.

First determine what you want to accomplish with your press release. Is your objective publicity for your book? Then your job is to come up with a reason why a newspaper or a magazine editor would want to run your story or interview you. What sort of information or intrigue can you offer—something controversial, a solution to a common societal problem, a human interest story or something important or entertaining with a local slant, perhaps?

Answer the newspaper editor's burning question, "So What?" Tell him, through your press release, what is unique about your story or your book and how what you have to share is beneficial and to whom. Don't be afraid to weave in a little humor if it's fitting to your topic. And if you can tie your book topic to a holiday or a world news situation, all the better. Most author press releases are designed to announce a new book or an event related to a new book. Unfortunately, for authors, book launches and book signings are commonplace, these days. Consequently, we must be even more creative and clever when it comes to writing a news release.

Start by coming up with a title that reaches out and grabs the editor's attention. Let's say that you are pitching a book featuring how to fix up your home to sell. How about this, "New Book Helps Homeowners Get More Cash For Their Homes."

For a book on doggie dress-up, you might address the *Pet Corner* or *Patter on Pets* column in newspapers nationwide with this lead, "Dogs Are Leading the Fashion Parade" or "Is Your Dog Making a Fashion Statement This Spring?"

When I'm ready to write a press release to promote this book, my title might be: "Most People Go Wrong When They Write a Book." Or "Ten Common Mistakes Most Authors Make."

A press release is not a one-size-fits-all letter. You may have to write several versions of your press release to attract different types of editors. As an example, perhaps you have written a book on collecting gum ball machines and other candy dispensers. You may focus your press release on the largest collection of Pez dispensers in a certain city for a local newspaper. You might reminisce about the manufacturing of early gum ball machines for the senior section in various newspapers throughout the states. Or create a press release for the entertainment section of newspapers nationwide featuring a few celebrities who collect candy dispensers.

When writing your marvelous press release, think *benefits* not *features*. A feature is a selling point that describes the book, a benefit tells readers how the book will help them in some way. They want to know, "What's in it for me?" In a press release for my book, *The Mainland Luau*, if I say, "This book includes eight different methods of roasting a whole pig," this is a feature. A benefit might be, "Learn how to present an authentic Hawaiian luau and become the most popular host in your neighborhood."

The following is a feature of the book you're reading: "Tips, techniques and resources for hopeful authors." Here's how I might present a benefit, "Learn the ropes and live your dream of becoming a successful author."

Stay abreast of trends and fashion your press release to conform. For example, you may have noticed late in 2004 that ponchos were making a comeback, yet you couldn't find a pattern for knitting a poncho. But wait! You've written a book of simple things to knit and it includes a few poncho patterns. That would have been the time to send your press release to newspapers nationwide.

249

You may notice a lot of articles and commentary lately in newspapers everywhere focusing on the economy. What better time than now to introduce your new (or even older) book, *Money Matters, Budgeting Techniques for Today's Family*.

A press release is not an advertisement and it should not read like one. A press release should be newsworthy. Avoid pitching a product. Pitch a story, instead. Point out a need and show how your book can fill it.

Sometimes it's difficult to come up with fresh ideas for a press release or a promotional brochure. This is why I suggest soliciting customer feedback. Others may describe your book in an entirely different way than you typically do. Listen to your readers. Glom onto their words and use them to sell books.

Approach the right person with your excellent press release. Do your homework and find out the name of the appropriate editor and how that particular publication prefers to receive the press release and when. Some editors will request a press release be sent by mail two weeks before an event, for example.

Include your contact information in case the editor has additional questions and make sure it is imbedded within the press release so folks reading it will know how to reach you. Also provide a photograph of yourself and the cover of your book.

Note: Keep your press release to one page.

What can you expect when you submit a press release?

- It may be published as is.

- The editor may call you with additional questions.

- A reporter might call and ask for an in-depth interview and ultimately write an article about you and your book.

Of course, there's always the off chance that the press release will be ignored. It's common to fall between the cracks in this age of great communication. So be sure to follow up with an email or phone call if you haven't heard from the editor within three or four weeks (one week for time-sensitive material).

## Sample Press Releases

This is an example of a press release for an event:

April 28, 2002     Contact: James Johnson—xxx-xxx-xxxx

**For publication between June 10 and June 14**

**Subject: Book Signing for *Robin's Robins*, a children's book**

*Robin's Robins* is the charming, adventure-packed story of a lonely little girl who befriends a pair of abandoned robins who ultimately bring her out of her shell. It's a toss up as to whether Robin or the robins instigate the exploits that take the trio to places formerly unknown to Robin or to any other neighborhood children, for that matter. Join in as Robin and the robins rescue Mr. Farley's goose, help an injured kitten, replace a nest of misplaced eggs and befriend the most terrifying creature in the woods. Age appropriate for children 8—10 years old.

Author James Johnson will be signing his book at:
Greta's Book House
1314 Sunset Lane
Chandler, WY
Saturday, June 15
2-4 p.m.
Reading at 3:00 sharp

Bring your children, grandchildren, nieces, nephews and neighborhood children of all ages. Free gifts for every child.

This is an example of a new book announcement:

August 1, 2006    Contact: Patricia Fry—(xxx-xxx-xxxx)

**For immediate release**

Re: *Publishing Expert Shares Success Secrets With Hopeful Authors*

More people today than ever before are becoming authors. Unfortunately, most of them fail in their quest for even minimal success.

Veteran author, Patricia Fry, is on a mission to help the millions of hopeful authors out there to manage the publishing maze. Her new book, "The Right Way to Write, Publish and Sell Your Book," provides the information, resources and gentle nudging that new memoir-writers, novelists and other budding authors need in order to succeed.

Fry's 33 years in the industry are evident in the solid advice she offers throughout this 300-page book. You'll learn how to write with more clarity, choose a good editor, locate the right publishing model for your project, write more effective query letters and book proposals, successfully promote and sell your book and handle the business side of authorship.

Fifteen industry reviewers can't all be wrong; they each gave this book a 5-star rating. And it's no wonder; this is a book like no other, as it covers all publishing options in depth—both the pros and cons. Only after studying this book, is a first-time author equipped to enter into the world of publishing.

Contact Patricia Fry for more information, to conduct an interview or to request a review copy of "The Right

Way to Write, Publish and Sell Your Book." *Matilija Press, 323 E. Matilija St., Suite 110-123, Ojai, CA  93023. www.matilijapress.com.*

## Media Kit

Send or hand a media kit to a book reviewer, a journalist or a magazine editor who is interested in reviewing your book or interviewing you. A media kit usually includes:

- A review copy of your book (or a description of the book, including ISBN).

- Your bio.

- A few of your published articles related to the subject of your book.

- Previously published book reviews.

- Endorsements and testimonials.

- Awards related to the theme of your book.

- Book tour dates.

- A list of scheduled media appearances.

- Your photograph.

- Examples of questions they can ask you during an interview.

- Contact information.

If you are sending out quite a few media kits, you may not want to include a book in each one. Include, instead, a press release, your promotion piece/brochure and your table of contents. (See the Resource List in Chapter Sixteen for newspaper directory sites, market lists for periodicals, etc.)

## Sell Sheet

A sell sheet is a relatively new concept for book promotion. I consider it a one-page media kit, as it encompasses practically everything you've included in your media kit on just one page. Here's what to include:

- Title of your book.

- A small photo of the book.

- Contact information.

- A description of the book (including the ISBN, size, format and category).

- A brief synopsis.

- The price of the book.

- The name of your publisher.

- A few endorsements (if there's room).

Include the sell sheet in your media kit or send it independently to bookstores, specialty stores related to your book, retail stores (such as Wal-Mart) and so forth.

## Make News

I've suggested that you take advantage of trends and news to promote your book. If you can't find news that relates to your book, make news. I know someone who wrote a novel about a homeless family. He could make news, thus get exposure for his book, by spearheading an effort to find housing for a local homeless family, for example, help homeless people get jobs or start a free laundry service or clothing exchange program for the homeless. When this story appears in a newspaper or on a TV station, his book will surely be mentioned.

With the help of a few friends, I once presented a full-blown luau for 100 people and invited the press. This was a heck of a lot of work, but it resulted in a photo story on the front page of the Living section in our county newspaper. The story of this outlandish, exaggerated promotional ploy was so unique that it rated a chapter in Debbie Allen's book, *Confessions of Shameless Self-Promoters.*

A few years ago, I taught an eight-week writing/publishing module to a group of homeschoolers, which resulted in a published book. My objective in doing so was to provide a service to young authors on behalf of SPAWN. But there were unexpected residual benefits, as well. The local newspaper did a story featuring these youngsters and their self-published book. Of course, I was also mentioned and this publicity actually got me two wonderful new clients.

## Solicit Free Advertising

What is promotion, anyway? It's considered promotion any time your book is publicly mentioned. And promotion doesn't have to cost you a cent. In fact, with so many opportunities for free advertising, why pay for it? As we've discussed above, you can present your "ad" as news. All you have to do is tweak it. You can also promote your book through magazines, newsletters and Web sites. (Read more about promoting through periodicals in Chapter Thirteen.)

Become familiar with newsletters, magazines and Web sites in your genre, area of interest or expertise. Most of them have sections where people can make announcements or provide news bites. Announce your book signings, the free things you offer through your Web site or a fundraiser you're running related to the theme of your book, for example.

Write letters to the editor on topics related to your book along with your bio which, of course, mentions your book. Participate in online discussion groups on the theme of your book—parenting, arthritis, scrapbooking, fishing or woodworking, for example. Don't sit back and wait for an invitation to promote your book. Seek out opportunities for free publicity and take advantage of them.

## How to Make Sales Using Your Mailing List

A mailing list can be one of an author's best promotional resources. Start one the minute you decide to write a book and keep adding to it. Include friends, family, neighbors, coworkers, clients, your kids' teachers, members of your gym, former classmates, people with whom you serve on committees, folks you meet online and, of course, every person who expresses an interest in your book. Maintain this list and keep updating it.

Use your email and snail mail lists to announce a new book or to remind folks of a book you published last year. Send a promo piece with your Christmas cards. In fact, send your cards early so friends and family have time to order copies of your book for Christmas giving. Send a spring mailing with a charming card related to the changing of the seasons. Include information about your book and suggest that people order a copy to read during summer vacation.

Treasure your mailing list, for it is one of the most valuable tools in your promotional tool belt. And the value isn't just in immediate sales. You never know when a distant relative will respond to your mailing with an invitation to be a guest on a TV talk show he produces. A former client might come from nowhere and offer to purchase a thousand books to use as an employee incentive within his corporation.

I once got a call from a woman on my mailing list whose daughter was the chairperson for a huge fundraiser in Florida that year. She needed authors to participate. This turned out to be an all-expenses-paid gig that resulted in multiple book sales for me.

## Produce a Newsletter

Some authors produce newsletters in order to promote their books. A couple of years ago, Karen Stevens launched an enewsletter to support her organization, All For Animals. Her book, *All For Animals*, followed. Stevens' desire is to motivate and inspire people to express more compassion toward all animals. Not only does her newsletter help in this mission, it gives her a venue for promoting her book. And it puts her in touch with people who have compassionate animal stories for her next book.

For more about how to create an enewsletter read Christopher Heng's article at thesitewizard.com/archive/newsletter.shtml. Learn more about the software you'll need to create and distribute an email newsletter at enewsletterpro.com, newsletterease.com or any number of similar Web sites. To locate others, do a Google search using the keywords, "enewsletter," "ezine," "how to start a newsletter (or ezine)" or "ezine/newsletter software."

## Network, Network, Network

Networking is the coming together of people for the purpose of sharing information. When you discuss your project or publishing in general with other authors at a writers' conference, you are networking. When you tell a colleague about your latest book or you ask her who her publicist is, you're networking. Networking is a natural way to promote books. But it takes concentrated effort and a measure of protocol.

You must be willing to put yourself out there—to mingle, participate in small talk and even schmooze. Networking is a two-way connection. Sometimes you're on the giving end and sometimes you are the receiver. Good networkers do both well and find both equally important and satisfying.

Where does one network? Join networking organizations and attend writing club meetings, conferences and book festivals in order to network with other authors. Ask them how they sell books. Participate in activities and meetings associated with your topic in order to meet potential customers. But don't limit your networking efforts to certain venues. Talk about your book everywhere you go.

Network through online discussion groups and bulletin boards. It's amazing what you can learn by taking advantage of appropriate online opportunities. But don't take everything you read at these sites to heart. Consider those bits of wisdom and advice that resonate with you, but always check on their validity before investing. Whenever you are in doubt about a particular company, agency or individual, check it out by doing thorough Internet research and be sure to see if

257

it is listed at any of the warning sites. (Listed in the Resource Section of this book: Chapter Sixteen.)

For additional networking tips read the article, Networking Tips for Authors at spawn.org/editing/networking.htm.

## Get on Radio and TV

Many radio and TV stations feature talk shows whose hosts are always seeking interesting guest experts and authors to interview. You are, after all, considered an expert in the field related to your book. Start with your local TV or radio station. Find out what shows are aired and know ahead of time where your book topic would fit in. There are many radio shows across the nation whose hosts entertain by insult and ridicule. If yours is a controversial topic, you are a likely candidate for such shows. But be prepared—you may be made a spectacle instead of being treated like an honored guest.

Check the phone book Yellow Pages or call the station to find out the name of the program manager or producer. Either call and introduce yourself and your book or send a copy of your book (or a synopsis) and a photograph of yourself (for television). Tell the producer that you would like to be interviewed on MayBell White's Cooking Show or Doug Mabry's Anything Goes Show. Follow through and follow up and chances are, you will be invited to appear.

There are reportedly over 700 talk radio programs nationwide that feature interesting, intriguing, entertaining and controversial guests. To locate appropriate radio and television stations, refer to *Literary Market Place, Gales Directory of Publications and Broadcast Media* or *The Business Phone Book U.S.A*—available in the reference section of your public library. You can do your own search or you can pay someone anywhere from $200 to $700 to position you for radio and TV appearances. Buy an ad in *Radio-TV Interview Report* (rtir.com or 215-259-1070) or sign up at GuestFinder (guestfinder.com).

Some radio stations now charge guests—making it seem more like an infomercial than a guest appearance. Most of my colleagues advise against paying for air space at least until you've exhausted all free opportunities.

While you must dress and travel to appear on TV, you can conceivably do a radio interview by phone in your robe and bunny slippers. I recommend dressing for the occasion, however. Sit up straight in your chair and smile and you will come across sounding more alert and friendly. This is true. Record your voice speaking while wearing sweats and sitting slumped down in a chair. Then record the same words while dressed up, sitting up and smiling. You may be surprised at the difference.

Beware! Radio personalities hate dead air—that silence that occurs when no one is saying anything. While planned pauses can add to a live talk, silence can damage a radio show. When the host asks you a question, he or she generally hopes you will respond with more than a monotone word. Be ready with explanations, anecdotes and interesting information.

Express emotion, where appropriate—let your passion show. Enthusiasm, as you know, is contagious. If you aren't excited about your book, no one else will be.

An author I know told me recently that he felt foolish because he had become a little emotional while talking to a group of people about his book. The book features the story of the trials, struggles and joy in his relationship with his fiancé, who ultimately died after brain surgery and a long period in a coma. I asked him how many people were in attendance. He said, "Fifteen." I asked how many books he sold. He said, "Fifteen." Now that's highly unusual. In fact, I've never heard of a signing or presentation where everyone in the room bought a book. We decided that it was the author's show of emotion that prompted the one hundred percent success factor that day.

Don't be afraid to give. Let's say that you're talking about your book, *Teaching Old Dogs New Tricks*. Share stories from your book. Give some nifty tips for handling a certain behavioral problem. But let listeners know that there are many additional anecdotes and training techniques in the book. Give enough and you will spark customer interest. Withhold and you may lose those potential customers.

### Radio/TV Tips for Novelists and Children's Book Authors

What if your book is fiction? Can you get gigs on radio and TV? Certainly. But you, too, will need a hook—something of interest to a wide audience. Professionals suggest coming up with a nonfiction hook even for a historical novel, fantasy, adventure or children's book. A radio show host in Massachusetts might find your novel set in 1700 Plymouth a worthy topic, indeed. Your young adult adventure featuring a western theme might capture the attention of show hosts in rodeo towns throughout the U.S. Your children's book focusing on one or more character values could be of interest to many morning talk show hosts, particularly hosts of psychology or parenting programs. Maybe your novel presents a unique twist on a current controversial issue. This should spark numerous invitations to appear on radio or TV.

# Hone Your Speaking Skills

An author can't sell books that no one knows about. One way to spread the word about your book is to go out and talk about it. I speak publicly dozens of times a year and I generally sell books to about twenty to thirty percent of the audience.

Aggressive promoter, Debbie Puente urges authors to talk about their books wherever they go. She says, "I sell books at the ball park, the grocery store—everywhere I go, I sell books." But you must be a good conversationalist and have good speaking skills.

Speaking skills are also important for pitching publishers personally at conferences and on the phone.

Here are some tips—please, don't just gloss over these important tips. Read them, study them and put them into practice. I am constantly astounded by how many people continually break one or more of the following speaking qualities. So many of them are common-sense rules.

- Speak with a strong voice. Don't mumble or cover your mouth when speaking. Stand tall, speak to be heard and enunciate clearly.

- Use vocal variety. Vary the tone of your voice. Create high tones and low ones. Practice reading children's stories out loud to get a feel for vocal variety.

- Eliminate filler words. *Ah, um* and *er* are filler words. So are *so* and *and* when used to connect sentence after sentence. Banish from your vocabulary repetitive phrases that have become a habit—terms such as *you know* and *know what I mean?* and *clearly*, for example. Pause, instead. Practice omitting filler words and words of habit in all of your speaking opportunities, whether during conversation or on stage at the microphone.

- Use good grammar. Slang is pretty much accepted at many levels of intelligence and education these days. It's usually okay to use a bit for drama or to make a point. But avoid sloppy communication. Make proper grammar your rule.

- Make eye contact whether you're speaking with an individual or an audience. When speaking before a group, move your gaze around the room, letting your eyes rest on various individuals for a few moments or so. This is how you make everyone feel included.

- Don't apologize—it damages your credibility. If you make a mistake, ignore it. Just move forward with your excellent speech and no one will be the wiser. If, on the other hand, you arrived late for your presentation and there's an interesting story behind it, by all means entertain and inform your audience.

- Handle notes and props effectively. In fact, I urge you to avoid using notes. If you must use them, do so discreetly. Practice using props so that your movements are smooth and your timing is sharp.

- Repeat audience questions for all to hear. Don't you hate it when you are in the audience and the speaker responds to a question that you didn't hear? Involve the entire audience by repeating the question before you respond. It is your job as the speaker to make sure that everyone is on the same page and no one feels left out.

- Be well prepared. Practice your speech and then practice it some more. Avoid memorizing your speech, as it may sound canned. But certainly have a plan and a direction. I've been known to toss out a perfectly planned speech and wing it, instead. I can do that successfully when I'm highly familiar with the material.

- Learn to speak within a projected time limit. Often, you will be given a time slot during which to speak. It is imperative that you know how to comply. It takes practice to deliver a speech within a time frame. But the alternative isn't pleasant. How would you like to be interrupted before you get to the most important part of your talk? Worse, yet, what if the speaker in front of you runs over and uses half of your allotted time? I've had this happen to me a couple of times. Now, I always check with the program organizer and those who are on the schedule ahead of me to make sure that everyone is in agreement as to the time segments. If I'm concerned that the speaker ahead of me will disregard the time element, I'll offer to signal him when his time is almost up.

- Know your audience and prepare your speech accordingly. If you aren't sure where your audience stands or what their interests are, ask. I like to question an audience who has come to hear me talk about authorship, as to their level of experience and where they are in the publishing process. I may plan to speak about the various publishing options, but decide, based on audience feedback, to lean more heavily than I expected in the direction of self-publishing.

- Join a Toastmasters Club. Toastmasters is a self-help club for folks who want to improve their communication and public speaking skills. Toastmasters Clubs offer a venue for practicing public speaking and receiving valuable feedback. And it offers an environment where you will gain self-confidence. Find a Toastmasters Club near you by visiting toastmasters.org. Or write to Toastmasters International, POB 9052, Mission Viejo, CA 92690.

**How to Locate Speaking Opportunities**
Once you feel confident with your public speaking skills, begin setting up speaking engagements locally. Find service organizations listed in the city pages of your local telephone book. Ask your local Chamber of Commerce or City Hall for a list of service and specialty organizations. Organizations and associations are always seeking good programs for their weekly or monthly meetings.

If your book focuses on a specific theme, look for organizations related to this topic. For a book on gardening, contact garden clubs, the orchid society, the African violet society and the organizers of the annual lavender festival. If your book features true Christian stories, contact the usual service organizations, but also get in touch with local churches, Christian youth groups, senior centers, Christian schools and the ministerial association.

There you have it—this chapter alone gives you around three dozen ideas for promoting your book plus explicit details for accomplishing some of these ideas. And it's just a start. Read on to discover some of the more creative promotional ideas.

# Recommended Reading:
*Confessions of Shameless Self-Promoters* by Debbie Allen (Success Showcase Publishing, 2002).

# Chapter Thirteen

# BOOK PROMOTION

## GET CREATIVE

You're probably beginning to understand why not every promotional activity is going to be successful for every book or every author.

Study the promotional basics in Chapters Eleven and Twelve and the creative marketing ideas in this chapter and begin to build your personal promotions plan. I suggest choosing half-dozen major promotional ideas (sign with Amazon; have a Web site built; send press releases to appropriate Web sites, magazines and newsletters; create a blog; solicit book reviews; do a few book signings and write articles for magazines, for example). But also plan a few minor promotional activities to try throughout the year. You might send a couple of targeted mailings, rent a booth at a book festival, speak on a few occasions and do some seasonal promotion.

## Keep a Hot File

When I hear or read about a potential market for one of my books, I make a note and slip it into my promotions *hot file*. One day a week (usually on Sunday) I address these ideas. That's the day when I might send press releases using a fresh promotional angle to a new list of appropriate newsletters or to newspapers in a specific region. I might target two or three dozen libraries with information about my latest book. Or I may contact several writing Web site hosts and ask to be interviewed.

Barbara Florio Graham (Simonteakettle.com) is the author of three books. She says that she tends to promote her books all the time. In other words, she's always in promotion mode. She explains, "I include brochures and bookmarks in every mailing, even bill payments and letters not related to my work. It's surprising how many book orders have come from that simple effort."

I know another author who uses those pre-stamped envelopes that come with junk mail as a means to promote her book. She simply tucks her brochure or a flyer into the envelope and mails it off FREE.

## Give Customers More Than They Expect

Think about how you feel when you go to the store to buy an avocado and discover that you can get two for the price of one. Delight your customers by giving them something extra. I could package the luau book with uli ulis (feather gourds). My journal-keeping book for teens would make a wonderful gift if packaged with a journal book and a pen. Think about offering your novel with a reading light or combine your book of cat stories with a stuffed kitty or a packet of cat stationary.

Provide occasional perks. Send out press releases, mail notices and post announcements stating that during the month of June, you'll provide tickets to an upcoming play for customers who purchase your novel or that you'll give away calendars featuring photographs of dogs to everyone who buys your book on pet photography.

Some authors gift wrap their books for special occasions. When customers order your book, give them a place to check if this is a gift and the occasion. Wrap the book accordingly. Or do as Linda McGinnis does when she gets an order for her book, *The Art of Hairdressing Success*, and wrap your book in pretty paper for every customer.

As authors, we stay so busy trying to make a living, keeping up with our contacts, processing the enormous volume of materials we receive each day, coming up with new marketing ideas for our books and trying to maintain some order in our personal lives, that we sometimes miss promotional opportunities. This is why I urge authors to be in promotion mode all the time. If you're constantly thinking about your book, you'll be aware of opportunities when they come up.

Gloria is a marketing hound. She is always promoting and she sells a lot of books. She carries a copy of her historical novel in her purse and a box of books in her car. She keeps appropriate denominations of change in her wallet and she's never without a stack of business cards and brochures.

She shows her book to everyone she meets. When someone expresses an interest in her book, but doesn't buy it on the spot, she takes their business card and follows up with an email, letter or phone call. She's the only author I know who actually sold fifty copies of her book at her class reunion. She is also the only person I've ever met who can sell a novel to people who claim they never read the stuff. Gloria's mantra is, "There's a potential sale in every encounter."

I've been known to sell books on the streets of downtown Ojai. Often, a tourist will look a little lost or unsure. Sometimes they're just sitting on a bench looking at a map or a copy of our *Visitor's Guide*. If they don't ask me for help first, I volunteer to direct them.

Inevitably, they ask if I've lived here long. I tell them, "I'm a fifth-generation Ojai resident. In fact, I wrote the history of the Ojai Valley." I've sold many a copy of that book to tourists from the trunk of my car.

The same thing happens in the cemetery. I take my walk through the pioneer cemetery nearly every day and often meet descendants of folks buried there. I strike up a conversation and usually sell a copy or two of the Nordhoff Cemetery books.

Several months ago, I got a call from the local librarian who said, "There's a man here from Pennsylvania who wants to buy a copy of your Ojai history book." Instead of sending him to a bookstore, I drove down to meet him. He was so touched by my attentiveness that he bought two copies of the book.

A few years ago, a woman from a local pioneer family invited me to her family reunion. I spoke to the group about their ancestors' contributions to this valley, mingled with folks, ate with them and sold dozens of copies of my local history books.

Neighbors sometimes come to me to buy an autographed copy of a book as a last-minute gift. They wouldn't even know about my wide array of titles had I kept this a secret.

## Sell Books Through Articles and Excerpts

One of my favorite methods of promoting my books is through articles. Not only do I get to tout my book (usually in the bio at the end of the piece), I am positioning myself as an expert. And I even get paid.

Magazines will generally pay anywhere from $50 to $1,000 for a good article. There are also a lot of non-paying magazines. While I discourage freelancers and authors from writing anything for free, I wonder, isn't the opportunity to promote your book a form of payment? In some cases, it is.

Keep in mind, however, that an article is not an advertisement for your book and should not come across as such. In fact, most editors will reject anything that looks like an ad. Editors want articles that are timely, informative and/or entertaining.

I have sold numerous articles related to grandparenting and each time the byline reads, "Patricia Fry is the author of *Creative Grandparenting Across the Miles* (Liguori Publications, 800-325-9521)."

My article themes related to the grandparenting book include long-distance grandparenting, of course, and how to teach your grandkids money awareness, keeping family traditions alive even from a distance, traveling with grandkids, choosing gifts for grandkids, entertaining the grandchildren when they visit, how to stage a family reunion, how to be the best grandparent you can, grandparent as mentor and so forth.

I've also sold articles on journal-keeping to magazines including, *Today's Catholic Teacher, The Toastmaster, Teacher's Vision* and *Adventist's Journal*. In these articles, I typically give concrete information and tips on journal-keeping. I mention my book, *Write On! Journal-Keeping for Teens*, in the bio along with ordering information.

You've probably seen my articles in numerous writing/publishing-related newsletters and magazines. I've been published in *Writer's Digest, Authorship, National Association of Women Writers Newsletter, SPAWNews, PMA Independent, Writer's Weekly, Absolute Write, SPAN Connection, Book Promotion Newsletter, Publishing Basics, Writing World, Freelance Writer's Report, Writing for Dollars, Writer's Journal, Personal Journaling* and many others. In the bio, I mention at least one of my writing-related books, depending on the topic of the article.

Many magazines use excerpts. A chapter from your book on butterfly migration would surely be of interest to the editor of a children's magazine or a teachers' journal. You could probably sell excerpts from your book on depression to women's, men's, health, regional, religious/spiritual, association, ethnic and even teen publications. An excerpt is a good way to generate sales.

What about fiction? Hey, you can write articles related to and sell excerpts from your fiction book, too. Write a short story on any topic and include in your bio that you're the author of *My Way, By the Way*, a novel set around the movie industry in the 1930s. Offer excerpts from this book to entertainment, history, regional, nostalgia and women's magazines.

Don't forget about the opportunities for articles and excerpts on the Internet. I have to tell you that the pay isn't much, but the exposure is pretty grand in many cases.

Think ahead! This should be the mantra for all freelance writers and authors who wish to promote their books through articles. You can't look at your calendar and say, "Hey, it's October. I think I'll write something about my most memorable Thanksgiving for *Vermont Life Magazine*." Oh no! While some magazines need only a few months editorial lead time, other editors such as, Thomas Slayton at *Vermont Life*, outlined his Fall/Winter edition nearly a year ago. You could possibly send him your idea in October of 2007 for his 2008 edition.

Most article writers live in the fast lane—always planning for the future. We think Christmas in May and Easter in September. We must be aware of the trends and fads before they occur. This is the nature of writing for magazines. The editorial lead time for *Reunions Magazine* is six months. Send queries to *Robb Report* five months in advance. *Woman's World* has just a four-month editorial lead and *Wired* will accept material three months in advance. *Florida Review* needs ideas nine months ahead and *AARP The Magazine*, six months. *Woman's Life* plans their editorial line-up a year in advance.

So what should we be thinking about in October? Forget thoughts of pumpkin pie and Christmas trees. Focus, instead, on summer vacation, travel, barbecues, kittens, hot weather, water safety and class reunions.

It's especially important to consider the seasons when you have a book to promote. I like to submit query letters in May for an article designed to promote my grandparenting book for Grandparent's Day in September. I write articles promoting my luau book in December for publication in the summer. If your book would make a good Christmas gift item, you'll want to submit your articles for the November/December issues. This means that you will start sending out queries in the spring/summer or earlier.

Before submitting an article to a magazine, study a couple of issues. Note the style, focus, scope and tone of the magazine and pay attention to the topics they typically publish. Find out if they've run a piece on your subject within the last several months. If so, perhaps you can offer a new twist. Using the pet photography theme, maybe you notice that *Dog Fancy* published an article just last year on studio photography for pets. You might suggest an article teaching dog fanciers how to photograph their pets in unique natural settings or how to get that action shot.

Study the submission guidelines for each magazine, as they will differ from magazine to magazine. What is their preferred word count? Do they publish essays? Do they use pieces with expert quotes and lots of statistics? Do they seem to like bulleted articles? Do they prefer being contacted via email or regular mail? And specifically who do you contact? You may also be interested in their pay scale.

Most editors prefer receiving a query letter first. Once the article is requested, write it to that magazine's specifications. Learn more about submitting articles to magazines in my book, *A Writer's Guide to Magazine Articles for Book Promotion and Profit* (matilijapress.com).

## Let's Go Sell Books at a Book Festival

If you have a book to promote, sooner or later you'll probably participate in a book festival. There are hundreds of book and author festivals held throughout the world each year where you (or your publisher) can rent a booth and sell books. Organizations such as SPAWN often purchase booth space at book festivals in order to provide members with the opportunity to participate at a reduced rate.

Authors can secure booths at trade fairs and flea markets. I had a booth at our county fair one year and sold nearly 200 copies of my brand new local history book. I've also set up booths at arts and crafts fairs and various other community events.

I find that I do well at book festivals and craft fairs, but flea markets and garage sales are terrible venues for new books. I believe this is because of the mindset of the attendees. They're expecting to get a bargain. While an individual may not balk at spending $19.95 for a book in a bookstore, they are adamant against it at a flea market.

## What Does it Cost to Participate?

The organizers of major book festivals, such as the prestigious Los Angeles Times Festival of Books, charge around $900 per booth. But there are plenty of smaller book festivals, and probably some right in your own neighborhood, that charge anywhere from $100 to $400 for booth space.

## How Many Books Can You Sell at a Book Festival?

We'd all like a guarantee before getting involved in a book festival. The truth is that you could walk away $1,000 richer or it might cost you money to participate. Your success depends on several factors. While no one can second-guess the public's book-buying habits, there are steps you can take to ensure greater success. For example, it's important that you choose the right venue. In other words, bring the right books to the right place.

If I'm doing a book festival or craft fair close to home, I always bring my local history books. If I'm out of town, these books won't be of much interest to festival-goers. When I'm participating in the SPAWN booth, I always sell my writing/publishing-related books. Because we are a publishing organization, many of the folks coming to our booth are interested in writing and publishing.

I may sell anywhere from six to forty copies of my books at a book festival. There was one time, however, when I sold nothing. And it was because I chose the wrong venue. I joined a fellow author in his booth at a large book festival in Los Angeles. I had a metaphysical adventure story and books on writing. A large banner above this booth advertised that we were selling mysteries and children's books. And people came to our booth to purchase mysteries and children's books, not books on writing and spiritual matters.

A booth displaying a large variety of books attracts more attention than one with just a few titles. If your book has a dull, uninteresting cover, however, chances are that it won't be noticed. People are drawn first to books with colorful, eye-catching, appealing covers. Next, they seem to gravitate toward a book on a subject of their interest: horses, writing, history, poetry or a period novel, for example. Some people are attracted by catchy titles.

**Focus On Exposure Not Sales**
Sure, you hope for sales when you participate in a book festival. But what if you don't sell as many books as you expected or you don't sell any? It's certainly disappointing, but this doesn't mean that the festival was a failure.

A sale isn't the only way to measure success. Exposure has value, too. And a book festival is a good way to get exposure for your book—to make people aware of it. Anytime you display your book or talk about it, you're getting exposure. There are those sales you make on the spot—spontaneous sales. And there are those that come only after exposure. The point is to view each person you talk to as a potential customer. If he doesn't buy your book now, there's every possibility that he will in the future.

It's important that you hold to this belief. It will help you maintain a good attitude and a good attitude will go a long way toward making friends and making sales.

As I said, SPAWN frequently rents booths at book festivals and we typically invite members to come and sell their books. Here are a few examples of how this exposure has served our members over the years: One author got a consignment agreement with a large independent bookstore. Another member made contact with a radio show host and got a gig on her show. A new author hooked up with a columnist who was interested in interviewing him on the topic of his book. Several of our self-published authors captured the attention of traditional royalty publishers—some of these connections resulted in contracts. I remember one new author who received an agent recommendation for her next book project. And this year, a member got the thrill of a lifetime when someone he met at the SPAWN booth introduced him to Steven Spielberg to discuss his screenplay.

## Here's What to Bring to a Book Festival
## When You're Sharing a Booth

If you're participating in a booth with several others, find out from the organizer how much space you'll have and what you can and cannot bring. If your area of space (generally on a table) is eighteen inches by three feet and you have one title to display, you may want to bring a single book display stand, maybe a small standing poster showing off your book cover, fifty books (or so), promotional material and maybe even some candy or stickers to hand out. The SPAWN booth often offers visitors stickers that say, "I love books." I've also seen authors provide a display of advertising pencils as give-aways. Give people a reason to come to your area and something to remember you by.

Bring plenty of change in appropriate denominations. And, if you have a merchant account, bring credit card forms. When setting up your merchant account, make sure that you can charge customers' cards by hand—without having to use an electronic connection on the spot.

I generally round off the prices of my books for festivals. Rather than charge $15.95 plus tax, I'll ask $16 and I'll pay the remainder of the tax. Sometimes for my $6.50 book, I'll ask $7, letting the customer pay the tax.

I recommend offering books at a discount as a way to make the sale. Advertise that you're selling a $12.95 book for $10. Sell your $17.95 book for $15.00.

While virtually all book festivals have food and drinks for sale, you might want to bring your own water and lunch. Also bring sunscreen, a hat and a sweater. It wouldn't hurt to throw in an extra folding chair. Organizers typically provide two chairs per booth.

I recommend investing in a handcart or a luggage carrier with wheels to transport boxes of books. I once bought a small luggage carrier at a garage sale. It was dependable for years. Now I use a small, but sturdy fold-up handcart, which I call my wheelie dealie. I also have a nifty folding tote with wheels. It folds up small enough to fit into my luggage when I'm traveling, yet it will hold two dozen or so books. I use this handy tote to transport books from the hotel to the bookselling venue. Some people use small suitcases with wheels.

## When It's Your Booth

If you want a booth of your own, but have only one or two titles to sell, you might consider inviting others to participate with you. By sharing the cost of the booth, you stand a better chance of profiting. Additionally, people are drawn to booths that are interesting and inviting. A larger display of books will attract more people than just one or two titles will.

Choose your booth partners carefully. Avoid authors with books that compete with yours. But consider those with books of the same nature. A book for preschoolers and one for teens might be a good combination. A book of poetry and a book for young writers may compliment one another. A book featuring extreme sports and an action novel might be a good match.

Share a booth with someone who has a product rather than a book. If yours is a children's book, partner with a local toyshop owner or someone who makes wooden toys. Another way to attract attention is to wear a costume. If your novel is set in eighteenth century England, dress the part and decorate your booth appropriately. If the main character in your children's book is a clown, become that clown.

Book festival organizers generally provide one six- or eight-foot table per booth, one or two chairs and an identifying banner. Some supply canvas booth enclosures and table covers. You can sometimes get electricity for an additional fee.

Make sure that your booth is appropriately categorized. You might want the title of your book on the banner they provide or the genre/subject matter, instead of your publishing company name. Additionally, at some book fairs, the booth banners are tacked to the front of the tables. People can't see your banner when others are standing in front of your booth. I suggest making a large banner that you can post above your booth or at the back of it just in case you need the extra signage. Save banners from book festivals to reuse.

A small sign that says "autographed copies" will impress and draw some shoppers.

We find that a small folding table placed at the back of our booth comes in handy at book festivals. We use this table for beverages, the money box and other incidentals that we don't want cluttering the display table. Sometimes we configure our booth so as to invite visitors inside. We place the main book table and the folding table against opposite side walls of the booth, which provides more browsing area for potential customers. You can purchase a light-weight aluminum folding table at any office supply outlet. Sometimes you can rent additional tables at the event.

Bring large cloths for both tables—cloths that are long enough to hide extra boxes of books and other items that are stored underneath. Sometimes a cloth and skirt are furnished for the main book table, but not always.

Bring extra pens (at least five of mine walk away during every event), felt markers, tape, bookstands, scissors, paperweights (we use painted rocks), name tags and any advertising posters you might have. Don't forget your professional-quality promotional pieces and business cards.

**Display With Pizzazz**
Presentation is everything. If you have a sweet little book of poems, for example, wrap some of them in pretty paper and tie them with ribbon. This can make a most appealing display.

Plant seeds about gift-giving. Wrap a few books in appropriate gift paper. Put up signs that state, "Perfect Gift for Dad," "Easter Gift Idea" or "Do Your Holiday Shopping, Now."

Maybe your book cover is particularly lovely. Create some note cards featuring the cover. Offer them for sale separately or together with the book. Have gift bags made with the cover of your book on the front.

Bring a vase of flowers for your table or sprinkle the table cloth around your book display with confetti hearts or candy kisses.

If the booth is covered, hang posters and make sun catchers or streamers from your promotional material to hang here and there. If there's room, place an easel at the back of the booth (or, if allowed, in the front) and display your poster.

Get people to participate. Ask visitors to color in a section of a large paint-by-number picture. Give away promotional pencils or bookmarks to folks who answer a question correctly. Or have a drawing. (This is a good way to add to your mailing list.)

If you produce a free monthly or weekly newsletter, provide a sign-up sheet.

## Sell More Books at a Book Festival

A key to selling books at festivals is to connect with the potential buyer. When someone looks at my books on writing, I ask, "Are you a writer?" Invariably, we become engaged in conversation, which affords me the opportunity to give my sales pitch.

I once watched a man with a children's book ask everyone who walked past his booth, "Do you know a child who likes to read?" Most people stopped and he was able to engage them in conversation. Many of them bought his book. In fact, he sold out before the day was half over.

One SPAWN member typically sells a dozen or more copies of his children's book during a book festival by offering to read a page of it to kids walking by. He'll ask the parent, "May I read this poem to your child?" He engages the child in the poem by helping him/her relate to the words. This technique often results in sales for this author.

If someone expresses an interest in your book, but doesn't buy it, make sure they walk away with one of your professional-quality promo pieces and, if at all possible, get his or her card.

And this brings me to another important point. Know when enough is enough. I've seen authors oversell their books and turn potential customers away. Likewise, I've observed authors avoiding contact with people who, with a little nudging, might have bought their book. There's a happy medium in there somewhere and it's up to the author to discover it. How?

- Be observant.

- Learn to read body language.

- Know how to talk about your book.

- Practice your sales pitch.

- If you need help with any of the above, join a Toastmaster's club.

A book festival can be a worthwhile endeavor, but you have to be well-prepared and willing to stretch and grow.

Locate book festivals through these online directories: lights.com/publisher/bookfairs.html or loc.gov/loc/cfbook/bookfair.html.

## Seek Out Special Venues

Special venues might also be considered niche markets for your particular book. There are oh, so many ways to make sales. Here are some that have been successful for other authors.

One author I know wrote a book featuring dessert recipes for diabetics—sweets without the sugar. She and her husband went on a cruise and were quite surprised to learn that there were no dessert choices on the menu for diabetics. This author requested a meeting with the head chef. She showed him her book and he prepared one of her recipes the next evening. The diabetic dessert option was so well received that he added the dish to the permanent menu. This author also negotiated to have the title of her book printed on the menu for travelers who were interested in purchasing it.

Another author I know went door-to-door with his book. He told me, "I thought people would think it was cool to have a local author going around selling his book and it worked. I met new people and made some friends." Did anyone buy the book? According to this author, they sure did. He said, "Some people bought four or five copies."

One children's book author hit the 250,000-copy mark in sales in less than four years by traveling to bookstores and libraries giving readings. She also gets exposure by donating books to children's hospitals. An article in the *Los Angeles Times*, announcing the book when it came out, didn't hurt, either.

There's a program called Character Counts in many schools throughout the U.S. This multi-faceted program includes reading requirements—books related to character issues such as honesty, trustworthiness and responsibility. If you have a children's book that fits into this niche, you might be able to sell numbers of copies through this organization. Charactercounts.org/members.htm.

Get your book listed in a Directory of Authors who do school visits. Learn more at authorsillustrators.com or call 503-297-8136.

Consider piggyback marketing. This means partner with another author who has a similar or complementary book and do a combined mailing or a seminar together.

Do a book signing at an unusual venue: Starbucks, a local military installation, Sam's Club, at a dog show, during a county-wide historical celebration or at an appropriate sporting event, perhaps.

For additional book promotion ideas read *Novel Ways to Promote Your Novel*, www.matilijapress.com/articles/promote_novel.htm.

## Seasonal Promotion
Take advantage of the seasons to promote your book. Pitch your mystery novel or a barbecue how-to book for Dad or Grandpa on Fathers Day. Promote a book of poetry for Mothers Day, Grandparents Day or Easter.

Of course, December provides the biggest holiday promotion opportunity of all. Here are some ideas for making Christmas sales that you may not have thought of:

1: Remind your family and friends about your book and suggest how they might use it as a gift. They could include a book on gardening in a gift basket with gardening tools, bulbs and packages of flower or vegetable seeds. They might give a local history book to a new neighbor. A book of delightful stories or poems is always a good gift idea for several people on anyone's Christmas list. This goes for a novel, too.

2: Mention your books at work and club meetings—bring them in, pass them around and take orders.

3: Send Thanksgiving cards this year with a discount coupon for copies of your books that are purchased during the month of December.

4: Sell something with your book. Include a mug, a package of hot cocoa mix and a cinnamon stick with your novel or package your book, *Doggie Dress-Up*, each with a dog cape. Of course, you may have to charge more to cover costs.

5: Ask appropriate specialty store proprietors if they would display and sell your book for the holidays. Provide your own point-of-purchase display. My *Young Writer's Handbook* does well in children's book stores, the library bookstore and gift shops. A book for kids on how to live with diabetes might be a hot seller at local drug stores and hospital gift shops. If your book does well, the proprietor may want to carry it year-round.

6: Take your children's book to school. Offer to read from your book or create a play from your book with the children taking on the character roles. Send order forms home with each child.

7: Invite neighbors in for a poetry or novel reading. Create an atmosphere related to the theme of your book and find a way to have plenty of audience participation.

8: Arrange to speak before various civic organization meetings this month. Rather than pitch your book, share the story around your publishing experience, talk about why you wrote the book or teach from the book. Of course, plan to sell books in the back of the room after the meeting.

## Boost Sales—Produce Spin-Offs

What's a *spin-off*? It's a by-product or a follow-up to the original. Within the context of a book, it might be a sequel or any number of other writings related to the theme of your book.

The point of a spin-off is to generate more sales. Not only will you have additional items to sell, but each book, pamphlet, guide or list that you produce is a marketing tool for the original book.

Let's say that you've written a book on raising healthy children. You might follow up with pamphlets featuring how to develop the habit of exercise in youngsters, good-for-kids snacks, recipes for healthy families or an activity workbook for kids featuring healthy life choices, for example.

Follow a book on growing a kitchen herb garden with one on selling herbs at local farmers' markets or how to make herb teas or herbal remedies.

Spin-off books or pamphlets can boost sales for fiction books, as well. If your novel depicts life in a small town in Oregon, follow up with a book featuring bed and breakfast inns in that state or create a mystery for readers to solve based on some of the characters in your original book.

Maybe you've compiled a book of poetry. Next, produce a pocket calendar or greeting cards highlighting some of the lines from your poems.

Plan carefully before launching your spin-off. Ask yourself:

- Who is my audience?

- What have my readers asked for?

- Is there something I should have included in my original book?

- How will I distribute the spin-off item?

- Is it cost-effective to produce another book/pamphlet or other items?

After I produced my 360-page local history book, folks started asking for more. I complied by writing a fifty-five-page book featuring the history of the local pioneer cemetery and profiling the earliest burials there. I also wrote an in-depth history of one of our oldest local private schools. Many people who bought the original history book also purchased the others.

Debbie Puente endorses a culinary torch. Someone wanting her book, *Elegantly Easy Crème Brulee and Other Custard Desserts*, will most likely buy the torch, which is used in caramelizing the sugar on top of the crème brulee. And someone with the torch will probably need her book.

Before thinking about your next book, consider writing a spin-off to promote your original book.

## Evaluate Your Efforts

Which of your promotional efforts is most effective? Track them and find out. This is valuable information to have. And the results of your tracking system may vary from book to book. I've learned that, while articles and book reviews sell my grandparenting and the journal-keeping books, press releases are by far the most successful promotional technique with regard to the luau book. I have to say that my Hawaiian distributor also contributed to high sales of that book. However, it is my Web site and personal appearances at conferences and book festivals that seem to sell my writing/publishing-related books. My credentials as a freelance writer/author also help to move these titles.

# Dealing With Promotion Burn-Out

There may come a time when you are sick of talking about your book. You'll get doggone irritated with having to work for every sale—you sometimes feel as though you are begging. It's humiliating and it's tiring. What happened to all of the enthusiasm that you entered into this field with? It's temporarily gone. In its place is a sad case of *burn-out*.

Don't fret. This isn't fatal, nor is it permanent. But it does come with the territory. What to do? When you feel yourself bordering on burn out—if you get to the point where you don't even want to look at your book—take a break.

Take a time-out. Do something else for a few days. Go on a trip. Meet friends for lunch and shopping. Put your energies into something that you enjoy—preferably something creative. Start your next book or shift gears and do some gardening, painting or carpentry. When you return to the task of promoting your book, you'll feel renewed and refreshed. Really, you will.

## Recommended Reading:

*Jump Start Your Book Sales: A Money-Making Guide for Authors, Independent Publishers and Small Presses* by Marilyn and Tom Ross (Writer's Digest Books, 1999).

# Chapter Fourteen

# BOOKKEEPING
## TIPS FOR AUTHORS

There's no getting around it; if you're the author of a book, you're in business. If you're selling books, you must keep records. Whether you're collecting royalties or working with retailers, wholesalers and distributors yourself, it's important that you account for every expense and earning. Keep accurate and complete records for your own sanity and to appease Uncle Sam.

## Do You Know Where Your Manuscripts Are?
It's not difficult to keep track of one manuscript. Most likely, you can recall the exact date that you sent it to X publisher. Do you remember when you approached Y and Z publishers? Shouldn't you have heard back from them by now? By the way, was it a book proposal or just the query letter that you sent? Uh-oh. It's starting to get complicated.

You wouldn't operate a retail business without documentation. Can you imagine having to recall each business transaction occurring in a supermarket at the end of every month? Neither should you leave the details of your writing/publishing business to memory. Log each submission as you make it. Note publisher comments or instructions when you receive them. Maintain an accurate record of every transaction related to each manuscript. When a publisher calls to remind you that he requested three sample chapters, you should be able to tell him the exact date that you sent them. If you wonder whether or not it's time to follow up on a submission, you can check your records to find out.

Since I am constantly circulating article and book manuscript submissions in various forms, I maintain a separate ledger book for queries and one for proposals and manuscripts. In the *query ledger*, I list, on one line, the date a query is sent, to whom, the working title of the book or article and then there's a column on the far right of the page for comments: "No" means the idea was rejected, "Yes" indicates that the proposal or manuscript was requested—in which case I log this in the *proposal and manuscript ledger*. I might also note in that column that the publisher sent an email August 29, 2007 saying he received the query letter and is considering it.

I keep track of royalty payments, payment for articles and fees from clients in a separate section of the query ledger. Here, I log the date of payment, from whom, for what and the amount. My accountant figures my article and client earnings separately from my royalty earnings. So, for ease at tax time, I use highlighters in different colors to identify each category—pink for article payments, blue for royalties and green for payments from clients.

In the proposal and manuscript ledger, I allow several lines of space to log the date the proposal or manuscript was requested, the date it was sent, publisher name and name of the project. Here, you might also keep track of the publisher's request for sample chapters and the date those were sent, the date the contract arrived and when you returned it, when you sent illustrations for the book and so forth.

I start a ledger book for each of my books as soon as they are in production. If it's a self-published book, I start the ledger as soon as I incur my first expense related to that book. I keep a running log of expenses. These include the cost of editing and printing, cover design and obtaining the ISBN and bar code. I don't log expenses for postage, envelopes, paper and other supplies here. But I do save receipts for these incidentals in a file folder to tally at the end of the year. When self-publishing, the task of adding up major production expenses can help you to determine your suggested retail price.

If yours is a POD "self-published" book or you have a traditional royalty publisher, you'll still want to document expenses. Log costs related to editing, publishing and promotion. Promotion costs might include, brochures, a large mailing, booth space at a local flea market, invitations for a book signing, ads in a couple of appropriate newsletters and the cost of having a Web site built. By keeping track of major expenses related to your book, you can more realistically evaluate the success of this project. Comparing expenses against earnings creates a pretty accurate measuring stick.

In each *book ledger*, I reserve several pages for logging sales. I take advantage of the vertical columns on the ledger sheets, providing one each for the date of the sale, number of books sold, to whom, tax collected on the sale and the total amount of the sale (without tax or shipping). I have two columns for the transaction amount. One is for retail sales (full-price sales to individuals) and one for wholesale sales (those to bookstores, amazon.com, distributors, etc). I do not log a sale until it is paid in full.

Reserve several pages for miscellaneous orders. I call these my *Books Out* pages. This is where I log books shipped to random customers with an invoice. I get orders from bookstores all over the U.S. Most are not regular customers, so I log my transactions with them in this area of miscellaneous orders. I might deliver a book to a neighbor who promises to pay me later. I log this on the miscellaneous orders page. Transfer these transactions to the sales page when you are paid. And be sure to mark "Paid" next to the original entry.

Prepare a section in your account book for regular customers. This would include bookstores, gift shops and other places of business that carry your books. I allow each customer at least two pages. I use tabs to identify each customer page and I write the business name, address, phone, fax, email and contact person at the top of their first page. Here, I document date of each delivery, number of books delivered, invoice number and amount owed. When they pay the invoice, I mark

# SAMPLE QUERY LOG

© WILSON JONES    G7902 ColumnWrite ®

| | Initials | Date |
|---|---|---|
| Prepared By | | |
| Approved By | | |

| Date | Publisher | Book | Response |
|---|---|---|---|
| 11/20/04 | ABC Publishing | Coffee House Blues | |
| " | Irish Holmes Publications | " | Yes/send Prop. |
| " | George Thompson Pub. | " | Holding 2/13 |
| " | XYZ Press | " | No |
| 12/27/04 | Angel Productions | Princess and Char Man | Bad Address |
| " | Clancy Publishing House | " | No |
| " | Bear Brand Books | " | Holding 3/2 |
| 1/2/05 | Clambake Press | Coffee House Blues | Yes/ send Ms. |
| 1/10/05 | Irish Gold Publishing | Here Comes Harry | No |
| 1/12/05 | Where It's At Pub. | Princess and Char Man | No |
| 1/22/05 | Howdy Publications | Art of Becoming a Clown | No |
| 2/1/05 | Encinal Press | Art of Becoming a Clown | Yes/50 pages |
| " | Harding Publishing | " | Holding 5/12 |
| " | Colinga Pubs. | " | No |
| " | Canadian Publications | " | Out of Bus. |
| 2/12/05 | Prince Publishing | Coffee House Blues | |
| 2/22/05 | XYZ Press | How to Entertain at Home | Yes |
| 2/23/05 | Golden Press | How to Entertain at Home | NO |
| 3/5/05 | Bear Brand Books | Art of Becoming a Clown | |

286

# SAMPLE MANUSCRIPT LOG

© WILSON JONES    G7502 ColumnWrite ®

| Date Req | Date Sent | Publisher | Book/Proposal | Response |
|---|---|---|---|---|
| | 11/20/04 | Grand Pubs | Coffee House Blues/Prop | No |
| | | | | |
| | 12/28/04 | Sillliman/Wresten | Princess/Char Man/Prop | No |
| | 1/12/05 requested sample chapters sent 2/22 | | | |
| | Sent tracer 4/30 | | | |
| | | | | |
| 1/3/05 | 1/7/05 | Irish Holmes Pubs. | Coffee House Blues/Prop | No |
| | | | | |
| 3/5/05 | 3/22/05 | Encinal Press | Art of Bec. Clown | Yes |
| | Sent first 50 pages | | | |
| | Req. entire ms 4/13/05 | | | |
| | Sent 4/25/05 | | | |
| | Received contract 6/2/05 | | | |
| | Signed contract 6/17/05 | | | |
| | Received $100 advance | | | |
| | | | | |
| 5/1/05 | 5/10/05 | Clambake Press | Coffee House Blues/book | |
| | Req. manuscript | | | |
| | and marketing plan | | | |
| | 7/13/05 tracer | | | |
| | 9/22/05 still holding | | | |

the entry paid and note the date. I also cross reference this with the physical invoice and I log the payment in the sales section of the ledger.

I use duplicate invoices. Upon delivery (or shipping) one copy goes to the customer and one goes into a file folder for that particular book title. Each book has its own file folder. When I receive a purchase order from a bookstore or distributor, I staple it to the invoice. Once the invoice is paid, I place it in a folder marked, "Sales."

I treat amazon.com orders a little differently. I keep a separate folder for their purchase orders. Whenever I receive an accounting and a check from them, I reconcile it against the purchase orders, staple the POs to the check receipt and accounting form and file this in the sales folder. I log the sales in the appropriate book ledger and mark the appropriate ledger entries "Paid."

I reserve several pages in the accounting book for logging promotional books. That is, books that I give away for promotional purposes— review books, donated books and those given to friends and key players in the production of the book. Log how many books you gave and to whom.

I have an inventory page where, at least once a year, I log the number of books distributed, whether sold, donated or given away for promotional purposes. This way, I can keep a running tally of books in stock.

## Record-Keeping for Uncle Sam

As I mentioned earlier and as I'm sure you've been advised, keep receipts. I simply toss my receipts in a file folder marked "Receipts" and the current year (2008, for example). I vow each year to tally receipts every few months or so in order to stay ahead of the tax season frenzy. But so far I have not managed to do so.

Keep receipts for all of the expenses incurred while you are working on a book. This might include, research materials, cassette tapes used for recording interviews, your page layout and cover designer, editor, mileage for trips related to your book and telephone expenses. Also log expenses involving writers'/publishers' conferences, supplies and equipment (paper, ink cartridges and a new FAX machine), and organizations you joined that are related to either writing/publishing or the topic of your book. Keep receipts even though you log some of these things in your ledger book. Save receipts even when you're unsure as to whether it is a legitimate deduction. Your accountant will let you know what is and what isn't acceptable.

Most likely, you cannot deduct the new suit you bought for your book signing or the limo you rented to bring your parents from the airport to the event. But save your receipts just in case. Your accountant might find a loophole that mine hasn't discovered, yet.

I strongly urge you to stay on top of things. Do not deposit or even file a check until you have accurately logged it. Update your log books either daily, as information comes in, or weekly. I ship almost daily and I log relevant information at the same time. I toss correspondence from publishers and receipts in a basket and log/file this information at least weekly.

## Donating Books is Good Business

Don't be afraid to give books away. This is a legitimate business expense. It's also a good way to generate sales. In order to get your book reviewed, you must send free copies to appropriate reviewers. To get publicity for your book, donate copies. While not every copy given results in sales, many do.

In 1999, I donated copies of my newly revised Ojai Valley history book for the silent auction at the city Christmas party. (As chair of the Historic Preservation Commission, I was one of about 150 invited guests.) I had also sent promo pieces to City Hall a few weeks earlier letting staff know about the revision and my array of other books for sale. During his speech that night, the city manager introduced my new contribution to the heritage and history of the valley. He went on to say that I was the most prolific and diverse writer he knew and he announced some of my other book titles.

This was a good reminder to me that you never know when your efforts, diligence and generosity are going to pay off.

Last year, my high school reunion was held, not in the city where we graduated, but fifteen miles inland in the Ojai Valley (where I live). I gave the class president a copy of my Ojai history book. Later, he got up and spoke to the crowd of 200 about some of our classmates who had either been successful or who were involved in something interesting. One fellow was spotlighted because he had ridden his motorcycle cross-country in a record number of days. And I was introduced as the only author from the class. The class president gave the titles of some of my books and I ended up selling several on the spot. I've discovered many times over that it pays to give and it's also wise to carry books around in the trunk of your car.

## How to Protect Your Review Copies From Theft

Over the years, I've heard that sometimes book reviewers will turn around and sell the review copies sent to them by authors. I chose not to believe that this actually happens. And then I met an author who caught a reviewer red-handed. His book had been out for all of a week. He had sent only one review copy. Later during that week, the author decided to conduct a search to see if his book was listed on amazon.com. It was. But along with new copies posted for sale, he saw a link to a used copy. He investigated and sure enough, there was one of his brand-new books being offered for sale at a discount as a secondhand book. In the author's mind, there was only one person who could possibly be responsible for placing this book for sale. He checked and he was right. Of course, he confronted the book reviewer who apologized profusely.

I was astounded and still a little suspicious about the validity of this story, until … Yes, until this actually happened to me. I had just come out with the first edition of this book in 2006 when I decided to do a Google search on the title. Lo and behold, there it was—a strange link pointing to my book. I clicked and found myself at a discounted book site. My brand-new book was listed for sale at a deep discount. What? It wasn't even up on amazon.com, yet. An investigation led to one of the few people who had received free review copies from me. You'd better believe that I e-confronted this thief and he even responded by admitting to his crime. He said he had never done anything like this before and he sure was sorry—sorry he got caught.

To keep this from happening to you, stamp "review copy" on the front of the book or on the flush edges of the pages before sending it out.

## You and the IRS

When do you begin to claim your earnings and expenses? When is yours considered a viable business? According to the IRS, a business must have a clear business purpose and profit motive before the owner can claim business expenses.

I claimed my expenses and earnings for several years before I actually made any money with my writing. I considered myself a writer—this was my profession, but, while I was still raising kids, I really wasn't making any money. My expenses were minimal and my earnings were even less. But I was earning a little money, so I felt it was honorable to claim it. I really didn't like that the expenses overpowered my earnings, but that was the reality of the situation. When I established my publishing company, in 1983, that changed.

I have hired a tax preparer ever since. And I recommend that you do, too. It's almost impossible to keep up with the changing laws for the ordinary tax return. Throw in the complexities of operating a business, and things can get pretty complicated. If, of course, you are comfortable with things financial, do it yourself. As with production tasks, when contemplating your business tasks, I suggest that you do the things you do well and hire out the rest.

I write, teach, promote, work with other authors, do simple bookkeeping, take care of my publishing business and leave almost everything else to others. Heck, I don't even clean my own house anymore.

From what I understand, you should keep receipts for seven years. I am so paranoid about being questioned by the IRS that I have kept every record related to my business since 1973. For more information about taxes and your small business visit irs.gov/smallbiz or call, 800--829-3676. Ask for a free copy of *publication number 3207. The Small Business Resource Guide CD-Rom 2004.*

## Welcome to the Shipping Room

I got a surprise a couple of years ago when I visited the post office. I used to ship up to nine of my 80-page books or five of my 180-page books in a 9 ¼ x 6 ¼ x 2 ¼ size Priority Mail Box turned inside out. I could then ship the books media rate. Or I would put books inside the Priority Mail Box, slip the box into a Flat Rate Envelope and send it priority for $3.85 no matter how many books were shipped or how heavy the package.

But now, those nifty Priority Mail Boxes have "Priority" stamped on the inside as well as the outside. This means we cannot ship in that box using the much cheaper media rate. Not only that, they have new restrictions as to the thickness of the materials you can ship in the Flat Rate Envelope. Bummer.

The post office does offer Priority Mail Flat Rate Boxes, both domestic and global. Use these boxes when you have several books to ship.

I generally send books media rate (or book rate) when I'm paying for shipping. When I charge a customer for shipping, I always send the book first-class or Priority Mail. Some people argue that media rate packages take too long to arrive. And sometimes that's true, so plan ahead. I shipped about thirty-five books to St. Louis, Missouri from California last October for a book festival at a cost of around $7.00 (media rate) and they arrived in St. Louis just six days later, a few days before I got there.

When I ship just one book, I use a bubble mailer. They weigh less, thus cost less to mail than the fiber-filled mailers. When I send more than one book, I use recycled boxes for as long as I have them. But at some point I always run out of them, so I recently went in search of boxes that I could purchase for small shipments of books. Here's what I learned. At the time of this printing, the best price on bubble mailers can be found at packitright.net and the best prices on boxes by bulk are at papermart.com. I use mainly size 9 3/8 x 7 ¼ x 2 ½.

Pack books so they are tight in the box. You don't want them doing the boot scootin' boogie or the electric slide while en route. Books packed too loosely will scrape against one another and become marred. Use plenty of newspaper, bubble wrap or Styrofoam peanuts when packing books to prevent them from sliding. My preference, when it comes to shipping, is to wrap sheets of bubble wrap around a stack of books which are then placed in an appropriate-size box. Fill in any leftover space using wads of the bubble wrap or Styrofoam peanuts.

If you have an accurate postage scale at home, you can calculate postage by weighing your shipment and going to usps.gov.

If you do a lot of shipping, it might be worth your while to rent a postage meter.

## Copyright Law and Contracts
You can't become a published author without some exposure to copyright issues and contracts. If you have absolutely no tolerance for things legal, run, don't walk, to the nearest attorney.

### Copyright Briefly Explained
One thing that most people fail to understand is that one cannot copyright an idea or words. It's the way the words are strung together that makes them unique, thus copyrightable.

Another thing that's hard to comprehend is that your writing is automatically copyrighted as soon as it is created. You don't have to register a copyright, but there are advantages of protection if you do. It is recommended that an independent publisher go through proper channels to file for a copyright. If you are working with a traditional royalty publisher, he or she will generally copyright the work in your name.

## How to Keep from Crossing the Libel Line

Hopeful authors often ask us here at SPAWN if they can get away with publishing a book featuring real people if they change the names. Some authors wonder if they can write a story that's derogatory to people who are still living as long as it is truthful. These are the sort of questions you want to discuss with an intellectual properties or literary law attorney.

I always advise erring on the side of caution. Anyone can sue for almost any reason. If someone feels that you have written something that is damaging to him personally or financially, he can take you to court—even if what you wrote is the truth and even if you have attempted to conceal that person's identity. And you can't hide behind a publisher, either. Most publishing contracts include clauses holding the author responsible in case of any libel suits.

## Understanding Publishing Contracts

Publishing contracts come in all types and styles. Some comprise a page and a half and are fairly straightforward, while others run on for pages and pages and seem filled with a lot of double-talk. I am not an attorney, but I recommend that you contact one anytime you receive a contract that you do not understand. Don't sign any contract that conjures up questions or that you cannot completely agree with. Often, we are so eager to be published and we work so long and hard to land a contract that, when one comes, we blindly sign. Contracts are negotiable, folks. And if you don't have an agent to help you navigate the deep crevices of a publishing contract, please hire a good attorney. This could well be the best $200 to $800 you spend in the process of becoming a published author.

For clarity on contract terms, visit textbookpublisher.com/contracts.html. This author has defined just about every term you will find in a contract including publication rights, royalties, ancillaries, subsidiary rights and so forth.

Lloyd J. Jassin is a book publishing and entertainment attorney. He also handles issues of copyright, trademark and Internet law. Read his articles at his Web site, copylaw.com. I particularly like his article on contracts at copylaw.com/new_articles/final.three.html. Herein, he coaches hopeful authors in how to negotiate a book publishing contract. Jassin is also coauthor of *The Copyright, Permission and Libel Handbook* (Wiley & Sons).

## Recommended Reading:

*Kirsch's Handbook of Publishing Law* by Jonathan Kirsch ($2^{nd}$ edition/ revised, Silman-James Press, 2005).

*Literary Law Guide for Authors* by Tonya Marie Evans and Susan Borden Evans (FYOS Entertainment, LLC, 2003).

*The Copyright, Permission and Libel Handbook* by Lloyd J. Jassen (Wiley and Sons).

# Chapter Fifteen

# THE
# WRITER'S
# LIFE

Most people think that, as writers, we have a lot of time on our hands. They imagine that we spend our days sitting around entertaining fanciful thoughts while waiting for inspiration. They don't understand this strange need to write—the drive that makes it impossible to not write. They don't know the sense of responsibility we feel to our readership or the hard work involved. In fact, few people think of writing as a profession.

I believe this is why we writers are drawn to conferences and writers' groups—to associate with people who share our passion and understand our sacrifices.

I work six or seven days most weeks from 5 a.m. until 5 p.m. in my home office. I know other writers who put in eight-hour days, five days a week. And some freelance writers and authors hold down fulltime jobs and write after regular working hours. A cross-country truck driver I know is writing a fantasy novel on his days off. He is among the countless people who hope to someday establish a writing career. Thousands of people become writers in retirement. And I know plenty of fulltime moms who write every chance they get—some are earning a comfortable living through their writing.

It's hard to explain to a non-writer that, no matter how much time you spend writing, it never seems enough. While absorbed in a writing project, it's excruciatingly difficult to walk away from the computer to run an errand, answer the doorbell, settle a squabble between preschoolers or let the cat in (out, in, out…). And it is sometimes difficult to sleep at night when you're eager to return to an exciting writing project.

At the other end of the spectrum is the newbie writer who finds it hard to discipline herself to write. She allows even mundane household chores to lure her away from her writing project. She caves in to the temptations of a sunny day and warm temperatures. But the worst culprits of all, when it comes to creating distractions for writers, are well-meaning friends, relatives and neighbors.

Non-writers simply don't understand (or refuse to respect) your need for time and solitude. They don't take your writing seriously. What you're doing isn't real work, is it?

Aunt Sue loves the idea that you're no longer working downtown. She can call you anytime to chat because she knows that you're at home. Even though you've told the neighbors that you are doing freelance writing now, they still stop by whenever they see your car out front. Your many friends and former coworkers expect you to be available for lunch and shopping just about anytime. You're no longer working, after all.

The second most difficult task in disciplining yourself to write regularly is to retrain your friends and family. You must help them to understand that writing is your career now. I learned, many years ago, when I was trying to condition my own family and friends to respect my writing time, that, when I began to take it more seriously, so did they.

It also helps to negotiate. Say to your sister, "I can't go to lunch today, but how about coming by later this afternoon and we'll have tea?" or "Let's go shopping Saturday together." Or say to your mother, "I'm working on a deadline, Mom. I'll have to call you back. Is 4:30 this afternoon okay?"

You'll meet people socially who ask what you do. When you respond with, "I'm a writer," immediately they want to know what you've published. Most people aren't impressed to learn that you wrote the new brochure for a local artist or that you had an article published in *Mold Today Magazine* or *Chess Life* (even though you were paid $50 an hour for this work). They won't even ask for your autograph when you tell them that you are working on a novel or that you are a published author, if your publisher is virtually unknown. Don't expect to get a whole lot of respect just because you're a writer.

If you truly yearn to feel like a celebrity and be treated like one, write a local history. No kidding. If it hasn't been done yet, and you have an interest in your hometown, write a book about it, promote it widely throughout your community and you will be amazed at the kudos that will rain down upon you.

I first published my Ojai Valley history book in 1983 and still people (even strangers) recognize me or my name and proceed to tell me how much they enjoy or appreciate or treasure that book. I love the attention and the validation. And this brings us to a question that every writer wrestles with. At some point we wonder, "Am I a hobby writer or a professional writer? When can I consider myself a writer?"

## When Can You Call Yourself a Writer?

It's easy to say, "I'm writing a book." But, for some reason, it's difficult to accept the label, *writer*. When is it appropriate to consider yourself a writer rather than someone who is writing a book in his spare time or who submits articles to magazines? Can you claim this moniker once you decide to write for a living? When you've completed a book? After you've had something published? After you've had several things published?

This varies from individual to individual and depends on one's level of confidence and commitment. I consider someone a writer when he has committed himself to a career as a writer. This might be someone who has set up a framework and is diligently seeking clients for a freelance writing business. It could be someone who has published her first book and is out there seriously promoting it. Or it might be an individual who is earnestly submitting articles to magazines with a business model in mind.

Until you feel comfortable wearing the title, *writer*, you can say to people who ask, "I'm doing some writing." Or "I'm writing a book."

## Learn to Pace Yourself For Greater Performance

If you're like most people, you perform better at certain times of the day. You might be fresher and feel more alert in the morning. Perhaps you are better with intricate details later in the evening when the household is quiet. It is a wise writer who recognizes his/her daily high achievement and low functioning periods and arranges their schedule accordingly.

I work better in the early morning. I go into a lazy slump after lunch and that's when I typically spend an hour or so running errands, taking a walk or pulling a few weeds in the garden. By evening, I'm generally rather spent. But I can still accomplish certain work-related tasks. This is when I do simple research, read some of the many publishing-related newsletters I receive each week and so forth.

If you find yourself staring into the computer like a zombie at certain times of the day, you may be trying to work during your low functioning period. Don't fight it. Right it! Adjust your schedule so that you are writing during your high achievement period and handling the more mundane tasks when your energy is low. You may discover a productivity level you never knew existed.

Believe it or not, getting away helps to increase your level of productivity. Remove yourself from your work for a few hours, a few days or more and you will return with a new outlook. It's amazing how the simple act of distancing oneself from a project can give one a more realistic, less emotional perspective. Whenever your creative edge seems to have left, step away for a while. You will come back with fresh ideas and a viewpoint to match.

## The Aftermath of Authorship

Most authors experience a mixture of joy and remorse during the first few months after publication. We're joyful of our accomplishment, but sorely miss the process of writing. In fact, one reason why many books fail is that the author succumbs to her writing withdrawal symptoms.

She too quickly turns her attention from promotion to writing her next book.

If you still have the writing bug after publishing a book, go ahead and write. But don't lose your focus. Apply your efforts, energy and expertise to writing promotional material for your book.

If you have another book boiling up inside you and your desire to get it out is so strong that you can't not write, create a plan. Schedule several hours each day spent promoting your new book and treat yourself to an hour or two every afternoon for the new project. If writing is so much a part of who you are, don't deprive yourself or you will resent the task at hand, which is to promote your newly published book. If you are like me—crazy in love with writing—it is important to know that you can write no matter what else is going on in your life.

## Watch Out for Burn-Out

There are two types of writers: those who can't find the time to write—who procrastinate themselves out of a writing career—and those who write for so many hours each day that their posture when standing resembles their posture when sitting.

Here's what I suggest and you KNOW I'm right:

- Get plenty of sleep. Most of us really do need eight hours.

- Eat regularly and make your meals nutritious. Keep a good variety of fruits and vegetables on hand.

- Exercise every day. You'll be amazed at what a thirty-minute walk can do for your energy level and your sense of creativity.

- Use ergonomically correct equipment and posture while working.

- Take regular breaks. (My chiropractor says ten minutes for every hour of sitting.)

- Seek mental stimulation and inspiration. Read. See good films and socialize with interesting people.

- Expand your creative endeavors. Sew, knit, garden, do woodwork or take up art. Even those of us who are involved in a creative pursuit need a creative outlet.

- Acknowledge your spirituality.

- Volunteer—yes, help others. It does a heart and a world good.

There you have it—a guide to successful authorship in frank, explicit detail with numerous anecdotes to illustrate the process and highlight the ramifications of various publishing decisions. Go forth into the world of authorship armed with the knowledge and skills you've gleaned from this book. Embrace only the most realistic expectations. Only then will you succeed. Oh yes, and enjoy the journey. Otherwise, what is the point?

## Recommended Reading:
*The Writer Within You: A Step-by-Step Guide to Writing and Publishing In Your Retirement Years*, by Charles Jacobs (Caros Books, 2007).

# Chapter Sixteen

# RESOURCES

## FOR HOPEFUL
## AND ALREADY SUCCESSFUL AUTHORS

**Articles for Authors**
These sites post numerous informational articles relating to all aspects of writing, publishing and book promotion.

www.matilijapress.com/articles.htm
www.matilijapress.com/forwriters.html
www.spawn.org/articles.htm
www.writing-world.com

**Author's Agents**
Find an agent through recommendations, on the acknowledgements page of published books similar to yours and through these online and print directories.

Online Directories
The Association of Author's Representatives (AAR) is the primary organization for literary agents. Members must adhere to strict guidelines. Most professionals recommend that you choose an agent who is a member of AAR.
www.aar-online.org

Agent Research and Evaluation Company database has a lot of information for a fee.
www.agentresearch.com

Writers Net lists over 600 agencies along with numerous articles and other information about hiring and working with an agent. www.writers.net/agents.html

<u>Print Directories</u>
*Guide to Literary Agents* (Writer's Digest Books)

*Jeff Herman's Guide to Book Editors, Publishers and Literary Agents 2005: Who They Are! What They Want! How to Win Them Over* by Jeff Herman (Writer's Inc.)

*Literary Market Place* (In the reference section at your local library.) www.literarymarketplace.com

**Author's/Publisher's Resources**
These sites offer information, resources and support for authors and independent publishers.

Patricia Fry's site
www.matilijapress.com/forwriters/wordsforwriters.html
www.matilijapress.com/forwriters/resources.html
www.matilijapress.com/publishingblog

John Kremer's site
www.bookmarket.com

Midwest Book Review site
www.midwestbookreview.com/bookbiz/pub_res.htm

Dan Poynter offers an enormous helping of information and resources on publishing and self-publishing—some for free and some for a fee. www.parapublishing.com

Small Publishers Artists and Writers Network (SPAWN) posts dozens of articles, an extensive resource list, complete archives for SPAWNews and the *SPAWN Market Update* and more. www.spawn.org

## Books for Authors
<u>Agents</u>
See Author's Agents (above)

<u>Book Promotion</u>
*1001 Ways to Promote Your Book* by John Kremer (Open Horizons, 6<sup>th</sup> edition, 2006)

*A Writer's Guide to Magazine Articles for Book Promotion and Profit* by Patricia Fry (Matilija Press, 2002)

*Beyond the Bookstore, How to Sell More Books Profitably to Non-Bookstore Markets* by Brian Jud (Reed Press, 2003)

*Book Marketing From A-Z* by Francine Silverman (Infinity Publishing, 2005)

*Confessions of Shameless Self-Promoters* by Debbie Allen (Success Showcase Publishing, 2002) (McGraw Hill, 2005)

*Grassroots Marketing for Authors and Publishers* by Shel Horowitz (AWM Books, 2007)

*Jump Start Your Book Sales: A Money-Making Guide for Authors, Independent Publishers and Small Presses* by Marilyn and Tom Ross (Writer's Digest Books, 1999)

*Over 75 Good Ideas for Promoting Your Book* by Patricia Fry (Matilija Press, 2000)

*Ten Ways to Make Your Book Outsell Another* by Judy Cullins

*Your Guide to Marketing Books in the Christian Marketplace* by Sarah Bolme (Crest Publications, 2006)

<u>Book Proposals</u>
*The Fast-Track Course on How to Write a Nonfiction Book Proposal* by Stephen Blake Mettee (Quill Driver Books, 2002)

*How to Write a Successful Book Proposal In 8 Days or Less* by Patricia Fry (revised, Matilija Press, 2005)

*Write the Perfect Book Proposal* by Jeff Herman and Deborah M. Adams (John Wiley and Sons, Inc. 2001)

Directories of Publishers
*Literary Market Place* (Found in the reference section at your library.)

*Writer's Market* (Purchase for around $30 at most bookstores.)

Grammar and Writing Help
*Associated Press Stylebook and Libel Manual* (Addison Wesley)

*Chicago Manual of Style* (The University of Chicago Press)

*Grammar Traps* by Stephen Dolainski (Paragraph Publishing, 2004)

*How to Say and Write it Correctly* by Dr. Santo J. Aurelio (Synergy Books, 2004)

Poetry
*How to Make a Living as a Poet* by Gary Mex Glazner (Soft Skull Press, 2005)

*Poet Power, The Complete Guide to Getting Your Poetry Published* by Thomas A. Williams (Sentient Publications, 2002)

The Publishing Industry
*The ABC's of POD: A Beginner's Guide to Fee-Based Print-on-Demand Publishing* by Dehanna Bailee (Blue Leaf Publications, 2005)

*The Fine Print* by Mark Levine (Bridgeway Books, 2006)

Publishing Law
*Copyright Companion for Writers* by Tonya Evans-Walls (Legal Write Publications, 2007)

*The Copyright, Permission and Libel Handbook, A Step by Step Guide for Writers, Editors and Publishers* by Lloyd J. Jassin and Steve C. Schechter (Wiley & Sons, 1998)

*Kirsch's Handbook of Publishing Law* by Jonathan Kirsch (Silman-James Press, 2005)

*Literary Law Guide for Authors*, Tonya Marie Evans and Susan Borden Evans (FYOS Entertainment, LLC, 2003)

Self-Publishing
*Complete Guide to Self-Publishing: Everything You Need to Know to Write, Publish, Promote and Sell Your Own Book* by Marilyn and Tom Ross (Writer's Digest Books, 2002)

*The Self-Publishing Manual* by Dan Poynter (15$^{th}$ printing, Para Publishing, 2007)

*The Well-Fed Self-Publisher* by Peter Bowerman (Fanove Publishing, 2007)

**Book Design**
SPAWN Member Directory
Use search feature
www.spawn.org

The Agrell Group
www.theagrellgroup.com

Linda McGinnis
mcginnis@snowcrest.net

**Book Production**
Bar Code
Bar Code Graphics

312-595-0600
www.barcode-us.com

Fotel
800-834-4920
sales@fotel.com
www.fotel.com

Books in Print
For ABI form:
R.R. Bowker
630 Central Avenue
New Providence, NJ 07974
888-269-5372

info@bowker.com
www.bowker.com
www.bowkerlink.com
www.booksinprint.com

## Copyright
US Copyright Office
Library of Congress
101 Independence Ave., SE
Washington, DC 20559-6000
www.loc.gov/copyright

## ISBN
International Standard Book
Number
R.R. Bowker
630 Central Avenue
New Providence, NJ 07974
888-269-5372
877-310-7333
Isbn-san@bowker.com
www.isbn.org

## Publishers Cataloging in Publication (PCIP)
Quality Books
800-323-4241
www.quality-books.com

The Donohue Group, Inc.
860-683-1647
www.dgiinc.com

## Book Promotion
Listed here are a few Web sites
and other resources to help you
promote your book.

## Become a Media Guest
www.guestfinder.com

## Radio-TV Interview Report
www.rtir.com
215-259-1070

## Book Fairs
Directory of Book Fairs
www.lights.com/publisher/
bookfairs.html

www.loc.gov/loc/cfbook/
bookfair.html

## Books
See list above.

## Book Videos
Circle of Seven Productions
www.cosproductions.com

## PR Tips
Publicity Insider—sample pitch
letters and more
www.publicityinsider.com

## Publicists
Circle of Seven Productions
www.cosproductions.com

Marsha Friedman
Publicity that Works
www.publicitythatworks.com

Penny Sansevieri
www.amarketingexpert.com
858-560-0121

Newsletters
*Book Promotion Newsletter*
(Fran Silverman)
www.bookpromotionnewsletter.com

*SPAWN Market Update* Join
SPAWN to have access to this
meaty newsletter.
www.spawn.org

**Distributors and Wholesalers**
(also see Chapter Eleven)
Distributor and Wholesaler
Directories
www.pma-online.org/
distribute.cfm

Dan Poynter lists numerous
distributors in his book, *The
Self-Publishing Manual* and he
offers more extensive lists for
sale. www.parapublishing.com

*Literary Market Place*
(Reference in the library)
www.literarymarketplace.com

John Kremer's List
www.bookmarket.com/
distributors.htm

Library Distributors
These companies distribute
books to the library market.

Quality Books
www.quality-books.com
800-323-4241

Unique Books
uniquebks@aol.com
www.uniquebooksinc.com
800-533-5446

General Distributors
Here's an example of a general
book distributor.

Independent Publishers Group
814 N. Franklin St.
Chicago, IL 60610
312-337-0747
www.ipgbook.com

Regional Distributor
Here are two examples of
companies that distribute books
just to a particular area or region.

Sunbelt Publications
1250 Fayette St.
El Cajon, CA 92020
www.sunbeltpub.com

Raincoast Book Distribution
9050 Shaughnessy St.
Vancouver, BC V6P 6E5

Specialty Distributors
Rittenhouse Books
511 Feheley Dr.

308

King of Prussia, PA 19406
www.rittenhouse.com
Medical and healthcare books.

DeVorss and Company
552 Constitution Ave.
Camarillo, CA 93012-8510
www.devorss.com
Inspirational and new thought books.

Wholesalers
These are the two major book wholesalers in America.

Baker and Taylor
255 W. Tyvola Rd. Ste. 300
Charlotte, NC 28217
800-775-1800
btinfo@btol.com
www.btol.com

Ingram Book Company
One Ingram Blvd.
La Vergne, TN 37086-1986
800-937-8100
www.ingrambook.com

**Editorial Services**
Patricia Fry
www.matilijapress.com/consulting.html
plfry620@yahoo.com
805-646-3045

The Writers-Editors Network
www.writers-editors.com

Victory Crayne
Specializes in Fiction
www.crayne.com
victory@crayne.com

Embree Literary Services
Specializes in Full Book Production
Mary Embree
maryembree@sbcglobal.net
805-643-6279

**Forms**
Book
*Business and Legal Forms for Authors and Self-Publishers by Tad Crawford* (Watson-Guptill Publications, 2000)

Online
www.copylaw.com/forms/forms.html

www.textbookpublishers.com/contracts.html

**Fulfillment**
Bookmasters
www.bookmasters.com

Book Clearing House
www.bookch.com

Pathway Book Service
www.pathwaybook.com

**Grammar and Writing Help**
Online
Grammar Now
www.grammarnow.com

Sharp Writer
www.sharpwriter.com

Vocabula Review
www.vocabula.com

Books
See listings under "Books,
Grammar and Writing Help."

**Grants For Writers**
Funds For Writers
www.fundsforwriters.com

Writers' Emergency Assistance
Fund
American Society of Journalists
1501 Broadway, Ste. 302
New York, NY 10036
www.asja.org

**Law and Copyright**
www.Copylaw.com

Intellectual Property Owners
Association
http://ipo.org

Volunteer Lawyers for the Arts
www.vlaa.org

(See books listed under "Books
for Authors, Publishing Law")

**Library Directories**
*World Guide to Libraries* (In
the reference section at most
libraries) www.galegroup.com

American Library Association
See their online directory.
www.ala.org

www.librarydirectory.com

http://travelinlibrarian.info/libdir

**Magazines and Newsletters**
In Print
*Foreword*
231-933-3699
www.forewordmagazine.com

*Freelance Writer's Report*
603-922-8338
www.writers-editors.com

*SPAN Connection*
For members of SPAN
7119-475-1726
www.spannet.org

*PMA Independent*
For members of PMA

(Independent Book Publisher's Association)
310-372-2732
pmaonline@aol.com
www.pma-online.org

*Publisher's Weekly*
646-746-6758
www.publishersweekly.com

*The Writer*
www.writermag.com

*Writer's Digest*
www.writersdigest.com

Electronic Publications
*Book Promotion Newsletter*
www.bookpromotionnewsletter.com

*Publishing Poynters*
www.parapub.com/news.html

*SPAWNews*
Free online newsletter
Small Publishers, Artists and Writers Network
www.spawn.org
(click on Free Newsletter)

*SPAWN Market Update*
Posted at the SPAWN Web site for members only. Join SPAWN.
www.spawn.org

**Merchant Account Services**
Echo (Electronics Clearing House, Inc.)
www.echo-inc.com

Total Merchant Services
www.merchant-account-4u.com.

USA Merchant Account
www.usa-merchantaccount.com

**Newsletters (how to)**
www.thesitewizard.com/archive/newsletter.shtml

www.enewsletterpro.com

www.newsletterease.com

**Newspaper Directories**
www.newspapers.com
www.newspaperlinks.com
www.onlinenewspapers.com
www.thepaperboy.com

**Online Bookstores**
www.amazon.com
www.barnesandnoble.com
www.borders.com
www.fetchbook.com

**Organizations**
PMA (The Independent Book Publishers Association)
www.pma-online.org

SPAWN (Small Publishers, Artists and Writers Network)
www.spawn.org

SPAN (Small Publishers of North America)
www.spannet.org

**POD Publishing**
Data base of POD publishers.
http://dehanna.com

www.sfwa.org/beware/printondemand.html

(See books under "Books and The Publishing Industry.")

**Postage and Shipping**
www.usps.com

www.upperaccess.com/rate%20charts.htm

**Printers**
Action Printing
Adam Kempf
akempf@actionprinting.com
920-907-7809

360 Digital Books
Linda Castner
lcastner@360inc.com
866-379-8767
www.360digitalbooks.com

RJ Communications
Bob Powers
www.booksjustbooks.com

Star Print Brokers
Nancy Starkman, President
425-603-1777
nstar@starprintbrokers.com
www.starprintbrokers.com
Contact for quotes in the U.S.
Canada and Asia

For lists of printers:
www.gain.net
www.literarymarketplace.com
www.spawn.org/printers.htm

**Proofreading and More**
Professional Secretary
Bonnie Myhrum
bmyhrum@wideopenwest.com

**Public Speaking**
Books
*The Quick and Easy Way to Effective Public Speaking* by Dale Carnegie (Pocket Books)

Organizations
Toastmasters International
POB 9052
Mission Viejo, CA 92690
949-858-8255
www.toastmasters.org

312

Opportunity
Speaker Bank
www.speakerbank.com

**Publisher Directories**
*Literary Market Place*
Public library reference section
www.literarymarketplace.com

*Writer's Market*
Available at most bookstores

**Publisher Online Directories**
www.literarymarketplace.com
www.writersmarket.com

**Publishing Professionals and Experts**
Patricia Fry
Matilija Press
www.matilijapress.com
plfry620@yahoo.com

Dan Poynter
Para Publishing
805-968-7277
danpoynter@parapublishing.com
http://parapublishing.com

Marilyn and Tom Ross
719-395-8659
marilyn@marilynross.com
www.selfpublishingresources.com

**Research**
www.askanexpert.com
www.publishers.org
www.everyonewhosanyone.com
www.expertcentral.com
www.expertclick.com
www.google.com/alerts
www.infoplease.com
www.parapublishing.com

Check Site Traffic
www.alexa.com

**Reviewers**
Find many additional book reviewers in Literary Market Place. Also refer to Chapter Eleven of this book.

Book Reporter
www.bookreporter.com

Danny Yee's Book Reviews
http://dannyreviews.com

Get Book Reviews
www.getbookreviews.com

*Midwest Book Review*
Jim Cox 278
Orchard Dr.
Oregon, WI 53575
608-835-7937

*New Letters* (Reviews literary titles) www.newletters.org

*New York Times Book Review*
Charles McGrath
229 West 43$^{rd}$ St.
New York, NY 10036
212-556-1234

## Search Engines
Google.com
Altavista.com
Yahoo.com

## Specialty Sites
Learn more about your writing specialty by visiting appropriate Web sites.

For Children's Book Writers
Children's Writers Marketplace
www.write4kids.com

Society of Children's Book Writers and Illustrators
www.scbwi.org

Christian Writers' Sites
Christian Writers Fellowship
www.cwfi-online.org

Christian Writer's Guild
www.christianwritersguild.com

Professional Association of Christian Writers
www.christianwritersinfo.net

Sites for Fiction Writers
www.fictionfactor.com
www.fictionwriters.com

Sites for Poets
www.everypoet.com
www.poetry.com
www.poetry.org

Science Fiction Writers
Science Fiction Writers of America www.sfwa.org

## Statistical Information
Publishing Industry
Book Industry Study Group
www.bisg.org

Bowker
www.bookwire.com

Para Publishing
www.parapub.com/statistics

General
Bureau of Labor Statistics
www.bls.gov/home.htm

www.pollingreport.com

## Supplies
Book Displays
Fixturecraft Corp.
331 Centennial Ave., Ste. 201
Cranford, NJ 07016
http://fixturecraft.com
800-275-1145

Shipping
www.packitright.net
866-572-2548

Paper Mart
800-745-8800
orders@papermart.com
www.papermart.com

## Tax Help for Authors
www.theartrepreneur.com/
financialplanning

Tax Mama
EvaRosenberg
www.taxmama.com
818-993-1565

www.writetools.com/taxes.html

## Warnings for Authors
Preditors and Editors
www.anotherealm.com/
prededitors

Storm Warnings
*Freelance Writers Report*

Warnings for Writers
www.todays-woman.net/poetry-
scams.html

Whispers and Warnings
www.writersweekly.com/
whispers_and_warnings.php

## Web Design
CogniText Web Development
and Marketing
Virginia Lawrence
www.cognitext.com
818-886-4281

## Wholesalers
(See Distributors and
Wholesalers.)

## Writers Conferences
http://writing.shawguides.com

# Glossary

**ABI** – Advance Book Information. A publisher fills out the ABI form in order to have his book included in R.R. Bowker's *Books in Print* and other important directories.

**Acquisitions editor** – The editor to whom an author directs query and manuscript submissions.

**Advance** – An amount a publisher pays to the author before he writes the book. Typically, the author gets half when he signs the contract and half upon satisfactory completion of the manuscript. The advance amount is then deducted from royalties.

**Agent** – An author's representative. An agent shows the author's manuscript around to publishers and negotiates on his/her behalf. Agents generally receive 10-15% of the royalties.

**Anthology** – A collection of written works published under one cover.

**Appendix** – Supplemental material placed after the text in a book.

**Back matter** – Material placed in the back of a book. This might include an appendix, the index, glossary, epilogue, ordering information and so forth.

**Bar code** – A system of bars printed on the back cover of a book which, when scanned by a bookseller, identifies the book, the publisher and the price of the book.

**Bestseller** – A book that generates high sales during a specific period.

**Bibliography** – A list of books and other materials that the author referenced while writing his book. The bibliography is usually placed in the back of the book just in front of the index.

**Bio** – A sentence or more which generally reflects an author's credentials as a writer and in the subject matter of the book.

**Blog** – A Web log – an online Journal.

**Book** – Some experts say that a book is a book when it is bound and contains at least 49 pages.

**Book fair/festival** – An event where authors and publishers display and sell their books.

**Booklet** – A bound book with 48 pages or fewer.

**Book proposal** – A carefully developed plan for your book sent to publishers and literary agents. A book proposal usually includes a synopsis, author bio, marketing information, a competitive analysis of similar books, a detailed chapter outline and sample chapters.

**Book Rate/Media Mail** – A reduced mailing rate through USPS for shipping books.

**Books In Print** – A complete directory and database of books which have been issued ISBNs.

**Book Trailer** – A video designed to promote a book.

**Bullets** – Dots or other symbols used to accentuate items appearing in a list.

**Byline** – The author's name as it appears with his published piece.

**Camera ready** – Graphics and text are in place and ready for printing.

**Cataloging-in-Publication (CIP)** – Information supplied by the Library of Congress and printed on the copyright page of a book for librarians' use. (See PCIP.)

**Chapbook** – A small book or booklet of poetry or stories.

**Clip** – Samples of your published work.

**Comb binding** – Plastic binding for loose leaf pages.

**Content editing** – Editing a book for content, flow and organization.

**Co publishing** – Subsidy publishing.

**Copyediting** – Editing for grammar, punctuation, typos and spelling errors.

**Copyright** – Legal protection for intellectual properties such as books.

**Copyright page** – Usually the second page to appear in a book. This is where you note your copyright information, Publishers Cataloguing-in-Publication (PCIP) or Library of Congress information and ISBN.

**Cover Letter** – A brief letter of introduction that accompanies your book proposal or manuscript.

**Creative nonfiction** – Nonfiction for which the author takes some artistic license. Also known as literary nonfiction.

**Distributor** – A company that represents your book for sale. A distributor generally has sales reps. They buy your book from you and sell it to a specific market such as libraries; throughout a specific region or related to a particular topic.

**Ebook** – An electronic book which can be read on your computer screen, printed out and read or enjoyed using a handheld reading device.

**Editing** – The process of correcting or altering text.

**Edition** – The incarnation of a book. The first edition indicates the first printing and all subsequent printings as long as the text is unchanged. When you revise and reprint the book, this is considered the second edition.

**Editor** – Someone who edits written works.

**Electronic submission** – An email submission to an editor or publisher.

**Epilogue** – An addition to the text which is designed to provide the reader with additional information.

**Ezine** – An electronic magazine.

**Foreword** – A message to the reader usually written by an expert in the subject of the book, or another author. The Foreword (not forward) is placed in the front matter of a book.

**Front matter** – Pages appearing in the front of a book before the main text begins. This might include the foreword, preface, dedication and disclaimer.

**Galleys** – Pre-publication copies of a book.

**Genre** – Can refer to the general classifications of writing such as nonfiction, poetry, novel or to the categories within those classifications.

**Ghostwriter** – You can hire a ghostwriter to write a book or other material for you. The writer's name generally does not appear on the finished copy.

**Glossary** – A glossary defines words the author has used throughout the book and, perhaps, other words related to the topic of the book. The glossary is part of the back matter of a book.

**Index** – An index is an alphabetical subject list designed for easy reference. It appears last in a book.

**In print** – This is the term used for books that are still available to purchase.

**International Standard Book Number (ISBN)** – A number that identifies a particular book and the publisher. ISBNs are required for books sold in the retail market. R.R. Bowker is the U.S. agency for distributing ISBN blocks.

**Introduction** – An introduction is generally written by the author as a means of preparing his readers. It appears just ahead of the first chapter.

**Invoice** – A bill or statement.

**ISBN** – (See International Standard Book Number)

**Library of Congress** – The national library.

**Literary Market Place** (LMP) – A reference book and database listing publishers, literary agents, printing companies, bookstores and others involved in the publishing industry.

**Manuscript** – A book in typed or handwritten form—before it has been printed and bound.

**Media Mail** – See Book Rate

**Memoir** – A personal history.

**Multiple submissions** – When you send two or more article or book ideas or manuscripts to an editor or publisher at the same time.

**News release** – (See Press release.)

**Out of print** – A book that is no longer available for sale is considered out of print.

**Pamphlet** – A small unbound publication.

**Perfect binding** – A book binding option for a paperback book. A perfect bound book has a spine.

**Plagiarism** – The practice of copying the writing work of someone else and claiming it as your own.

**Platform** – Your accumulated expertise in your subject. Your degree of notoriety. Your following. Your way of attracting readers.

**POD** – (See Print-on-Demand.)

**POD "self-publisher"** – Generally you pay this publisher to produce your book.

**Preface** – A preface is part of the front matter of a book and generally contains a message from the author—why he wrote the book, how the research was conducted, etc.

**Premium** – A book or other items given away as a promotional tactic.

**Press kit** – A promotional package created by the author or publisher to distribute to book reviewers, bookstore managers, reporters and others. A press kit generally includes a press release, author biography, testimonials, former published book reviews and so forth.

**Press release** – A letter sent to newspapers and magazine editors designed to announce your book or a book signing or to entice the editor to publish a story about you or your book.

**Print-on-Demand** – A digital printing process for books and other written materials. Since items are printed one at a time, you can generally order as many or as few as you want.

**Promotion** – The act of marketing your book for the purpose of making sales.

**Proof reading** – Careful and thorough reading of a manuscript in order to catch grammatical errors and typos.

**Proposal** – (See Book proposal.)

**Publicist** – You can hire a publicist to promote your book for you.

**Purchase Order** (PO) – A request from a distributor, wholesaler or bookstore buyer who wishes to purchase your book for resale.

**Query letter** – A letter of introduction to your book or an article. Send a query letter to publishers, magazine editors and literary agents to pique their interest in your project.

**Review** – A written evaluation of a book.

**Revise** – To change aspects of your book.

**Royalties** – A percentage paid by a publisher for books sold.

**Saddle stitch** – Another term for the folded and stapled binding style.

**Self-publishing** – The process of financing and managing the production of your own book.

**Signature** – A printed sheet of paper folded to page size and bound together into a book. A signature might contain 16 pages, 32 or 48.

**Simultaneous submissions** – The process of sending the same manuscript to more than one publisher at the same time.

**Spiral binding** – Wire binding which secures loose leaf pages.

**Subsidy press** – A publishing company that requires payment for producing your book. Most POD publishers are subsidy presses.

**Synopsis** – An overview of your book. A synopsis is part of a book proposal.

**Table of contents** – A list of chapters in order with their page numbers—always placed in the front of a book. (The index is an alphabetical subject list appearing in the back of the book.)

**Testimonials or endorsements** – Favorable comments about your book made by experts in your field or other authors. Testimonials are sometimes published on the back cover of a book or on a "testimonials" page inside the book.

**Title page** – The first page that appears in your book. The title page is a right-facing page and generally includes the book title, subtitle, author's name and the publishing company name and contact information.

**Wholesaler** – A company that purchases books from publishers for resale to bookstores and libraries. Wholesalers do not have sales reps. They are not distributors.

# Index

*1001 Ways to Promote Your Book*, (Kremer) 115, 304

AAP (see Association of American Publishers)

AAR (see Association of Authors' Representatives)

*AARP The Magazine*, 269

*ABC's of POD* (Bailee), 55, 305

ABI (see Advance Book Information)

About the author, for book proposal, 61, 62, 78-83; for novel, 79-80; example, 80-83; for book, 189

*Absolute Write*, 24, 268

Acknowledgements page, make book marketable, 106; find an agent, 135; for fiction, 187; for nonfiction, 188; defined, 189

Acquisitions editor, addressing, 25, 140-143

Action Printing, 312

Adams, Deborah, 83, 159, 305

Advance (against royalties), 17; explained, 20, 156-157; agent negotiations, 132; warning, 133; 198

Advance Book Information (ABI), 206, 217; contact, 316

*Adventist's Journal*, 268

Advertise, free, 255

Afterword, 190

*African Voices*, 233

Agent (see Authors' agents)

Agent Research and Evaluation, 135, 302

Agrell Group, 306

ALA (see American Library Association)

Allen, Debbie, 255, 263, 304

Alexa, 313

Allworth Press, 223

Amazon.com, for book titles, 68; 87; for book sales, 91; your competition, 94; discounted books, 166-167; for research, 170; 237; submit your title, 239; promote book, 232, 264; link to Web site, 242, 244; 264, sales, 288; 290, 311

Ambassador (wholesaler), 236

American Library Association, booklist, 208; 235, 310

Appendix, description, 190-191

Arrow Publications, 28

Articles, for authors, 302

Article writing, to promote books, 105, 267-270; test book, 161-162; 218

AskanExpert.com, 90, 313

*Associated Press Style and Libel Manual*, 180, 305

Association of American Publishers (AAP), book sales, 84

Association of Authors'
   Representatives (AAR), 135,
   302
Attorney (see Intellectual
   properties attorney)
Audience (see Target audience)
Aurelio, Santo J., 305
AuthorHouse, 20
Authorme, 24
Authors' agents, 8-9, 30;
      what they want, 57; 131;
      why use one, 132-136;
      royalties, 132-133;
      contracts, 132-135;
      escalator, 133;
      intellectual properties
      attorney, 133;
      warnings, 133-136;
      example, 134-135;
      resources for locating, 135-
      136; working with, 136-137;
      140; locate, 302-303
Author's guidelines (see
   Submission guidelines)
Author's Guild, book statistics, 14
*Authorship*, 268
Authors' mistakes, 16-19, 99
*A Writer's Guide to Magazine
   Articles*, (Fry), 304

Back matter, 190-191
Bailee, Dehanna, POD database,
   47; book, 55, 305
Baker and Taylor (wholesaler),
   221, 232; library sales, 235;
   236, 237, 309
Ballentine, 131

Bancroft Press, 27, 28
Bantam Dell, 28
Barbour Publishing, 28, 29
Bar code, self publishing, 21, 34,
   45; POD publishing, 48;
   ordering 209; 284, 306
Bar Code Graphics, 209, 306
Barefoot Books, 30
Barnes and Noble, 48, 204;
   submitting books, 220; 237,
   311
Barrett, Jim,
   one-sentence challenge, 70;
   platform example, 104
Baycrest Books, 28
*Beyond the Bookstore* (Jud), 304
Biblio Book Distribution, 221
Bibliography, for marketability,
   106; 120, 181, 188; defined,
   191
*Bibliophilos* (reviews books),
   233
Binding, comb-binding, 198;
   choices, 201;
   saddle stitching, 201, 204;
   for libraries, 236-238
Blog, to promote book, 111;
   software, 243;
   start one, 245-246
Blue Leaf Publications, 55
Bly, Robert, 198
Bio (see About the author)
Bolme, Sarah, 304
Book, build marketability, 4-5,
   57; 105-106; classification,
   30; sales, 84; special interest
   item, 107-108; research

using, 165-167; organize, 162-164; timeline, 192; how to finish, 192; set price, 209

Bookazine (distributor), 221

Book Clearing House, fulfillment, 240

Book cover design, 202-204; cost, 202

Book design, 45, 198, 202-204; cost, 202

Book fair (See Book festival)

Book festival, 7; meet publishers, 41-43; how to dress, 43; selling books, 270-277; merchant account, 243; 270-277; cost, 271; 281; transport books, 273-274 handouts, 276; sell more books, 276-277; locate, 277; 307

Book Industry Study Group, 219, 314

Bookkeeping, 154, 283-293; examples, 286, 287

Bookmasters, fulfillment, 240

*Book Marketing From A-Z* (Silverman), 304

*BookPage*, 230

Book promotion, 1, author's responsibility, 4; build promotion into your book, 4-5, 57; 99-115; make news, 105-106, 254-255; through articles, 267-270; seasonal, 278-280; what publishers want, 101; for fiction, 100; plan, 108-113, 264-265

*Book Promotion Newsletter,* 268, 308, 311

Book proposal, write one first, 7, 10; 16, 18; how to write one, 56; why write one, 56-58, 60; when to write one, 57, 58; nonfiction, 60-61; novel, 61; formatting, 62-64; cover letter, 60-61, 63-64; sample cover letter, 64-66; title page, 66-67; synopsis, 70-78; sample synopsis, 72-78; about the author, 78-83; about the novelist, 79-80; sample about the author, 80-83; marketable topic, 84-86; target audience, 86-93; target audience for fiction, 91-92; sample marketing section, 93-94; competition, 94-98; sample market analysis, 96-98; promotion, 99-115; build marketability for fiction, 100, 105-108; build marketability for nonfiction, 106; book promotion plan, 108-113; chapter outline, 116-130; organize book, 116; organize children's book, 117; send to publisher, 130; work with agent, 132

Book reviews, 10, 211, 229-234; libraries, 245;

Book reviewers, reject some books, 3; charge fee, 10; 313

Bookselling stats, 1, 2, 84, 99, 104, 112
Books For Cooks, 219
Book signing, 223-238; what to wear, 226; handouts, 227
*Books in Print*, described, 22; check competition, 94; check titles, 68, 206; include your book 216-217; 220; contact info, 306
Bookstores, number of titles, 2; POD/self-published books, 3, 9-10, 46, 49; number of, 86-87; sales, 99; get book into, 104; sales statistics, 112; research, 166-167; get into bookstores, 213, 217-229; work with bookstores, 221-223; discount, 222; consignment agreements, 222; wholesalers, 236-237
Book trailers (videos), defined, 245; contact, 307
Borders Books, 48, 108, 204; submitting books, 220-221
Bowerman, Peter, 306
Bowker, RR, 8; order ISBN, 206; ABI form, 206; Books In Print, 216-217; contact info, 307, 314
Breakaway Books, 30
*Bridget Jones Diary*, 28
Bridgeway Books, 55
Britton, Betty Middleton, 108

Brodart (wholesaler), 236
Browning, Elizabeth Barrett, 198
BuilderBooks, 29
Build promotion into book, 4-5, 57; fiction, 100; 105-108
Bureau of Labor Statistics, 314
Burn-out, promotion, 282; writing, 300-301
Burton, Elizabeth K., why she writes, 12; POD technology, 46, 215
*Business and Legal Forms for Authors and Self-Publishers,* 223
*Business Phone Book USA, The,* 258
Button, Clair, 228

Carstens, Harold, 58
Carstens Publications, 58
*Celestine Prophecy*, 154-155
Chapter outline, for book proposal, 116-130; fiction, 116; nonfiction, 116; examples, 119-120, 121-130
Chapter summaries (see Chapter outline)
Chapter titles, 118
Character Counts, 278
Chick lit, 26, description, 28; titles for, 69
*Chicago Manual of Style*, 305
Children's books, 13, 15, 17, 30; book proposal for, 59; target audience, 92; special interest item, 107-108;

organizing book, 117; 136, 148, 161; parts of book, 187 192; bookstore, 219; book signing, 226; author sites, 313

Christian Books, 17, 27, 19, sales, 84; 92, 148; reviews, 233; 239; public speaking, 263

Christian author sites, 314

*Christian Home and School*, 230

Circle of Seven Productions, 245; contact information, 307

Clichés, 183-184

Colbert, Teddy, 225

Commercial fiction, 26-27

Competition (see Market analysis for Book Proposal)

*Complete Guide to Self-Publishing* (Ross), 306

*Confessions of Shameless Self-Promoters* (Allen), 255, 263, 304

Contemporary Press, 29-30

Contracts, 6, 8, 18, 20; warning, 33, 47; POD described, 48-50; 56, 131; working with agent, 132-135; explained, 133; when you're issued one, 156-159, 293-295

Copper Canyon Press, 30

Co-publishing (see Subsidy publisher)

Copyright, self-publishing, 21; plagiarism, 167; 188;

forms, 206-207, 210; send books, 211; 293-294; libel, 294; contact info, 307

*Copyright Companion for Writers* (Evans-Walls), 305

Copyright page, 187; defined, 188

*Copyright, Permission and Libel Handbook, The* (Jassin), 295, 306

Cover design, self-publishing, 21, 34, 45; POD publishing, 48, 207

Cover letter, 60, 61, 62; writing, 63-64; example, 64-66; 208

Cowley Publications, 17

Cox, James A. 234

Crawford, Tad, 223

Creative nonfiction, 28

Cropsey, Sande, why she writes, 12; 214,

Cullins, Judy, 304

Dan River Press, 47, 154

Da Vinci Code, 27

DAW Books, 17, 30

Deaconess Press, 148

Dedications page, 187; defined, 188

Del Rey Books, 27

DeVorss and Company (distributor), 238

Digital Printing (see Print-on-Demand)

*Directory of Authors*, 278

Disclaimer (for your book),

defined, 189-190

Distributors, 3, 208, 212;
library, 234-236;
bookstore, 236-237;
defined, 237;
work with, 237-238;
payment, 236, 239;
listings, 238-239;
directory, 308

Dolainski, Stephen, 194, 305

Donate books, 289-290

Donohue Group (library
wholesaler), 210, 236;
contact information, 307

Ebook, defined, 35-36; produce
one, 200

Echo, merchant account, 244, 311

Editor, hire one, 9; fees, 49; POD
published books, 53, 130,
158; fees, 49, 130, 147, 178;
176-179; defined, 177;
choose one, 177-179; self-
editing,178-187; 199

Editing, it's necessary, 9; POD
publishers, 49; 176-184; self-
editing, 178-187; mistakes,
180; tips, 182-187

Editorial guidelines (see
Submission guidelines)

Elder Signs Press, 58

Endorsements (for your book),
61, 187, 188; defined 189

Epilogue, 190

Escalator, 133

Equilibrium Press, message to
authors, 101

Espresso Book Machine, 52-53

Evans, Richard Paul, 198

Evans, Susan Borden and Tonya
Marie, 198, 295,

Evans-Walls, Tonya, 295, 305

Excerpts, promote book, 267-
270

Expertcentral.com, 170, 313

Expertclick.com, 170, 313

Exposure, for your books, 223-
225, 272

Fairview Health Services, 148

Fairview Press, 148

Faithworks, distributor, 238

Fantasy, 17; described, 28; 136,
187, 236

*Fast-track Course on How to
Write a Nonfiction Book
Proposal*, (Mettee), 98, 304

Fat Cat Press, 27

Fell, Frederick, Publishers, 18

Fiction, successful, 14; 17;
categories, 26-27; genres,
27-28; build promotion
into, 57; book proposal for,
61-62, 100; title for, 69-70;
about the novelist, 79-80;
target audience, 91-92;
chapter outline, 116;
organizing book, 116-117;
146; research, 164-173;
parts of book, 187-192;
reviews, 232-233; sell
excerpts, 268; promote
through articles, 268

Fiction author sites, 314
Fictitious Business Name, 205
Fidlar Doubleday Printing, 312
Fielding, Helen, 28
*Fine Print, The*, 47, 55, 305
*First Line, The*, 233
*Florida Review*, 269
Foreword, 188; defined 189
*Forthcoming Books in Print*, 68, 94
Fotel, 306
Free advertising, 255
Freelancewriting.com, 24
*Freelance Writer's Report*, 268; contact information, 310
Friedman, Marsha (Publicity That Works), 307
Front matter (for your book), 188-190
Fulfillment services, 239-240
Funds for Writers, 310

Gale Group, 235
*Gale's Directory of Publications and Broadcast Media*, 231, 258
Galley, 208
Genre, 26-30, 142, 160, 161, 231
Glazner, Gary Mex, 15, 305
Glossary, for your book, 188; defined 191; for this book 316-323
Google, locate publishers, 26; locate writers' conference, 36-37; locate titles, 68; find statistics, 90; 167, 168, 160; find book review opportunities, 231; locate newsletter sites, 257; 314
Google Alerts, 231-232, 313
Gothic, 27
Grafton, Sue, 27
Graham, Barbara Florio, 265
Grammar, 178-187
Grammar Now, 310
*Grammar Traps*, 194, 305
Grand Canyon Association, 29
Grand Central Publishing (formerly Warner Books), 17, 131, 155
*Grandparents Magazine*, 233
*Grassroots Marketing for Authors and Publishers* (Horowitz), 304
Greenwillow Books, 28
Grey, Zane, 198
Grisham, John, 27
GuestFinder, 258, 307
Guidelines (see Submission guidelines)
*Guide to Book Editors, Publishers and Literary Agents* (Herman), 303
*Guide to Literary Agents* (Writer's Digest Books), 135, 303

Handouts, for publisher, 39, 42; for book signings, 227; promote through, 246-247; for book festival, 276
HarperCollins, 28, 159,

Hay House, 29
Heacock Literary Agency, 136,
Health Communications, 154
Hemmingway, Earnest, 198
Heng, Christopher, 257
Herman, Jeff, 83, 159, 303, 305
Hill Street Press, 27
Historical fiction, 27; titles for, 69;
    promoting, 100; premium
    item, 107; 207, 234, 266
*Historical Novel Society*, 234
Hoffman, Mabel, 85
Holbert, Christine, 62, 146,
Horowitz, Shel, 304
Horror, 28, 136,
Hot file, for promotion, 264-265
Houghton-Mifflin, 8,
How-to books, 29, 71, 89, 160,
    188, 189
*How to Make a Living as a Poet*
    (Glazner), 15, 305
*How to Say and Write it
    Correctly*, (Aurelio), 305
*How to Write a Successful Book
    Proposal in 8 Days or Less*
    (Fry), 305

*Iconclast,* 232-233
Independent Publishers Group,
    238, 308
Index, description, make book
    marketable, 106; 120, 188;
    defined, 191
InfoPlease.com, 90
*Information Please*, 90
Ingram (wholesaler), check book

sales, 91, 94, 219; get into
    bookstores, 221, 232
*InnerSelf Magazine*, 234
Intellectual Properties Attorney,
    54; and agents, 133, 136; and
    contracts, 294-295
Intellectual Property Owners
    Association, 310
International Digital Publishing
    Forum (IDPF), 35
International Standard Book
    Number (See ISBN)
Interview, techniques, 169-173;
    via email, 171-173
Introduction, for book, 161; write
    one, 162-163; 188; defined,
    189
Invoice, 221; bookstores, 222-
    223; 288
IRS (also see Taxes), 291, 292
ISBN, self-publishing, 21, 34, 45;
    POD publishing 48; ordering
    information, 206, 307;
    assign number, 207;
    prepublication reviews, 208-
    209; 216, 284,
Island Heritage Publishing, 32,
iUniverse, 20

Jackson, Jennifer, 136
Jacobs, Charles, 301
Jaffe, Azriela, 111-112
*January Magazine*, 233
Jassin, Lloyd J., 294, 295, 306
Jenkins Group, 87, 104
Jennie's Garden Books, 219

JIST Publishing, message to
authors, 101
Jud, Brian, 304
*Jump Start Your Book Sales*
(Ross), 282, 304

Katco Media, 28
King, Stephen, 215,
Kirkus Discoveries, 209
*Kirkus Reviews*, 209, 229
Kirsch, Jonathan, 295, 305
*Kirsch's Handbook of
Publishing Law* (Kirsch),
306
Kremer, John, 113, 115;
distributor list, 238; advises
promotion, 241; 303, 304,
308

Le Baigue, Catt, 136,
Levine, Mark, 47, 55, 305
Libraries, number of, 86-87;
for research, 166; 234-236;
mailing list, 235; web site,
235; promote to, 264
*Library Journal*, 208, 229
Library of Congress, 211, 216;
contact, 307
Liguori Publications, 32
Literary agent (See Authors'
agent)
Literary fiction, 27
*Literary Law Guide for Authors*
(Evans), 306
*Literary Market Place*,
described, 22, 135, 158,

207; locate distributors and
wholesalers, 212; locate
fulfillment, 240; 303, 305,
308
Loft Press, 17
*Los Angeles Times*, book review,
229
Los Angeles Times Festival of
Books, 175, 271
Lost Horse Press, 62, 146
Love Inspired, 28

Maass, Donald Literary Agency,
136
Mailing list, for promotion, 204;
make sales, 255-256,
Mainstream fiction, 27
Make news, promotion, 105,
254-255
Manuscript, formatting, 62-64;
66-67
Margins, for manuscript, 66, 193
Marketable topic,
authors mistakes, 16; choose
one, 84-86, 99
Market analysis, 61;
how to write, 94-98;
example, 96-98;
Marsh, Jeff, 52
McGinnis, Linda, 265, 306
Medallion Press, 28
Media kit, 253,
Media mail (book rate), 292
Memoir, 29, 49, 71, 86, 117,
132, 197
*Memoirs of a Geisha*, 27

Merchant accounts, 243-245; contact, 311

Message Boards, for research, 169, 170; for networking, 257

Metaphysical, book, 148; bookstore, 219

Mettee, Stephen Blake, 98, 304

Michner, James, 27

Midwest Book Review, 234, 303

Morgana Publishing, message to authors, 101

Morrow, 131

*Mothering Magazine*, 233

Mountain View, 148

Myrhum, Bonnie, 312

Mystery, 26, 27, 58; titles for, 69; 223; review, 233

Mystical World, 219

Mystic Ridge Books, message to authors, 101

Myth Busters, for authors, 8-11

Narrative nonfiction, 28

National Association of Women Writers, 268

National Writers Union (NWU), 135

Networking, 257-258

New Horizon Press, 28

Newsletters, to promote book, 111-112; writing one, 256, 257

Newspaper Directories, 311

News release (see Press release)

Nonfiction, write one first, 13; successful, 14; 17; description, 28-30; parts of book proposal for, 60-61; title for, 67-69; build marketability, 105-106; chapter outline, 116; organize, 116-117; research, 164-173; parts of book, 188-192; spin offs, 281

Novel, 13, description, 27; book proposal for, 57, 59; parts of book proposal, 61, 62; title for, 69-70; about the novelist, 79-80; target audience, 91-92; build promotion, 105-107; special interest item, 107-108; organizing, 117; 131; read what you write, 160; promote through radio/TV, 260; promote, 279; spin off, 280

Novella, 26; word count, 27

*Novel Ways to Promote Your Novel* (article), 278

Nursebooks, 29

NWU (See National Writers Union)

Oats, Carol, 27

Olmstead, Robert, 47, 154

One-sentence challenge, 70-72

Online bookstores, 311

Open Horizons, 115

O'Reilly, Bill, 111

Organize book, how to 116-117
*Over 75 Good Ideas for Promoting Your Book* (Fry), 304
Overview (see Synopsis)

Page layout (see Book design)
Pandora's Books, 219
Partners Book Distributing, 221
Patterson, James, 202
Paulist Press, 17
PayPal, 244
PCIP (see Publisher's Cataloging in Publication)
Pelican Publishing Co., 18, 27
Penguin Putnam, 30
Permission, to quote, 106
*Personal Journaling*, 268
Plagiarism, 167
Platform, 37-38, 58, 59; defined, 61; 62, 80; explained, 102-105; example, 102; how to build, 105
PMA, 24, 238, 311
*PMA Independent* (newsletter), 24, 268, 310-311
PO (See Purchase order)
POD "self-publishing" services, 3, 5, 6, 9-10, 20; explained, 21; working with, 33-34; facts, 44-55; history, 45-46; complaints; 46-49; cost, 49-50; lure of POD, 50-53; the right choice, 53-55; promotional package, 104-

105; 208, 213; book reviews, 229
POD publisher database, 45, 55
POD (Print-on-Demand) technology, 3, 33, 44-45, 46, 50; for self-published book, 198; 200,
*Poet Power* (Williams), 15, 305
Poetry, 13, selling, 15; 17, 29; book proposal for, 59; get reviewed, 232-233; promote, 279; spin offs, 280; sites, 314
Postage, 312
Potomac Books, 17
Powers, Melvin, 57-58
Poynter, Dan, 10, 205, 212; specialty stores, 228; 238, 303, 306, 308, 311, 313
Preditors and Editors, 314
Preface, 188; defined, 189
Premium item, 107,
Prepublication reviews, 10, 207
Prepublication sales, 204; solicit orders 210
Press release, sending, 101, 105; 218; for book signing, 225; how to write, 247-253; sample, 251-253; in media kit, 253; 264
Pricing (for book), 209
Printer, print-on-demand, 44-45; 207; price quote, 200-201; request for price quote, 207; locating, 207; choose, 210; list of, 312
Print-on-Demand (See POD)

334

Promotion (see Book promotion)
Proofreading, 312
Proulx, Annie, 215
Publicist, 103; hiring one, 112-113; directory, 113; 214; contact information, 307
*Publicity Insider*, 307
Public speaking, improve skills, 260-263; opportunities, 263; resources, 312
Publisher's Cataloging in Publication, 188; ordering, 209-210; library use, 236; contact information, 307
Publishers Group West, 238
*Publisher's Weekly*, subscribe, 23; Espresso Book Machine, 52-53; 229; contact, 311
Publishing, profits, 14; specialties, 16-17; promotional assistance, 104
*Publishing Basics,* 268
Publishing industry statistics, 1, 2; number of books published 2006, 8; 14; ebooks, 35; book sales, 84; number bookstores/readers, 86-87; books represented by agents, 131; 156-157, 195, 200, 219-220, 232; resource list, 314
Publishing professionals, 313
Puente, Debbie, example of platform, 103; working with publicist, 214; demonstration, 225; 260; spin off, 281

Punctuation, 180-181
Purchase order, bookstores, 221-222; 288

Quality Books, 209-210, 211; library sales, 235, 237; contact information, 307, 308
Query letter, 16, 18; mistakes, 19; 20, 24, 25; introduction to, 58-59; 130; to agent, 137; to publisher, 138-144; defined, 140-144; format, 140-141; margins, 140; email, 141; addressing, 141-143; what to include, 143-144; simultaneous, 144; response, 144-146; rejection, 146-147; examples, 148-153; 160

*Radio-TV Interview Report*, 258, 307
Raincoast Book Distribution, 308
Random House, 17, 131
*Reader's Guide to Periodical Literature*, 166
Record keeping (see Bookkeeping)
Red Dress Ink, 28
Redfield, James, 154-155
Rejection, 87, 145, 154-155
Religious books (see Christian books)
Research, how to, 164-173; using books, 165-167, 170; computer, 168; resources, 313

Resources, 302-315

Return policy, 48-49, 222
Returnable insurance, 48-49
Request for price quote, 200-201,
    207
*Reunions Magazine*, 269
Reviews, (see Book reviews)
Review copies, protect, 290-291
Rittenhouse Books, 238
RJ Communications, printing, 312
*Robb Report*, 268
Romance, 26, 27, 28; promoting,
    100; 148; reviews, 234
*Romantic Times Book Review*,
    234
Rosen, Judith, 52
Ross, Marilyn and Tom, 84-86,
    96, 282, 306, 313
Royalties, 14, 17, 20; working
    with agents, 132-133; in
    contract, 156-157
Rubie, Peter Literary Agency, 136

Sable Publishing, 28
St. Martins Press, 27, 131
Sample chapters, nonfiction 61;
    fiction, 62
Sansevieri, Penny (A Marketing
    Expert), 307
SASE, 24, 62, 145
Schlesinger, Dr. Laura, 111
Science fiction, 17; defined, 27;
    30, 58, 136, 148, 187, 236;
    sites, 314
Scriblerus Press, 18,
Seal Press, 28

Search engines, 313
Seasonal Promotion, 278-280
Seized By the Tale, 230
Self-addressed-stamped-envelope
    (see SASE)
Self-help book, 17, 29, 30, 71,
    89, 95, 148, 188
Self-publishing, 3, 5, 6; and
    bookstores, 9-10; earning
    potential, 14: description, 20,
    21; advantages/disadvantages,
    34-35; 45-46, 195-212; why
    self publish, 195-196; is it for
    you? 196-200; versus
    traditional publishing, 187,
    199-200; timeline, 205-212;
    book reviews, 229
*Self-Publishing Manual*, 10,
    205, 212, 306
Self-publishing timeline, 205-212
Sell sheet, 254
*Sharp Writer*, 310
Shaw Guide (Directory of Writers
    Conferences), 37
Shipping, books, 198, 292-293,
    312; supplies, 314
Silverman, Fran, 304, 308
Simon and Schuster, 2, 131, 132,
    245
Simultaneous submissions, 144
Small Press Distribution, 238
Small Publishers, Artists and
    Writers Network (see
    SPAWN)
Soho Press, 29
SPAN, 24, 86, 312

*SPAN Connection*, 24, 310
*SPANet*, 85
SPAWN, 7, 23, 24, 100, 101, 102, 111, 114, 137, 143, 175, 203, 207, 223, 244, 255, 270, 272; contact info, 303, 312
SPAWNDiscuss, 24
*SPAWN Market Update*, 23, 100, 148, 168, 303, 308, 311
*SPAWNews*, 23, 245, 303, 311
Speaking (See Public speaking)
Special interest item, 107-108
Specialty bookstores, 9-10
Specialty stores, 228-229
Special venues, 277-278
Speculation, writing on, 157
Spencer, Russ and Kathlyn, 44
Spielberg, Steven, 272
Spin offs, 280-281
*Spirituality and Health Magazine*, 230
Star Print Brokers, 312
State Board of Equalization, 207, 211
Steele, Danielle, 27, 202
Steeple Hill Women's Fiction, 17
Stevens, Karen, example of platform, 103; newsletter, 256
Strider Nolan, 18,
Subheadings, 117
Subject line, 141
Submission guidelines, 17-18; locating, 24; 60, 63, 100, 101; for agent, 136-137;

publisher's, 138, 141; 147, 148
Submission service (see Manuscript submission service)
Subsidy publisher, description, 21; working with, 33. (Also see POD "self-publishing" services.)
Sunbelt, distributor, 230, 308
Sundowners, 148
Supplies, shipping, 314; book display, 314
Synopsis, 61, 62; how to write, 71-74; example, 72-78

Table of contents, for book proposal, 61; for book, 116-117; 187; defined, 188
Tan, Amy, 27
Target audience, 4, 16, 61, 70; determining yours, 86-93; for fiction, 91-92; for children's books, 92; get to know, 102
Taxes (also see IRS), 291-292; help for authors, 315
*Teacher's Vision*, 268
*Ten Ways to Make Your Book Outsell Another* (Cullins), 304
Testimonials (see Endorsements)
Thirty-second commercial, 39-41
Thriller, 28, 136
Title, choosing, nonfiction, 67-70; fiction, 69-70; for chapters, 118

Title page, 61, 62; how to write, 66-67; 187; defined, 188

Toastmasters International, 263, 277; contact information, 312

*Toastmaster Magazine*, 268, 312

*Today's Catholic Teacher*, 268

*Today's Christian Women*, 233

Total Merchant Services, 244, 311

Tracer letter, 154

Traditional royalty publisher, 2, 3, 6, 8-11; working with, 16-21; defined, 21; locating, 22-24; Web sites, 24-26; choosing, 30-36; meeting with, 36-43; what they want, 57-58, 50, 101; promote your book, 104; accepting self-published books, 198-200, 213

Trailer, (see Book trailer)

Treble Heart, 148

True crime, 17, 26, 28-29, 104; get reviews, 233

Twisted Shift, 28

Unique Books (library wholesaler), 236, 308

University of Nevada Press, 29

USA Merchant Account, 244, 311

Vanity publisher (see Subsidy publisher)

*Vermont Life*, 269

Video, book, (see Book trailers)

Vision Quest, 219

Vocabula Review, 310

Volunteer Lawyers for the Arts, 310

Warner Books, (See Grand Central Publishing)

Warnings for writers/authors, 314-315

Washington Book Distributors, 238

Web design, 241-243; cost, 244; 315

Webster, Edward D., 70, 109

*Well-Fed Self-Publisher* (Bowerman), 306

Western, 26, 27, 148

Wholesalers, 212; library, 234-236; bookstore, 236-237; defined, 237; work with, 237-238; payment, 236

WhoooDoo Mysteries, 148

Williams, Thomas, 15, 305

Wilshire Book Company, 57

Windward Publishing, 18

*Wired*, 269

*Woman's Life*, 269

*Woman's World*, 269

Word count, publisher's requirements, 20, 66-67, 118-119; determining, 193

*World Guide to Libraries*, 310

Write for magazines (see Article writing)

*Write the Perfect Book Proposal* (Herman/Adams), 83, 305

*Writer, The*, 311

Writer.com, 24

Writers' conferences, 12, meeting publisher, 36-41; locating, 36-37; 175-176, 281, 315

*Writer's Digest, Magazine*, 218,
     268, 311
Writer's Emergency Fund, 310
*Writer's Journal*, 268
*Writer's Market*, 9, 22, 43; how
     much should I charge pages,
     168; magazine listings, 231;
     305
*Writer's Net, 303*
WriterSpace, 24
*Writer's Weekly*, 268
*Writer Within You, The* (Jacobs),
     301
Writing, your motivation, 11-14;
     success, 13-14; disciplining
     self, 173-175, when are you a
     writer, 298-299
*Writing For Dollars*, 268
Writingforum.com, 24
*Writing World*, 268

YMAA Publication Center,
     message to authors, 101
Young adult novel, 17; sales, 84;
     142, 160, 236
*Your Guide to Marketing Books
     in the Christian
     Marketplace* (Bolme) 304

Zumaya Publication, 46